W9-CCD-647

This Advance Reader's Edition is an uncorrected version of the book. All quotations from the text should be checked for accuracy either against a finished copy of the book or, if not available, with the Palgrave Macmillan Publicity Department.

# THE INEVITABLE CITY

# THE
# INEVITABLE CITY

**SCOTT COWEN**
WITH BETSY SEIFTER

FOREWORD BY
**WALTER ISAACSON**

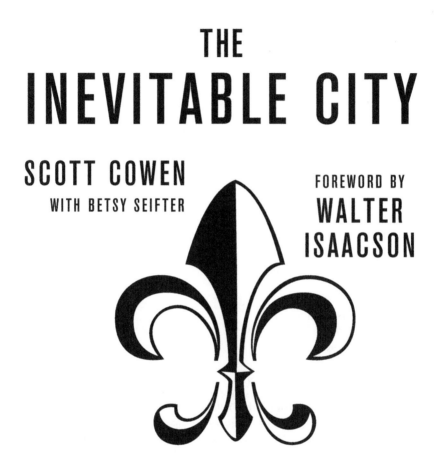

## THE RESURGENCE OF NEW ORLEANS AND THE FUTURE OF URBAN AMERICA

palgrave
macmillan

THE INEVITABLE CITY
Copyright © Scott Cowen, 2014.

First published in 2014 by
PALGRAVE MACMILLAN®
in the United States—a division of St. Martin's Press LLC,
175 Fifth Avenue, New York, NY 10010.

Where this book is distributed in the UK, Europe and the rest of the world,
this is by Palgrave Macmillan, a division of Macmillan Publishers Limited,
registered in England, company number 785998, of Houndmills,
Basingstoke, Hampshire RG21 6XS.

Palgrave Macmillan is the global academic imprint of the above companies
and has companies and representatives throughout the world.

Palgrave® and Macmillan® are registered trademarks in the United States,
the United Kingdom, Europe and other countries.

ISBN: 978–1–137–27886–9

Library of Congress Cataloging-in-Publication Data is available from the
Library of Congress.

A catalogue record of the book is available from the British Library.

Design by Newgen Knowledge Works (P) Ltd., Chennai, India.

First edition: June 2014

10 9 8 7 6 5 4 3 2 1

Printed in the United States of America.

*To all New Orleanians and the Tulane Community for their grit, resilience, and determination to overcome adversity*

*With special thanks to my adorable wife, Marjorie, for her unwavering support, patience, ability to keep me grounded, and sage advice*

*New Orleans is the inevitable city on the impossible site.*

—Peirce Lewis, Professor Emeritus of Geography, Penn State University

# CONTENTS

# ACKNOWLEDGMENTS

THE WRITING OF THIS BOOK HAS BEEN A LABOR OF LOVE FOR ME but it would have not occurred without a superb team of people helping me along the way. Besides my wonderful family, especially my wife Marjorie, and my Tulane colleagues, this book would not have become a reality without Betsy Seifter, my friend and collaborator. Throughout the process Betsy was a confidant, writer, creative partner and researcher. Betsy found my voice and a way to make my stories come to life. She deserves a tremendous amount of credit for the end product but none of the criticism for anything a reader may dislike.

The book also significantly benefitted from the work of Heide Winston, my Special Assistant for Civic Engagement and Research. Heide was our primary fact-checker and reader of the manuscript throughout the process. Her thoughtful comments and questions resulted in an improved book. Jason Ashlock, former President of Movable Type Management and my literary agent, was very helpful in framing our original proposal and connecting us to Palgrave Macmillan. Likewise, the Palgrave Macmillan team of Donna Cherry, Christine Catarino, Allison Frascatore, Tracey Lillis, Samuel Bayard with Davis Wright Tremaine (representing Palgrave), and especially senior editor Emily Carleton made several valuable contributions to the project.

I also want to acknowledge and thank Walter Isaacson for his moving Foreword and James Carville, Vartan Gregorian, Lisa Jackson and Michael Lewis for reading and commenting on the manuscript. Their support inspired me to continue the journey and to make the book something they and other New Orleanians would be proud of.

I am also indebted to my many colleagues at Tulane who assisted me on this project. There are dozens who deserve mention, all of whom know who they are, but I do want to give a special thanks to the staffs of the Cowen Institute for Public Education Initiatives, Communications and Marketing, Center for Public Service, and Government and Community Relations.

Finally, I want to acknowledge and thank the amazing organizations and individual people mentioned in the book, for without their resilience and great desire to persevere against all odds there would be no story to tell.

# FOREWORD

A FEW DAYS AFTER HURRICANE KATRINA, I GOT A CALL FROM Governor Kathleen Blanco asking me to be vice chairman of the Louisiana Recovery Authority. I flew from my home in Washington to Baton Rouge, where we boarded a National Guard helicopter to tour New Orleans. The devastation was so bad that I was unsure if people would ever come back.

But by my next visit, a few weeks later, a few restaurants had reappeared, like crocuses. They were filled with people who wanted to see kindred spirits who had returned. I went to Upperline, where the owner, JoAnn Clevenger, was holding court. That night, over Sazeracs, a few of us plotted ways to entice others back. The method we chose, this being New Orleans, was to throw a party. We enlisted Wynton Marsalis to join the cause, and we decided to hold it on Martin Luther King weekend that upcoming January as part of a series of events that would culminate with the official reopening of Tulane University. We intuitively knew that Tulane and its president, Scott Cowen, were the key to the city's revival, and the return of its students would mean the return of vitality.

The party and related events were jammed, since everyone was eager to catch up and swap tales. It culminated with an inspiring speech by Wynton in Tulane's magnificently domed McAlister Auditorium, which he punctuated with riffs on his horn. "Tough times force us to return to fundamentals," he said. "And there is nothing more fundamental than home."

This is a book about home, and thus it is a book about fundamentals. Most important, it is about the fundamentals of leadership. I've been writing about leadership my entire career, starting as a reporter in New Orleans and then at *Time* and as a biographer. Scott Cowen is among the best leaders I've known, and he turned out to be the greatest New Orleans had in the aftermath of the storm. He was steadfast, cool, and never lost his humor or optimism. He saw the crisis as an opportunity.

Tulane became the primary engine of the town's revival and, in the process, transformed itself into a unique institution in a unique place. It also set an aspiration for the whole city. The goal was not just to restore what had existed before the storm but to build something better. With Tulane in the lead, New Orleans seized that opportunity.

Some feckless folks flinched, even left their jobs at schools and hospitals and opted for a less challenging life elsewhere. But New Orleans is a city that engenders a deep love, and most of its denizens followed Scott's example and came back. After the waters receded and the earth began to heal, a large cadre of everyday heroes was willing to engage, month after month, in building a better city.

These included the Tulane students who were in McAlister Auditorium listening to Wynton Marsalis. They had been dispersed around the country for five months. Those who chose to come back to Tulane, rather than transferring to more sedate enclaves, were the type who relished serving others. Because of Scott's leadership and their eagerness, Tulane became the foremost university in America for instilling the concept of service into what it means to get a great education.

Another group that came back was the city's Teach For America corps members. I met with a gathering of them in a hotel soon after the storm. Since it was unclear if and when the old school system would reopen, they were all given the chance to be reassigned elsewhere. Instead, almost all of them stayed and took on a grand mission: to build a new type of school system that would be better than the old one. Instead of shrinking, the size of the Teach For America corps in New Orleans quadrupled in the next three years. New Orleans became a magnet for idealistic educational entrepreneurs. It offered the chance to invent a city school system from the ground up. For anyone infected with the spirit of school reform, to pass up the opportunity to go there was like missing the chance to fight alongside Henry V at Agincourt.

They charged into the breach with Scott, who chaired the education committee for the city's recovery commission.

One issue New Orleans faced was which neighborhoods should be rebuilt. As Scott describes, that question got entangled in the city's complex racial dynamics. Most notable was the issue of the Lower Ninth Ward. I felt it was wrong to send people back to a place that was below sea level and where the levees might not be ready for a few years. We developed a plan that would buy up property in that area and offer "Road Home" incentives to resettle in the safer parts of town. But many residents of that proud community objected, understandably. As Wynton had reminded us, there is nothing more fundamental than home.

I got a better appreciation of the emotions of the Lower Ninth Ward residents when one of the planning proposals suggested that my own family neighborhood of Broadmoor, which had flooded badly, might be turned into parkland. It was a wonderfully diverse and mixed central city neighborhood, filled with whites and blacks, rich and poor, all enriched by the friendships and frictions that come when different groups live together. Years ago, my parents helped start the Broadmoor Improvement Association, with the goal of having a racially balanced organization that would work to keep the neighborhood mixed rather than tipping white or black. Now the association had a critical new mission: Save the neighborhood from tipping into oblivion. A rally, replete with jazz bands and food stalls, was held in the yard of our family home, and it spilled out into Napoleon Avenue. Broadmoor became the model for neighborhood rebuilding. It came up with a plan that tied together a revitalized school, library, and community center into an education corridor, and the neighborhood is now back with all of its glorious diversity.

Scott has written three books in one. He weaves together a charming personal memoir, a study of urban rebuilding, and a leadership text. As you read this book, you will understand, in both a personal and an analytical way, how great leaders act. They have vision, and they have the grit to translate vision into outcomes. They know how to inspire and also how to listen. They have passion, but they leaven it with empathy and humility. They have the realism to face facts and the determination to do the right thing. They don't quit. And they know the importance of achieving leadership's most important balance: being resolute in your principles yet also willing to find common ground with others of good faith.

Walker Percy, the Louisiana novelist whose wry philosophical depth and lightly worn grace produced such novels as *The Moviegoer*, had a theory about hurricanes. He believed that people are at their happiest when a hurricane is about to hit. When you're mired in the everydayness of ordinary life, he explained, you're likely to be afflicted by what he called "the malaise," a free-floating despair that comes from feeling disconnected from the world. We feel alienated, detached. But not when a hurricane is about to hit! Then we're focused, connected, engaged. We know what we're supposed to do, and we do it. Alas, after the winds recede and normalcy stalks back in, Percy said, the malaise and alienation settle over us again.

Hurricane Katrina was, I think, an exception to Percy's theory. It wrought such destruction that, even years after the waters receded, the alienation and malaise have not returned. Instead, Katrina continues to keep people in New Orleans engaged and connected to one another. There's an edgy creativity that comes from the shared aftertaste of danger, and there's a sense of community that comes from being in the same boat. The city remains rife with enticing challenges that attract young people from around the country.

On that first helicopter ride I took into New Orleans after the storm, I had tears in my eyes. I was not sure that the city would ever revive. But miraculously, it did. Actually, it was not a miracle. It was the product of hard work, of love, of creativity, and of leadership. It's an inspiring tale, full of lessons for every community—or every company or family or individual—who will ever face a challenge. And now, in this book, which also starts with the sounds of a helicopter, you get to read an insider's tale of how it happened.

—Walter Isaacson

# Introduction

# FIND YOUR PURPOSE

## September 2, 2005

I'M STANDING ON THE BANKS OF THE MISSISSIPPI RIVER ON A
humid afternoon, in the sodden grass of what used to be a football field. The
air is very still; leaves hang limp on the trees. Then I hear it: the ratcheting
sound of a helicopter, followed by a hot wind whirling down from a blur of
blades. We've been hearing choppers all week, watching them hover over the
city like crazed dragonflies, but this is our chopper, aiming for our ragged
band clustered around the dump truck we commandeered to get us out of
the city.

At least we hope it's our chopper. Two have already come and gone, the
first missing us entirely despite our shouts and waves, the second landing
on the batture, the mudflats between the edge of the river and the base of
the levee. We crashed the dump truck through a chain-link fence to reach

it—a TV helicopter, it turned out—then drove back up the incline to our first position.

We raise the Tulane banner over our heads, waving like mad. The copter hangs in the sky above the football field. It's coming down: I see nearby trees bending under the force of the mechanical wind, and I'm back in basic training. I have a familiar, paradoxical sensation of alert numbness. I don't feel anything, yet I'm all eyes, all ears.

The helicopter descends onto the field and the crew helps one of my senior staff members aboard. It's my turn, but I can't move. I feel a huge sense of anxiety and guilt. I want to get back in the battered motorboat we've been using to get around the campus and go out into the city and rescue people.

"Come on," someone says.

**Image 1**  Cowen in water

With flood waters surrounding the Reily Student Recreation Center on the uptown campus and the nearby neighborhood, Tulane loaned a boat to a group of neighbors who had landed in a helicopter on the roof of the Diboll Parking Garage. Talking with them is Scott Cowen, back to camera, while Tom Casey, a Tulane electrician, holds the boat.

(*Courtesy of Louis Mayer*)

I have to leave, for the sake of the school. There will be no school if we don't start rebuilding now.

I climb up and the chopper lifts away, headed west to an airport in Patterson, Louisiana, where a trustee has arranged to have us picked up in his private plane and flown to Houston. I look down. A muddy sea spreads everywhere, its surface broken by the faint remnants of a landscape: the roofs of houses, the tops of fences, the crowns of trees.

Where are the people?

Where are the bodies?

It's the first moment, after five days of heat, darkness, rising water, hunger, thirst, that I really understand the magnitude of what has happened.

By the time we reach Houston, I've composed myself. I can do that, just shut it off, which has proved useful many times in my life. Immediately we're whisked off in a plush, air-conditioned limousine. Next to me is Anne Baños, my chief of staff and all-purpose lieutenant, the one who somehow wrangled the helicopter and now this limo; the one who arranges everything, even in hurricanes. I lean back in the seat and close my eyes.

"Where are we going?" I ask.

"The Four Seasons."

I bolt upright. "We have a whole school to save, and no money to do it with. We can't stay at a fancy hotel. Let's go to a Sleep Inn—anywhere with a bed."

"It's all right," Anne says. "They're giving us rooms dirt cheap."

I lean back and close my eyes again. Okay, then.

We get to the hotel, where I finally strip off the grimy khakis and the yellow polo shirt that I've lived in for the entire week, ever since addressing the incoming freshmen at orientation. I shower. I eat something. I lie down on the soft bed with the down pillows. I listen to my heart pound.

I think I should call Marjorie—she's at our summer home on Long Island—but it's the middle of the night. I'll wait until morning.

I pull on some shorts, take the elevator down to the fitness center, and get on the treadmill. As I start slowly walking, I glance at the screen built into the instrument panel. What I see on TV is what the rest of the country has been watching all week: masses of people crammed into the Superdome and spilling into the streets around the Convention Center. Some of them look as though they are literally dying. You can feel the heat, you can smell the stench. There are people begging for water, there are old people slumped in wheelchairs and babies crying with hunger. It's then that I begin to lose it.

A middle-of-the-night exerciser stops what he's doing and comes over to my treadmill. "You okay?"

It seems horrible to be okay, to be on a treadmill at the Four Seasons, when so many people are suffering. I tell the man yes, I'm okay and head back up to my room, where I call my wife, middle of the night be damned. I'm really crying now. I tell her, "I don't know what to do...I don't know what to do."

The stress of the last five days is hitting me—sleeping on the floor, raiding the cafeteria, dunking in the rec center's Olympic pool to get relief from the unbearable heat. Meanwhile our two major campuses are underwater, students and faculty are god knows where. At this moment, there is no Tulane University.

Marjorie says in her calm way, "What do you always do when you don't know what to do?"

My mind's a blank.

She says, "You make a list."

EVERYONE IN NEW ORLEANS HAS A KATRINA STORY, one they keep retelling all these years later. Everyone's story is, in part, the same.

The sky was so blue.
Hurricanes were nothing new.
The day after, it wasn't so bad.
Then, the water rose.
It was surreal. It was horrible. The smell. The bodies.

Everyone's story is also different, depending on circumstances. There are the ones who lost family, and friends, and all their earthly possessions; the ones who ended up in shanty housing in a score of states; the ones who killed themselves or landed in jail; the ones who came back, and the ones who will never come back.

My story is different too. I live Uptown, in the President's Mansion on the Tulane campus. I saw no bodies, lost no friends; even my belongings came through intact. I was never personally at risk, except maybe in those first chaotic days on campus, when our facilities staff chased off looters and it seemed like anything could happen. But I carried a weight of responsibility for thousands of lives and for a 172-year-old institution. Before Katrina, Tulane was the largest private employer in New Orleans; for a time after Katrina, it was the largest employer period. To bring Tulane back would mean bringing New Orleans back.

As president of the university, I had the opportunity—the obligation, really—to lead the way to transformative change across the whole spectrum of civic life. Since 1998, when I accepted the post of president, I've also been a consultant and board member for organizations of every kind, touching every aspect of this iconic city that has become my adopted home—all of which is another way of saying "I was there," as witness to the rebirth of the city and as an active participant in one of the largest experiments in urban renewal the country has ever seen.

And that's the story I'm going to tell. It's a story about jump-starting the university and rebuilding the city despite a miserably inadequate response from the federal government; about quelling racial animosity after the storm and partnering with Dillard, a historically black college, in the recovery effort; about salvaging the education system, creating high-performing charter schools that have helped kids from drowned neighborhoods and wrecked homes finish high school and go to college or get a job; about projects like Grow Dat, an urban agricultural experiment, and Roots of Music, a program that teaches middle schoolers how to play in brass bands (but only if they keep their grades up). It's about landmark battles—over the destruction of the housing projects, the abandonment of the historic Charity Hospital for a new hospital center on expropriated land, and the erosion of the *Times-Picayune*—that seem like lost causes but have ultimately yielded surprising benefits and unexpected growth.

The resolve that formed in that dark night in a Houston hotel was the wellspring of all the transformational changes up ahead. Leadership begins inside you, with a vision of the future, which then becomes—as my wife suggested—a "list": the concrete steps that give your vision flesh. *The Inevitable City* focuses both on the nature of leadership, especially in a time of crisis, and on the concrete practices that, step by step, can change communities and the world. The book is also a description of, and prescription for, what it will take to rebuild urban America, told through stories and experiences related to the rebuilding of New Orleans.

After two opening chapters that recount the events following the storm, first at Tulane and then in the city at large, the book lays out the chief areas of renewal in the great surge of innovation and effort of the post-Katrina years. These are the crucial building blocks of any great city: education, health, social innovation, economic development, public safety, environment, and culture. This foundation has been reconstructed in New Orleans over the last nine years, often with the help of the university, which, standing apart from the political fray, brought a dispassionate and practical voice into the heated debates that developed.

A note on the handling of time in the book: within chapters, each devoted to one area of rebuilding, I begin in "the present," that is, the years 2012 and 2013, the period of the book's composition, and then move back in time to the critical moments in the resurgence of a particular domain—schools, housing, social innovation, and all the other building blocks of urban life. The time travel between "now" and "then" is testimony to how amazingly far we've come.

And the key ingredient to this extraordinary rebuilding effort has been leadership.

*What is leadership, and why does it matter? Leadership is about making a significant positive difference in the lives of organizations and people. It involves envisioning a future that does not currently exist and working with others to realize it. The journey from vision to outcome is a long one that requires giving of yourself, empowering and inspiring others, being willing to give and take, and finding the courage to act and the determination and will to succeed. To effect transformational change is often difficult and chaotic, but leaders always act to ambitiously optimize a situation, aiming for the best possible in a highly imperfect world. They recognize good ideas, understand and respect conflicting points of view, and actively engage with others. Most important, they don't quit till they get it done.*

One theme threads through all the leadership decisions, actions, and choices that went into this massive project of renovation: In aiming for a greater good, you have to pay a price, sometimes a steep one, not only in money but in lives derailed and hopes crushed. In the literature of leadership, from Sun Tzu's *Art of War*, to Machiavelli's *Prince*, to the latest business bible, there's a covert tension between operational thinking—get it done, find the money, make it happen—and social and moral considerations—who gets hurt, is it fair, is it right. Sometimes there is no clear moral equation, particularly in crisis situations; I'm even a little suspicious of those who are overconfident about their "rightness." But I do believe in what I would call principled decision making. In my mind, it's principled, and smart, to use deliberate, calculated means—rational thinking, strategic use of power, emotional persuasion, mutually advantageous partnerships—for the ultimate good of many.

While telling the story of the resurgence of New Orleans, in each chapter I focus on one particular element of leadership that guided my actions, as well as those of others, through events that unfolded after Katrina. But elements and their definitions don't fully capture the heart of the matter. Something more passionate and personal is behind all these recommendations and prescriptions. The truth is, New Orleans is a place I've fallen in love with. And loving what you are changing—really caring about making a difference—is the animating force behind all these tenets. Everyone has his personal version of this much-loved city, and this book is full of my own New Orleans, people, places, and events that have particularly affected me.

It's also, in part, about where I come from—literally, suburban New Jersey, but also the other kind of "where": dyslexia, a tough father, the army, a business degree, administrative jobs, and, ultimately, Katrina. Personal history is another animating force for meaningful action. Two early experiences that shaped me were my difficulties learning to read and write at a time when the diagnosis of dyslexia was unknown and the disapproval of my father, who saw me as deficient in will, or intellect, or both; in a sense, I had to fight my way to accomplishment. Ultimately, no matter what you do, it has to come from deep within who you are—your pain, and your solutions to that pain.

And a third force driving positive action is belief, whether spiritual, moral, or philosophical. For me, the source of conviction comes from my adopted religion. In Judaism, there's a phrase, *tikkun olam*, which means "repair the world." It's an ethical imperative that each person lives out in his own way, as opportunity presents. Katrina was my opportunity to live my creed and do the right thing.

Today, when I walk past the Superdome and remember the hopelessness of the crowds abandoned there at the height of the storm; when I walk through a neighborhood in the Lower Ninth Ward, with one shotgun house intact and the rest of the place still, all these years after Katrina, in ruins; when I talk to children in an elementary school whose daily lives tell them they'll never amount to anything, or see teenagers, the ones we in education call disconnected youth, hanging on the corner with no point to their day—I know exactly why we at Tulane create our institutes for social innovation and send our students out to hammer nails, grow gardens, read to preschoolers, paint murals, distribute needles, clean up trash. People *can* make things happen with their actions—specifically, those actions that reach across the divide between institutional, philanthropic, well-to-do America and the "other America" that lives in the shadows and on the streets. This vision of a united country—*e pluribus unum*—was, after all, the original American dream that made us strong and great. In New Orleans, we've tried to build a culture of inclusion and opportunity in the city, person by person, program by program. We've made a new, living version of the American dream.

*The Inevitable City* is the story of how we did it and how it can be done.

# Chapter One

# HARD CALLS

## DO THE RIGHT THING

IT'S 10 A.M. ON A SUNDAY AND I'M AT MY DESK, WRITING. OUTSIDE the window, across the street in Audubon Park, a group of Mardi Gras Indians are practicing for St. Joseph's Day, one of the lesser-known holidays on the New Orleans calendar. Mardi Gras is the biggest blowout of the year, but we celebrate a lot here—formal occasions like St. Joseph's Day and Super Sunday and informal ones like second-line parades and jazz funerals. People take to the streets all year long, swept up in tides of music and movement.

Looking out my window, I see that the Indians are wearing their costumes—extravagant scaffolds of plumes, rhinestones, and beadwork. They're riveting. Arms flung wide, feet stomping, the men execute peacock struts and ruffle their feathers. The tambourine shakes out a beat and strange words float in the air.

The Mardi Gras Indians are African American, with possible traces of Caribbean and Native American heritage, strains that are evident in the songs and dances. According to local lore, the impulse to dress up as Indians stems from a feeling of kinship with the Native American tribes who took in runaway slaves in the nineteenth century. Some of the chiefs say that another motivating force for the creation of tribes was opposition to the predominantly white Mardi Gras processions. Feeling unwelcome, African Americans made their own parade.

One of the complicated things about New Orleans is the racial divide: How divided is it? You talk to different people, you get different answers. On one hand, there's a lot of easy warmth and acceptance, a feeling of "we're all from here." There's also a strong multiracial element, with many genetic mixtures and many shades of skin color. On the other hand, there are occasional collisions along racial lines. Even so, it's not like elsewhere. The civil rights movement stopped short of New Orleans, at least in the sense of open hostilities. Everything down here is more subtle, more encoded, than elsewhere.

I should add that I'm not "from here." I'm originally from New Jersey, a place with very different social codes. I was also, for a long while, a transplant to Cleveland, Ohio, the rust belt city derided as "the mistake on the lake" but in fact a place of interesting textures and customs. Still, New Orleans is different: more intricate, more layered. There's something in the air, a complicated, liberating ethos of permissiveness, indulgence, acceptance, forgiveness. As my wife, Margie, puts it, she's never lived in a place where she's known so many people who've been in jail, not for violent crime but for white-collar misdeeds, shady dealings, minor corruption. People tend to shrug off other people's mistakes, as they shrug off their own. That's the way it is down here.

In my seven pre-Katrina years in New Orleans, I was, in a way, a tourist. But since Katrina, I feel more like I'm "from here." I've become engaged with everything New Orleans—the music, the food, the artists, the history; the hurricane parties, the Mardi Gras floats, the smell of jasmine, the glitter of the river. I've met remarkable people, like the late Jefferson Parish sheriff Harry Lee, who figured out how to get Tulane's database files out of a downtown building when the city was under martial law, and like Quint Davis, the mastermind and producer of the New Orleans Jazz and Heritage Festival, who almost singlehandedly brought the city's music—everything from the Mardi Gras Indians' chants to Professor Longhair's blues—to national prominence. And then there's Bob Breland, my regular cabdriver, whose colorful turns of phrase, careening sense of humor, and encyclopedic mind for city detail remind me of Ignatius from John Kennedy Toole's *Confederacy of Dunces*.

There are also the people I don't know personally but who make me feel like I know them. I was in the grocery store not long ago, and a woman in an extravagant hat, some sort of feathered thing sitting on the rim, passed by me in the aisle. She smiled warmly and said, "How ya doin', baby?" I smiled back and told her I was fine, how was she doin'? It's like old home week everywhere you go. In the pre-hurricane years, I grew to love this town. It was Katrina that changed the landscape, literally and figuratively, and gave me the chance to do something here.

I turn again to the window. The Mardi Gras Indians are still chanting, and I try to make out the words. *Hey Mama, hu tan nay, pock a way pock a way.* It's patois, mixing English with what sounds like non-sense words. We have a group of linguists at Tulane who are analyzing Indian songs to try to identify their roots in French, Spanish, and Native American dialects. We also have a group at the law school trying to copyright the costumes of the Indians as works of art, so that the tribes, some 40 of them, will benefit whenever they're displayed at art museums or on the web.

I love watching the Indians dance, but I'm aware that I'm only an observer. I see them framed in the window: They're out there, I'm in here. A lot of the life of the city, vivid, messy, exotic, is "out there," while I spend my time in offices and conference rooms. Maybe I've become more part of the city, a transplant with roots, but I'm still somehow separated from the culture—which may be one reason I've been able to do certain things, hard things, that people born and raised here couldn't or wouldn't.

Another reason I could do things is Tulane itself. New Orleans, already beset by multiple urban problems, was in danger of a disastrous decline in the aftermath of Katrina. Because the fate of the city was so closely tied to the university, I ended up playing a part in its rebuilding. Tulane's part of the story is about seizing an opportunity and assuming a responsibility that chance presented and, in the midst of chaos and paralysis, taking action. Action meant hard things: challenging tradition, breaking rules, disrupting the status quo, causing pain. But "before" wasn't ever coming back. Everything we did at Tulane was done in the belief that the cost, and there was always a cost, was worth it—because we had to change things, and fast, if we were going to have a future.

The story of the four months after Katrina is really two intertwined tales: what the university did to "build a village" in the flooded and anarchic city, so that students could come back for a spring term, and what happened in the city itself, where civic leaders tried to plan a new urban environment while half of the community was scattered across the entire nation. This chapter describes what we did at Tulane; chapter 2 takes up events in the city. Both narratives cover roughly the same time period: those critical months of posthurricane chaos.

I begin with what happened in the autumn of 2005, when the very idea of a future was in doubt.

IMMEDIATELY AFTER THE STORM, TULANE, like every other institution and business in New Orleans, was scrambling for basic survival. Though the situation was dire, it was also clouded with uncertainty—the fog of disaster. In the end, the facts looked like this:

- More than 1,500 people died in the Greater New Orleans area. Most drowned in their homes or expired in the 100-degree heat of their attics. Many hundreds more died from stress-related illness and inadequate health care in the year following the storm.
- More than 200,000 homes were destroyed, and many more were damaged.

- More than 1 million people—80 percent of the greater metro population—were displaced for at least six weeks, many for months. (And, according to some estimates, 100,000 have still, nearly a decade later, not returned.)
- More than 80 percent of Orleans Parish, or county, was flooded—a landmass equivalent to 7 times the size of Manhattan.
- The hurricane resulted in 22 million tons of debris, more than 12 times the amount of the 9/11 tragedy.
- Katrina has been ranked the most expensive disaster in the history of the United States.[1]

Tulane University was not immune to this devastation. Seventy percent of the main campus and all of the health sciences campus were flooded with water ranging from one to three feet in depth. The university experienced losses in excess of $650 million.

But we didn't know all this at the time; we were dealing with facts as they emerged, day by day, in the aftermath. I was the president; the buck stopped with me. And there were hard decisions to make, actions to take. It was not a time (if there's ever a time) for crowd pleasing or grandstanding or leisurely democratic consensus. It was up to me to decide what would be most effective, productive, fair, and beneficial for a broad range of people and interests.

*"Managers do things right, while leaders do the right things."[2] Doing the right thing is not a matter of correctness or following a blueprint; it frequently entails difficult, controversial decisions, because the "right thing" is often in the eye of the beholder. Yet doing the right thing is what separates true leaders from those who do not have the capacity or insight to search out what's required to resolve complex issues. Leaders ultimately are held accountable for their actions and measured by their achievements; and it's getting things right that determines success versus failure.*

The central theme of this chapter is leadership and the challenges it poses for those who can find the strength and will to effect positive change.

During all of September 2005, following the August 29 landfall of Katrina, the administrative staff was in emergency mode, hunkered down in a hotel room in Houston with a flip chart itemizing the day's top priorities. (Except, that is, for a three-day hiatus in Dallas to escape Hurricane Rita, which, coming less than a month after Katrina, felt like one hurricane too many.) We worked 20-hour days there, people sitting underneath tables and sprawled on couches, taking notes and working cell phones. We'd evacuated the school, at least, but its fate remained uncertain. There was a tremendous sense of urgency. I thought of the old joke: "How do you eat an elephant?" Answer: "One bite at a time." I took my wife's advice; I think of the flip chart as the concrete analog of her suggestion to make a list. We would get things done, one bite at a time.

I concentrated on Tulane, blocking out, as much as I could, the continuous tragedies elsewhere in the city. Some of my colleagues were not as good at compartmentalizing; some were separated from their families, some had lost their homes. I remember a key staffer, one of the administrative vice presidents, who was near meltdown: incapable of making a decision, not eating or sleeping, often on the verge of tears. I called him in and said, "I want you to know that I understand what you're feeling, but I have to ask you: Can you do the job?" He says my question knocked him out of his daze. After we talked, he shook off his paralysis, got down to work, and more than rose to the occasion. Others were not as resilient and, hard as it was, had to be replaced. There was so much to do, none of us could afford to feel things that intensely.

The first thing we did was decide to keep everyone on the payroll, despite the fact that we had no money coming in. It was clear people couldn't manage for months without a paycheck, and without a faculty and staff, we had no university. We'd get the money from reserves, loans, insurance proceeds, and eventually the Federal Emergency Management Agency (FEMA), though the latter became an almost impossible challenge.

Next was communications. David Filo, a Tulane grad who had cofounded Yahoo!, set up an emergency website where I conducted Live Chats with students, parents, and employees. Then we went after Tulane's database—our entire archive of information technology files had been left behind in a downtown high-rise. New Orleans was in lockdown, no one in, no one out, but Harry Lee, the Jefferson Parish sheriff at the time, the one with the magical connections, helped us arrange a raid: A self-designed SWAT team flew into New Orleans by helicopter and carried crates of discs down 14 flights of stairs to waiting trucks and then an airplane, which made it out of the city before curfew fell.

With email back in operation, we at least had a fully functioning virtual community. But physically, the displaced students, more than 13,000 of them, had to go somewhere for the semester. Higher education groups across the country leapt in with aid: Hundreds of colleges and universities offered placements, and most of them, in a move beyond generous, didn't accept tuition for the semester. That meant we could keep the tuition from the fall term to pay faculty and staff during the months of suspended operations.

Another make-or-break question was whether we could persuade students and faculty to come back to New Orleans by January 16, the start date for the second term. Here's where the wider anguish of the city, which had so affected me when I saw TV images on the treadmill in Houston, seeped into my make-a-list mind-set. The city—not news to anyone who has read the Katrina accounts—was a mess; it was no wonder people felt uncertain about returning. It was soon clear that FEMA couldn't manage itself out of a paper bag, and mocking graffiti ("Katrina survivor, FEMA victim," "FEMA Kills," "I've been FEMA-ed") sprouted all over town. The police couldn't handle the looting and crime, which continued long after the storm had passed, and rescue teams couldn't keep up with the bodies of those who'd perished, leaving scrawls on buildings ("1 Dead in Attic"[3]) to direct the coroner to where the corpses were.

City services were very slow to come back. Weeks after the storm, refrigerators full of rotting food still lined the streets; the smell of human waste hung over large portions of town; power hadn't been restored in many neighborhoods; and the New Orleans Parish School Board didn't open a single school in the fall term because of damage to buildings and the diaspora of so many students and teachers. Meanwhile, Ray Nagin, the mayor, seemed paralyzed: At the height of the crisis, he had failed to show up at the Superdome and the Convention Center to tell the huddled refugees what was going on in the city or provide the kind of encouragement and support so desperately needed. Since then he'd appeared in public only rarely, offering the occasional manic pronouncement ("New Orleans will be the new Las Vegas!") but no clear, credible plan of action.

Rage and despair were in the air, and conspiracy theories were beginning to flourish. Chapter 2 describes in detail the heated controversies about what, exactly, had happened in New Orleans and what, exactly, would happen next. In these early months, the media was often oil on the fire; reporters were on the prowl for the most dramatic and contentious storylines, and public figures weighed in with impassioned opinions. The *Wall Street Journal* published a piece suggesting Uptown businessmen who were opposed to rebuilding the flooded African American neighborhoods were plotting to reengineer New Orleans as a white corporate town.[4] Rapper Kanye West said, "President Bush doesn't care about black people." Movie director Spike Lee held similar views, given full expression in his 2006 documentary, *When the Levees Broke.* Civil rights activist Jesse Jackson and Mayor Nagin also subscribed to the view that covert forces at the highest corporate and government levels were conspiring against the majority black population.

I'm slow to believe in conspiracies, but I can personally testify to the government's incompetence and stonewalling, based on a meeting I had with Michael Chertoff, secretary of the Department of Homeland Security, which oversaw FEMA. FEMA, which had been folded into Homeland Security after 9/11, had lost status and funding because of the intense focus on terrorism. From a psychological perspective, natural disasters were a far less satisfying foe than jihadists, and preparedness for such disasters was spotty in many American cities. As with most complex events, there was no one cause for the collapse of aid and rescue in the aftermath of Katrina. But the mind-set of bureaucrats like Chertoff was certainly a major obstacle.

One day in early November, I sat in the steely light of Chertoff's office to make the case for a more flexible interpretation of the Stafford Act. The act was, in essence, a reimbursement regulation guiding FEMA's actions, and completely inadequate for a disaster of the magnitude of Katrina: It required contractors to engage in a long bidding process in order to repair damaged or destroyed property. This was time we didn't have, either at Tulane or in the city at large, if we were to save New Orleans from stagnation and despair.

I tried to impress on Chertoff the situation as I saw it, describing the devastation I'd witnessed, the potentially disastrous consequences of approaching the recovery with a business-as-usual mentality, the need to act boldly and flexibly. But Chertoff, a lawyer by background, would not, or could not, respond in a human way. All his answers were strictly legalistic and canned—he kept citing the language of the Stafford Act, as though scoring points—and his tone was officious. It was like talking to a robot. Finally, I stood up in frustration. "Mr. Secretary, this is getting us nowhere. Thank you for your time, but I'm leaving." I was at the door when he said, "Come back, sit down." We talked for another half hour after that, and his tone veered 180 degrees. He stopped issuing the standard message points and went into listening mode. I left with some hope of help, but it soon became clear that Chertoff was just pacifying me. Ultimately nothing came of the meeting.

His anxiety and defensiveness were not unusual: FEMA administrators, many of them lawyers, felt safer playing by the rules. But after Katrina, those rules were useless: We were operating in a new environment where information was inadequate and coordination was nonexistent. I don't believe there was prejudice or malice at the heart of the government's paralysis, simply incompetence and a paint-by-numbers mentality. Why else was a naval vessel, in the Gulf of Mexico and ready to come in to rescue people, prevented from entering the Mississippi River? Why else was a Coast Guard ship, supplied with thousands of gallons of diesel oil, forbidden by FEMA to send the fuel into Jefferson Parish? Why else were hundreds of other opportunities blown by some functionary who was following ineffective orders or, more likely, had received no orders at all?[5]

President Bush, that self-styled "decider," seemed as incapable of decisiveness as everybody else. I met him several times, not alone but with others—Mayor Nagin, city council members, business leaders—all of us trying to give him a picture of what was happening on the ground and what kind of assistance we needed. I found him easy enough to talk to and sympathetic, with a Texas twang and the habit of giving everyone a nickname. (I was "the big guy.") On the surface, at least, President Bush seemed moved by New Orleans' plight, but that was the totality of his reaction. He seemed unaware of basic facts; mere days after the storm, he congratulated Michael Brown, director of FEMA, for a job well done: "Brownie, you're doing a heck of a job."[6] Same story, in the end, as Chertoff: Whether it was apathy, incompetence, callousness, rigidity, or the unwillingness of his subordinates to respond, nothing happened.

But it was different for those of us on the ground. We could—had to, really—act on our own. My staff started watching the blogs, especially the sites with lots of traffic, and identified the key sources of anxiety for students and parents: housing, environmental issues, and city amenities like restaurants, businesses, and transportation. For faculty and staff, add that they had no place to send their own children to school now that the New Orleans educational system had virtually shut down.

My coworkers and I focused precisely on these issues, determined to stay in operational mode.

- *Housing:* We bought an apartment building and (the idea of a dean at the medical school) rented a cruise ship, anchoring it in the Mississippi.
- *Environment:* Mold remediation and building repairs went forward on schedule, helped by donor contributions because there were no FEMA dollars.
- *Amenities:* Pizza joints, grocery stores, and copy centers around campus were getting ready to reopen.
- *Schools for faculty and staff children:* This, unlike the other items on the list, turned out to be far short of a slam dunk. Our idea was to charter Lusher, a K–8 selective admissions school close to the Tulane campus, turning it into a K–12 school to accommodate all ages. (A previous attempt to charter the school had failed in the spring of 2005.) I put in a call to Kathy Riedlinger, the principal of Lusher, and proposed funding the reopening and expansion; in exchange, she would guarantee spaces

for all faculty and staff children at Tulane, Loyola, Xavier, and Dillard, temporarily exempting them from the usual admissions tests and giving remaining spots, if any, to children in the community. Kathy said, "We have water damage, we have no books, the school board's dysfunctional." I said, "Details, details."

The chartering of Lusher raised one big, uncomfortable question: Were we bumping neighborhood African American kids to make room for the privileged white kids of Tulane faculty? The answer, like everything in New Orleans, is complicated. After Katrina, I was appointed the head of the education task force on Ray Nagin's Bring New Orleans Back Commission, which immediately became known for championing open admissions in all city schools. That Lusher was a selective admissions school—a magnet school for kids with artistic talent—and also, not coincidentally, one of the best public schools in Louisiana, raised red flags: Was Lusher somehow discriminatory? Was Tulane saying one thing but doing another? As part of its expansion, Lusher also assumed control of Fortier High School, one of the most troubled schools in the city and almost exclusively African American. But in its reincarnation as a school for faculty and staff children, Lusher would be about 60 percent white.

It was one of those moments when, depending on your outlook, the needs of the university clashed with the needs of the city. In defense of the plan: Lusher was selective in its admission to begin with, so making it a feeder school for children of Tulane faculty and staff, many of whom lived in the neighborhood, was not such a radical step. Not only Tulane but our partner schools Loyola, Dillard, and Xavier, the latter two historically black colleges, would be able to send their children there. Lusher was already in a white part of town, so very few African American children were affected. There were far fewer African American kids in the schools generally after Katrina because of displaced families. And another way to look at the takeover of Fortier High School was that it was the turnaround of a failing school where, before Katrina, even the valedictorian couldn't graduate because of multiple failures to pass Louisiana's Graduation Exit Exam in math.

But however I frame it, it was a tough call. Was it moral? Was it worth the cost? Ultimately, we can't really know. Each time I do a hard thing, I hope that other choices will come along that might redress the balance sheet.

In chapter 4 I'll be describing education initiatives we launched post-Katrina to tackle the issues of equity sidestepped in the case of Lusher. These issues are permanent sore points in the renewal of New Orleans. The city has had a boom in recent years, directly tied to the post-Katrina influx of money and talent, and we're blossoming into a model for cities across the United States. In fact, the main story of this book is how the city's resurgence is reviving the dream of opportunity and upward mobility that has character-ized our nation from its founding. But I don't want to soften it: New Orleans is an inner city that ranks extremely low on every key measure: jobs, income, safety, health, education, literacy. The bottom line, as in all political mat-ters, is resource allocation—who gets what. We're one happy family in New Orleans, but we're also not; we're the Big Easy and the Big Uneasy. Every decision was going to be hard.

WHEN MARGIE AND I MOVED BACK into the President's Mansion on November 1, the city was still a shambles: drowned neighborhoods, shut-tered businesses, wrecked infrastructure. We couldn't sleep because of the silence—no familiar clang of streetcars running past our house—and Margie couldn't find basic staples, like bread and eggs, on supermarket shelves. I was aware, despite the blasted feeling all around us, that we were the lucky ones; that the wider city was full of stories of loss and desperation. Still, I felt a glimmer of hope about the university. Some basic services were in place, and we hoped to bring a reasonable percentage of our scattered students back. But the crucial question remained: Could we get the school up and running after such severe financial and physical losses?

We were going to have to cut our budget dramatically while maintaining the strength of our academic core and present our plan to parents, students, faculty, and alums as quickly as humanly possible. We created the renewal plan in a space of a few months, chiefly because a recent analysis of school and departmental performance had told us what was strong and what was not, financially and academically. Three of the five departments in the engineering school—civil and environmental engineering, electrical engineering and computer science, and mechanical engineering—were eliminated, and the remaining departments were combined with the sciences to create a new School of Science and Engineering. The men's and women's liberal arts and sciences undergraduate colleges, Tulane College and Newcomb College, previously separate, as well as all other undergraduate programs were merged into a single unit under the name Newcomb-Tulane College, eliminating duplication of effort and confusion regarding the home of undergraduate degree programs. Half of our athletic programs were suspended, along with a third of our doctoral programs.

In December 2005 we announced the necessary cuts and changes. There was an immediate outcry from (no surprise) virtually everyone adversely affected by the changes, including engineering students, Newcomb alums, doctoral students, dismissed faculty, and athletes. It hurt me to explain it, but facts were facts. We had to reshape the school if we wanted it to survive financially and with our academic reputation intact. A blog written by Ashley Morris, a computer science professor at DePaul University with a PhD from Tulane, was widely celebrated for its jazzy, angry riffs; one post in particular, "FYYFF" ("Fuck you, you fucking fucks") accused the federal government and various cities in the United States (Houston, Dallas, and New York, especially) of abandoning New Orleans.[7] One of Morris's posts from late 2005, entitled "R.I.P. Tulane Computer Science," listed the "shocking" elimination of programs, and another from May 2007, entitled "Scott Cowen Strikes Again," elicited a long string of posts about my ruthlessness. These were only a few of many personal attacks.

The medical school was another hard call. Because of the depopulation of the city and the reduced need for clinical services, we had to cut a number of faculty positions. Yet the people who remained in New Orleans were in dire need of health care—suffering from poverty, first and foremost, but also from conditions related to the storm, including stress-related pulmonary and cardiac disease.[8] One of the ironies of the disaster was that it launched a long-needed network of community health centers designed to reach underserved neighborhoods. Since Katrina, more than 90 such centers have sprung up around the city, eight of them Tulane's. Karen DeSalvo, an internist and geriatrician at the medical school, was a leader among those who started this movement. In the days after the storm, with permission from me, she picked a well-trafficked corner downtown, set up a card table, an ice chest with supplies, and a hand-lettered sign ("Tulane Community Health Center"), and staffed the place with Tulane interns and residents. Long lines snaked around the block as poor people, many of them homeless, sought care. Karen's was the kind of action, spontaneous, flexible, can-do, that the government seemed incapable of at the time.

Another big change the university instituted right after Katrina—maybe the biggest, viewed in hindsight—was the public service requirement added to the undergraduate core curriculum. In the aftermath of the storm, I began thinking a lot about the history of Tulane: who we were and who we might become. Going back to its beginnings in 1834—171 years before the storm nearly shattered us—there was another catastrophe, an epidemic of yellow fever that was decimating the population of the Gulf States. In response to this crisis, the Medical College of Louisiana, later renamed the University of Louisiana and then Tulane, was founded with the mission of researching and treating epidemic diseases—which is why our school of tropical medicine, the oldest such school in the United States, remains one of our strongest divisions. Wrestling with the idea of a "new" Tulane, I had the thought, as did others, that we needed to return to our roots—our founding mission of social service and responsibility to the community around us.

And I had the further thought that this was the moment, and this was the place, to address our worst social problems head-on, to aspire and be bold. The American Dream was faltering, and the cracks in our society were only widening as the decade went on and the recession hit. In New Orleans after Katrina, there was no ignoring the chasm between rich and poor, white and black, opportunity and despair; it was all on display.

These thoughts led me to create the Center for Public Service, through which every Tulane student enlists in a program serving the city of New Orleans, whether it's tutoring in the public schools, building houses in the decimated Ninth Ward, working with Native Americans to reconstruct lost dialects, or creating public gardens in urban neighborhoods. Making such service part of the core curriculum forged a connection between the university and the city that is rare in this country. As New Orleans native James Carville, now a professor of political science at Tulane, puts it, "The town *is* the gown." Such relationships are usually fraught with tensions about race, class, education, and, very often, real estate. But with the public service requirement, Tulane bridged many of these fault lines, linking its destiny to its home city. And in turn, it hugely enhanced our fundraising, providing money to fuel innovative projects all over the city. People eager to contribute to the rebuilding of New Orleans gave donations to us because, after Katrina, we were identified with social activism and engagement.[9]

The renewal plan was a lightning rod for anger, but the Center for Public Service, signifying our commitment to civic engagement, has been a home run; it's often cited as one of the most innovative programs of its kind at a major research university. The lifeblood of the program is our undergraduates, who are on the leading edge of movements for social justice and fairness and believe that, through their personal choices and actions, they can make the world better. Their idealism drives community change and urban renewal in a way that chief executives and committee members, however well meaning, cannot.

All of this brings me, in a circuitous way, back to Lusher. When we provided the means for faculty and staff to return to New Orleans, we set the stage for everything that came after, including a new commitment to solving the problems of any urban community, starting with ours.

*A first principle of leadership is Do the right thing, despite opposition. Leaders have the realism to face the facts, the wisdom to weigh the options, the will to make a decision, and the audacity to act. Which is another way of saying, Stand up and do what you think is best.*

Apart from my fight with the American Association of University Professors on the firing of tenured professors plus a few other things, like defending lawsuits and chasing FEMA for what it owed us, the months after Katrina didn't feature many showdowns. Mostly that period was devoted to making lists, adding up numbers, and getting things done. But bottom lines and organizational strategy don't appeal much to people who are on the wrong end of a decision—something much on my mind as I sat at my desk in December 2005 composing a letter to the students and others about the renewal plan. Many of the students were mad because their major had been cut or their doctoral program was being phased out and because no one had consulted them. I chose my words carefully, explaining that we'd had to abandon the university principle of shared governance for the more urgent goal of survival, especially since people were scattered across the country, and I emphasized that the restructuring made room for gradual transitions, substitute programs, and transfers to other institutions. Though I was effective at defending the plan, I was worried: Would it save the school? Would it, as we hoped, make Tulane better than it ever was?

Somewhere in the middle of my second paragraph, Margie came in and sat down in the chair she always sits in when she needs to discuss something important. She said, "Patrick wrote me."

Patrick was our house manager, a combination contractor, restaurateur, event planner, and booking agent who'd been with us since we came to New Orleans. He'd disappeared after the storm, and we'd heard nothing for months.

"And?"

"And he's not coming back."

This was a big disappointment. Convocation "Déjà vu"—the greeting to the incoming freshman that had been interrupted by Katrina—was only a few weeks away, and soon we'd be hosting events for visiting academics, politicians, celebrities. Patrick knew everyone and could do everything—arrange flowers, get the best prawns in town, book Wynton Marsalis. The whole first floor of the President's Mansion was public space, with reception rooms, dining areas, and a serious kitchen for serious entertaining. Margie and I had made a private apartment for ourselves upstairs, but downstairs was Patrick's domain.

"Where is he?" I asked.

"Alabama. He has family there."

"He's going to stay in Alabama?" It was hard to believe. Patrick was New Orleans through and through.

"He lost his house, and some friends died in the storm. He just doesn't want to come back."

I wondered how many Patricks there were out there, making the same decision. I said to Margie, "Can you start looking for someone?"

She nodded. "But it will take some doing."

I was going to miss him; he was capable and responsible but also funny, cheerful, and a great raconteur. I thought of him in Alabama—he'd become part of the diaspora of New Orleanians all across the South, many of whom might never return. One would expect the post-Katrina flight, given that it was in response to a natural disaster, would have fallen on everyone roughly equally, but race remained a factor—the flooded communities were mainly poor and African American, and the lack of resources meant fewer, or no, options.[10]

I went back to writing my letter to the mainly white, mainly privileged students of Tulane. I was "in here," at my comfortable desk in my comfortable house. Patrick was "out there," swept from safety by the chaos of Katrina. Could the school and the city, together, bridge that divide?

# Chapter 2

# CHOCOLATE CITY

## SEEK COMMON GROUND

I'VE JUST COME FROM A MEETING WITH MITCH LANDRIEU, OUR current mayor, on crime in the city. The statistics are shockingly bad, and we're trying to brainstorm about what to do. I sit down at my desk and glance at the *Times-Picayune.* COPS CONVICTED IN DANZIGER BRIDGE SHOOTINGS blares the front page, referring to an event that occurred years ago, only a few days after Katrina. I'm instantly reminded what we're up against in New Orleans: not just violent individuals, but a dark history of festering wounds.

Back then, of course, in the days after the storm, it was a unique set of circumstances. The fog of disaster hovered over New Orleans—people had no food, water, or power, and there was a pervasive sense of lawlessness and impending chaos. Many terrible events transpired, including the tragedy on the Danziger Bridge. The basics of that tragedy: Four New Orleans Police Department cops riding in a Budget rental truck drove onto the bridge; the officers later claimed to be responding to a report of gunshots in the area. People from the low-lying neighborhoods, now under ten feet of water, were crossing over the Industrial Canal to get to a supermarket on the other side of the bridge. The officers fired guns on the walkers, all of them African American, and all unarmed, killing two and grievously wounding four others. One of the dead was a mentally disabled man, shot in the back by an African American police officer. The first lawsuit wended its slow way through the Louisiana judicial system, ending in a mistrial because of irregularities in the prosecutor's handling of the case. In 2012, nearly seven years after the event, a federal judge has handed down sentences. The black police officer has been sentenced to 65 years; two others have received jail terms of 40 years, and a fourth, 38 years. A sergeant charged with conspiracy to cover up the crime, including planting a handgun at the scene and attempting to charge the mentally disabled man's brother with shooting at the police, got six years.

The blogosphere has responded with the usual cacophony: outraged citizens decrying the racist police, members of the force saying hey, it's black people killing black people and, besides, we have to defend ourselves. Everyone has an opinion. But the Danziger tragedy does underscore one enduring truth of New Orleans, sometimes called the homicide capital of the United States: Not only in the fog of disaster but, as statistics show us, in the ordinary murk of daily urban life fear and distrust are hair-trigger elements that can explode into violence at any moment.

It's ironic that the tragedy occurred in this particular place, given who Alfred Danziger was. A prominent Jewish lawyer who served as Huey Long's personal attorney—one can only imagine what gray areas he found himself in, serving a governor notorious for flamboyance—Danziger was one of the most socially responsible voices in New Orleans in the 1930s and 1940s. An advocate of flood control legislation, he was also a chief fundraiser for Dillard University, the historically black college created by white philanthropists for the education of African Americans in the Jim Crow era. The bridge named for Danziger carries seven lanes of Route 90 traffic across the

Industrial Canal; it's the widest vertical lift bridge in the world. And now it's linked with a police atrocity on a par with the Rodney King incident. In New Orleans, history—to borrow a line from Shakespeare—is "a mingled yarn, good and ill together."

One way of looking at Danziger Bridge is that Katrina opened up the floodgates of a complicated and troubled history; the poison of the past seeped through, and the wounds of race and poverty were brought to the surface. Every city in America has these wounds, but for the most part, we don't talk about them, or about what caused them, long ago, in the pre-Civil War and Jim Crow eras. In New Orleans, the first year after the hurricane was rife with dissension, suspicion, and antagonism—a background of discord that far predated the events of August 2005. How does a leader overcome deep, fierce divisions between groups of people in order to forge workable, durable solutions?

*Finding common ground, the leadership principle of this chapter, is the fundamental basis for any positive action. Effective leaders have the ability to find commonalities and bring people together because they are good listeners, can see all points of view, empathize with those who may oppose them, and find the connecting tissue of ideas that forms the basis of principled and fact-based decisions. They don't demonize, personalize, pander to, or belittle the thinking of opponents. And they don't attempt to find the least-common-dominator solution to an issue. Instead, they do what they feel is right and openly and candidly explain the rational basis for their decisions.*

I'm going to frame the main story of this chapter—events that occurred throughout the city when New Orleans "reopened" after Katrina, and the steps I took to find community and consensus in the midst of intense divisions—with a short trip into the city's past, because everything else is profoundly shaped by that history. Beginning in the eighteenth century, slavery in New Orleans took on a particularly complex structure because of the succession of Mediterranean colonial powers that ruled it—first French, then Spanish—and the cultural influences of Saint-Domingue (later Haiti), Cuba, and Africa, where the slaves originated. As the largest city in the South in the antebellum period, New Orleans was a center of human trafficking, where auctions were held and people were wrenched away from their families to work the sugarcane plantations, which were especially violent and repressive places for slaves. At the same time, perhaps because France and Spain were more worldly and tolerant than England, there was an unusual degree of racial intermingling and social acceptance in the city. Slaves could complain of abuses to the Spanish king, and, more important, they could arrange to buy their freedom, which led to a class of economically independent free men and women.

Racial mixing was another unique feature of New Orleans: There were many incentives to cohabit, involving, for white men, a scarcity of white women to partner with and, for women of color, the desire for economic security and status. It was also customary for white men to acknowledge paternity of and grant property to mixed-race children. The result was a society in which ethnic strains—not just "black" and "white," but French, Spanish, Italian, Irish, German, Native American, Caribbean, and African—intermingled, and words like *mulatto, quadroon,* and *mestizo* were coined to categorize the bloodlines, skin colors, and castes of an intricate melting pot.

All of these historical and cultural circumstances created the peculiar contradictions of New Orleans, a brutal slave-trading town but also a place where many people—Creoles, Cajuns, Native Americans—were racially mixed, and free people of color walked the streets. The Sunday celebrations of music and dance at Congo Square, where hundreds of unsupervised slaves were allowed to gather and people of various castes mingled together, is one symbol of the city's extraordinary ethos.[1]

During Reconstruction, New Orleans witnessed a brief period of something like equality under the aegis of the Radical Republican party: a black-owned newspaper, black doctors and lawyers, integrated schools, and sections of the city like Treme, the oldest black neighborhood in the United States, where the streets were a checkerboard of black and white households. In the state of Louisiana, the newly enfranchised African American majority elected a black lieutenant governor and a state legislature that was 50 percent black. The first black governor in the United States, serving for 35 days after the governor was impeached, dates to this period of relative racial balance.[2]

It was, in a way, the world we're still striving for—people of all colors living together with mutual respect and tolerance. But this Reconstruction society proved tragically short-lived, dismantled with brutal efficiency by white coalitions. As the saying goes, the Confederates lost the war but they won the peace; with the withdrawal of federal troops in 1877, state governments all across the South, including Louisiana, imposed repressive measures on African Americans. Literacy tests, a poll tax, and other forms of intimidation put an end to black participation at the polls, and lynchings served as visceral warnings: An archival photograph shows a body swinging from a tree with a placard hanging on it that reads "This Negro voted."[3]

It's an irony that Jim Crow first became codified as legal doctrine in Louisiana, and specifically in New Orleans, the most tolerant, permissive, and open city in the South. The 1896 Supreme Court case *Plessy v. Ferguson*, which established "separate but equal" as the law of the land, came out of an attempt by the Citizens' Committee, a coalition of black, Creole, and white New Orleans residents, to test what was known as the Separate Car Act, passed by Louisiana in 1892. Homer Plessy, an octoroon—one-eighth black—born a free man, agreed to buy a first-class ticket on the East Louisiana Railroad, traveling from New Orleans to Covington in the whites-only car. The sequence of events that followed was New Orleans street theater at its finest: Plessy, a quiet shoemaker, had been picked for the part because, even though he personally identified himself as a black man, he routinely passed as white. The Citizens' Committee actually had to arrange for him to be arrested: They tipped off the East Louisiana Railroad, which was opposed to the Separate Car Act because of the expense of maintaining an entire extra car for a single black citizen. The conductor was instructed to ask Plessy his race, and when he replied that he was "colored," to ask him to go to the colored car. Plessy refused, and an official waiting at Press and Royal

Streets in New Orleans forced him off the train and arrested him for violating the law.[4]

The entire episode was designed to raise the question "Who, really, is Homer Plessy?" In his own person, he showed that identity was too varied and complex to be controlled by state doctrine and that a law based on a binary code of black and white made no sense. Looking at him, you couldn't tell the difference. But in the 1890s, the "one drop" of African American blood Homer Plessy had inherited from his great-grandmother made him, according to the Separate Car Act, one color, period.[5]

The lawyers defending Plessy brought suit against the state of Louisiana, and ultimately the case went to the Supreme Court, which rejected the argument that Plessy's rights had been violated under the Thirteenth Amendment, which prohibits slavery, and the Fourteenth Amendment, which guarantees equal rights. Justice Henry Brown wrote that separation did not imply inferiority and that the Fourteenth Amendment was not intended to enforce social, as opposed to political, equality.

The *Plessy v. Ferguson* decision launched 70 years of discrimination in every facet of life, including education: Schools were resegregated and state colleges funded by federal land grants under the Morrill Act of 1862 had a whites-only rule, a policy that essentially created an underclass with little hope of rising out of poverty.[6] The intricate, intertwined society of New Orleans slowly gave way to a more typical stratification, in the South particularly, with racial categories growing ever more distinct and separate. And it's in this context that we must view the events of more than a century later, post-Katrina.

ON MARTIN LUTHER KING DAY, JANUARY 16, 2006, Mayor Ray Nagin gave his famous "chocolate city" speech, explicitly calling for an "African American city," the city that, he said, God wanted. Some people saw the speech as an attempt to tap into African American support in the face of the upcoming mayoral election. But whatever the motivation, it was racially divisive at the very moment when we needed to put aside identity politics and pull together.

**Image 2** Clinton Bush Cowen

Former Presidents Bill Clinton and George H.W. Bush with Scott Cowen at Tulane Commencement, May 13, 2006. In the months after the storm, Clinton and Bush worked together on a Katrina Fund that raised 130 million dollars.

(*Photo credit: Paula Burch-Celentano, Tulane University*)

From another angle, though, Nagin's speech revealed an oft-evaded truth about New Orleans: The melting-pot city has been largely abandoned by white people, who in the 1960s and 1970s, after *Brown v. the Board of Education* ended "separate but equal," fled to the suburbs, with the remaining white sections of town reduced to small, distinct enclaves. It's been said that in New Orleans, elevation is destiny: After the levees broke, wealthy white Uptown stayed mainly dry, while poor black neighborhoods built on swampland were obliterated by floodwaters. When Nagin said, "I don't care what people are saying Uptown or wherever they are, this city will be chocolate at the end of the day," he was describing a town that had suddenly, overnight, been reduced to black and white.

Ray called me after the speech—I knew him well from our work on the Bring New Orleans Back (BNOB) Commission—and asked me what I thought. I said, "Why did you give this speech? Aren't I and a whole lot of other people from Uptown busting our chops to help you rebuild the city?"

Ray said, "I'm not talking about you." I shot back, "Then who the hell are you talking about, and why?" There was silence on the line.

Ray had been elected, in large part, by Uptown, who saw him as smart and idealistic and, as a former cable company executive, a good manager. In political terms, he was a perfect crossover candidate, one who understood both minority experience and the mainstream. But the storm changed that for all of us: It was no longer easy to work together, or to "cross over."

A meeting months before, in Dallas, may have inadvertently planted the seeds for Nagin's outburst. I was among the 40 or so attendees, mainly white businessmen who were trying to help the mayor formulate a plan for recovery. Two friends of mine were also involved: Jimmy Reiss, chairman of the Regional Transit Authority, and Joe Canizaro, founder and chairman of a local bank and a real estate developer, who wasn't physically present but talked to Nagin by phone during the proceedings. Both of them got unfairly slammed in the media for statements they made at the time. Jimmy was quoted in the *Wall Street Journal* as saying that the city should be rebuilt "in a completely different way: demographically, geographically and politically."[7] In an article in the *New York Times*, Joe said, "I think we have a clean sheet to start again. And with that clean sheet we have some very big opportunities."[8]

A widespread reaction to these remarks was that these men were racists who wanted to reengineer New Orleans as a smaller, whiter city. As the waters of Katrina receded, there was a rising tide of distrust in the city, fed by provocative news reports and bits of hearsay. Floating around town were rumors of bombed levees, disaster profiteering, and political cronyism. Was Halliburton, the oilfield services corporation formerly run by Dick Cheney, making money off this? Why were there Blackwater operatives, quasi-military private security agents, in town? Was it all a plot to rid New Orleans of its black population?

Another element in the toxic brew was a private interview between Nagin and Louis Farrakhan, a civil rights activist and Muslim leader, which took place at the airport as the mayor was heading back to New Orleans immediately after the Dallas meeting. During the interview, Farrakhan asked Nagin whether, in fact, the levees had been bombed to flood out the black population. Farrakhan came out of the interview convinced that they had, based on what Nagin told him about a 25-foot crater in the levee walls. Nagin says otherwise: He told Farrakhan, no, the levees had not been bombed—but he also promised Farrakhan that he would defend the "poor and elderly," a tacit acceptance of Farrakhan's militant view that this was a war of rich against poor, white against black.[9]

Spike Lee echoed Farrakhan, saying that what had happened in New Orleans was, no question, a plot against black people. Such talk sounds extremist, even crazy—except that similar schemes have actually been carried out in the city. In 1927 an elite group of white bankers led by James Pierce Butler, head of the Canal Street Bank, decided to blast the levee at Caernarvon, south of new Orleans, and flood St. Bernard and Plaquemines Parishes in order to reassure investors that the city was safe from flooding after months of heavy rainstorms. As the waters continued to rise, crevasses flooded upriver and inundated the surrounding fields, relieving the pressure on downstream levees. Isaac Cline, chief of the regional bureau of the U.S. Weather Bureau, maintained that New Orleans was perfectly safe—but that didn't deter Butler and his associates from going ahead with their original plan. When upstream levees broke a day later, it became evident that the bombing was unnecessary as a flood control measure, raising serious questions of motive and intent. This much was clear: The destruction devastated two communities and exiled thousands of black sharecroppers, who were never compensated for their losses. Ultimately, they joined the Great Migration of 1910 to 1970, leaving for northern cities, never to return.[10] In 1965 Hurricane Betsy had similar disastrous results for the lowlying parishes where African Americans lived, and rumors flew then too—groundless, as it turned out—that someone had destroyed the levees to protect the prosperous French Quarter.

Given this tangled history, it's little wonder that, after Katrina, anxieties were running high. The media's skeptical take on the Dallas meeting, followed by Nagin's inflammatory chocolate city speech, set the stage for a collapse of communal resolve. Ray Nagin's recovery task force, the BNOB

Commission, in operation for about a year after the storm and charged with reinventing the city, was a follow-up to the impromptu Dallas gathering, and it was supposed to lead the way to a brighter future; but the seeds of suspicion had already been planted, and the shadows of the past persisted.

The commission's key recommendation for the physical rebuilding of the city came from Joe Canizaro's Urban Planning Action Committee, and it was an incendiary one: Don't rebuild in the hardest-hit neighborhoods—places below sea level, like the Lower Ninth Ward, New Orleans East, and Gentilly, all historically black—because they will inevitably flood again, and instead turn those low-lying areas into green space. The report included a map entitled "Parks and Open Space Plan," with green dots representing proposed parkland in each of the flooded wards.[11] What followed was a furious debate on the footprint of the city and how big the new New Orleans should be. At a commission hearing, one resident from the "bowl," the flooded neighborhoods below sea level, said, "How many people from my backyard are up there? I'm ready to rebuild and I'm not letting you take mine." Another said, "Over my dead body. Like I said, I didn't die with Katrina."[12]

You could say these responses were posttraumatic and hyperemotional, but again, from a historical perspective, the distrust was warranted. In the late 1960s, "urban planning"—a threatening phrase to many—had led to the construction of the I-10, a swath of freeway that cut right through the heart of Treme, with historic black neighborhoods razed to the ground. Now the commission's proposed redesign of New Orleans came with the threat of more obliteration and more discrimination. Representative Richard Baker, a Louisiana Republican, was overheard saying what many believed: "We finally cleaned up public housing in New Orleans. We couldn't do it, but God did."[13]

After Joe Canizaro's report on the flooded neighborhoods became public, this painful history erupted, splintering people into fierce factions: rich against poor, entrepreneurs against community activists, Republicans versus Democrats, trickle-down economists versus social innovators. I believe that the Urban Planning group, though probably headed for a collision no matter what, never meant to send a message of "Don't come back," but it failed to clearly enunciate its ideas, and the message got garbled. The Urban Planning committee, originally with Nagin's approval, also put a burden on people to "prove" their right to be there; basically, residents had to return to the most heavily flooded neighborhoods in order to achieve a critical mass in a given area and thus win building permits from the city. But return how, and to what? Apart from the fact that people had no money to travel, these neighborhoods had no utilities or grocery stores or temporary housing. (The FEMA trailer story was already becoming a long-running joke.) No health care. No schools. No services for the elderly, the disabled, the mentally ill. No jobs, and hence no money to live on in the interim. So in practice, the message appeared to be "Come on back, and good luck with that."[14]

In the end, Nagin simply dodged the issue of whether to rebuild in the low-lying areas; he returned to his initial repopulation plan, with phased reentry focusing on dry sections of the city. He avoided a definitive answer to the question of what to do with the flooded poor neighborhoods, basically allowing market forces—insurance companies, banks, and consumers—to decide the boundaries of the city and the fate of the Lower Ninth.[15] Again, it's impossible to really know Nagin's motives, whether political self-interest or a more emotional response to the pain of residents, but the results were clearly negative: No plan meant chaos, and eventually "Jungleland"—a Ninth Ward with odd outcroppings, like actor Brad Pitt's "Make It Right" houses in a huge swamp of snake-infested vegetation.

It's tempting to blame everything on Ray, but circumstances shape things more than we like to think. The troubled racial history of the town inevitably surfaced after Katrina, and if it hadn't been Ray with his chocolate city speech, it would undoubtedly have been someone else stirring the pot. At the same time, character matters. Leadership matters. Our job as civic leaders was to work with the difficult realities, including the realities of racial distrust, political dissension, and the traumatic effects of loss and dislocation.

To be fair, the BNOB Commission did try. A wealth of effort and a flood of words went into the documents issued by its various subcommittees.

Every report—Health and Social Services, Culture, Education, even Urban Planning—included passionate language about equity, social justice, and the unique opportunity, post-Katrina, to solve all the inadequacies of a failing inner city. Committee members were all thinking boldly and creatively; for example, the Cultural Committee envisioned a Jazz District downtown, the Urban Planning group proposed a light rail system connecting all parts of the city, the Health and Social Services group proposed introduction of city-wide electronic medical records.

All of us (and I include myself, as chairman of the Education Committee) were engaged in reimagining the city from scratch. It was like the SimCity scenario of postapocalyptic problem solving, only this was for real—this could change people's actual lives. Intentions, I believe, were good. To Ray's credit, he had the right instinct: Bring the strongest leaders and the best minds together to brainstorm their way to a renaissance.

And the commission had some successes. I think the Education Committee did better than some, for several reasons. First, despite the difficulties of reaching those in exile, there was a concerted effort to bring in the varied voices of the community, including interviews, public hearings, and web-based communications. Second, we may have framed our propositions more persuasively, using what I would call "visual" rhetoric. We had a steering committee of 20 people, a third of whom were African American, from organizations that were important in the community. At hearings about public education K–12, these committee members sat up at the front of the room, listening to concerns and answering questions. Just their presence—the fact that this was, in a sense, an in-group conversation—made the education recommendations much more acceptable than if some white guy (like me) simply handed down a bunch of proposals and reforms. But even these efforts would have failed if it weren't for a third, critical factor: We all had a common goal—to better educate our children, regardless of zip code.

Other subcommittees also organized around a common purpose that defused tensions and opened the door for future action. For example, the Health and Social Services Committee ultimately made headway with the community because of urgently needed services and a widespread consensus that health care needed an overhaul. The committee's recommendations included community health centers tailored to a diverse population; treatment for the uninsured across a number of hospitals now that Charity, the chief safety-net hospital, had been permanently closed; implementation of citywide electronic medical records, as mentioned; "healthy neighborhoods," with parks and fresh foods; and outreach on preventive care. The Culture Committee, with the agreed-on aim of preserving the city's rich artistic heritage, proposed rebuilding community resources for musicians and artists, plus a program of cultural ambassadors that would attract money and audiences to post-Katrina New Orleans. The Economic group emphasized supports for small businesses, local hiring, tax incentives and credits, and a wide-ranging set of initiatives to get funding and generate investment.

Yet despite everyone's efforts, the BNOB Commission largely failed to unify the community. The people of New Orleans were scattered across every state in the nation, and half were unable to return to the city in the first year. Many had no access to a computer. The commission produced handsome PowerPoint presentations and impassioned manifestos, but in many instances the audience couldn't hear us or see us.

And it wasn't only a failure of communication. As we thought up our great ideas, we were neglecting a stubborn reality. At this moment, people didn't want visionary improvements and urban renewal. They wanted their old neighborhoods back: shotgun houses, front porches, the corner convenience store, the church and school they knew. They wanted the network of relationships, the gathering places, even the old bus routes; they wanted their old jobs back.

The longing for "home" was, I think, at the heart of the anger over the urban renewal plans. The Urban Planning Committee was never going to achieve a commonality of purpose; in fact, it was headed toward a donnybrook, no matter what it proposed, because land has always been limited in New Orleans, sandwiched as it is on high ground between a bend in the river and Lake Pontchartrain. Was the high ground the only ground that should be redeveloped? Was the Urban Planning report really a way to say to hell with the black neighborhoods? Even if our approach had been savvier, I'm not sure there would have been a way, back in 2006, to satisfy the yearning for what the storm had taken away.

CITY PLANNING, LIKE ALL PLANNING, is rarely simple or rational, given the competing agendas and intense emotions amplified by layers of subterranean history. Policy makers often try to make it rational, giving precedence to statistics and bullet points over "irrelevancies" like really engaging with people. But in the immediate aftermath of Katrina, at a time of chaos and despair, it seemed particularly important to acknowledge the rage and the heartbreak while at the same time try to help those who'd been most hurt by the disaster. The essential question: Given that the Lower Ninth was on indefinite hold, how could we preserve the heart and soul of New Orleans, now that so many African American residents had been forced into exile and the inner city was depopulated?

We at Tulane struggled hard with the question of what the university could do, immediately, concretely, to address people's pain and strengthen the city's decimated core. We looked close to home, in the academic community—the source of so much of New Orleans' vitality—focusing particularly on the black academic community. And we endeavored to partner with the other universities, especially Dillard, to help one another recover.

Of the six universities in New Orleans, Dillard was the hardest hit by Katrina: Its campus in Gentilly was completely destroyed, every building, except (miraculously) the chapel, filled with six to ten feet of water. Dillard has a special place among the city's institutions of higher education because, along with Xavier University, it's classified as a Historically Black College and University (HBCU)—schools established in reaction to the post–Civil War whites-only policy of state universities, and a continuing force for upward mobility in the black community.[16] After Katrina, Tulane formed a consortium with the other area universities, including Dillard and Xavier and our next-door neighbor, Loyola, to strengthen all our chances of survival. Dillard and Xavier were particularly vulnerable to financial stress, on top of the flood damage they endured. Norman Francis, the president of Xavier—winner of the Medal of Freedom for his contributions in education, rightfully considered a national treasure in Louisiana, and the longest-sitting university president in the United States—was able to call on his many relationships to rebuild his university, which was also severely damaged but not quite to the same extent as Dillard.[17] Dillard was really another story.

At the helm was Marvalene Hughes, who'd arrived in July 2005 after an 11-year stint as president of California State University at Stanislaus; she'd been in New Orleans exactly two months when Katrina drowned Dillard's campus. Ironically, Marvalene had moved from California to New Orleans to avoid the threat of earthquakes. She'd already inherited a fiscal crisis involving a small endowment and shrinking enrollment. Even before the storm, she'd heard from trustees and alumni that the school should be moved to Atlanta, and post-Katrina, the pressure to relocate was intense.

I made a call to Marvalene, urging her to keep Dillard in New Orleans and offering a close partnership with Tulane in the period of recovery, including housing, classroom space, the use of facilities, and shared courses, plus enrollment at Lusher School for faculty offspring. Her one immediate request was that I fly with her to Atlanta to meet with her board of trustees and make the case for Dillard's staying. In the end, the two of us convinced the board members that Dillard should remain.

As for the rest, Marvalene mostly chose to go it alone—not really a surprise, given the history of HBCUs as separate but equal institutions. She moved to the downtown Hilton Hotel, where Dillard students also lived and where courses were offered for the spring term, and she embarked on a series of nationwide fundraising trips to solicit donations. Some students took advantage of the Tulane facilities, but many stuck with whatever courses Dillard was offering at the Hilton. Though enrollment fell because of cuts to faculty and curriculum, the essential goal had been accomplished: Dillard, a valued institution with a precious history, would remain in New Orleans.

Though Dillard only partly accepted Tulane's offer of help, the offer itself was one small step toward the healing of a painful wound—a much-needed recognition, however symbolic, of a distinctive racial identity that emerged from our nation's most shameful historical chapter. Separate is not equal, as the 1954 *Brown v. Board of Education* case finally established, and yet there is something about separateness that is valuable, particularly in redressing the national trauma of slavery. The enduring significance of HBCUs lies in helping young people see what they might become in a place of safety and nurturing, which may be a kind of inoculation against the persistent, deep-rooted prejudice of our nation.

Still, separateness is not our country's preferred answer to the question of diversity. The ideals of our nation are deeply wedded to the notion of a melting pot, where we're not chocolate or vanilla but "rainbow" and where we all have equal opportunity. Unfortunately, that ideal may remain beyond reach, not only because of the stubbornness of fixed identity but because of the glitch in our brains that's forever establishing pecking orders or flashing on stereotypes. Comedian Dave Chappelle has a skit about a racial "draft," where teams of African Americans, Hispanics, Jews, Asians, and Caucasians compete to adopt biracial celebrities, or, in a few instances, black icons who "pass" as white. Who gets Tiger Woods? (The black team!) Colin Powell? (The white team!) Lenny Kravitz? (Jews!) Chappelle is making fun but also making a point. Something in us asks, "Who are you? What are you?" It's basically the same question that Homer Plessy, with his "one drop" of African blood, posed. Mixtures and rainbows complicate things; they undermine stereotypes and unsettle minds; they threaten certainty.

During the LA riots of 1992, Rodney King famously asked, "Can we all get along?" The reason we can't lies in our divisions, our differences, our distrust. But in New Orleans we do, on occasion, all get along. One way the city holds onto both its diversity and its unity is through Carnival. The day before Ash Wednesday, Mardi Gras ("Fat Tuesday") is a celebration of indulgence before the onset of austerity at Lent. It's also linked to folk rituals of misrule in which social aggression is released as satire, play, topsy-turvy: Everyone's disguised, mischief is made, no one's punished, and no harm's done. The occasion for wayward eccentricity and expressiveness, Mardi Gras is also a celebration of communal joy and fellow feeling.

To me, New Orleans exhibits some aspects of a postracial vision, where everyone is simply his or her own wayward self, and some aspects of the media's preferred storyline, involving the melodramatic clash of black and white. The undertow of our national history and the lingering effects of a traumatic past will continue to affect African Americans, but there's also New Orleans itself, which encourages a shrug and a laugh, a "let the good times roll." Our politics in recent years, particularly under the stress of the recession, has splintered our nation into its component parts, and we tend to define ourselves in terms of color, creed, ethnic identification, party affiliation, economic class. But New Orleans is onto something with its openness, its amiability, its civility. As John T. Scott, a New Orleans artist, put it, "...the city has a oneness about it that very few places in the rest of the country have. New Orleans' promise is we can teach America how to be America, if anyone's listening."[18] And the message, if anyone's listening, is this: We're all capable of finding our common humanity and reaching for goals we all cherish.

But how, exactly, do we do it? What are the steps?

*In order to find common ground, leaders need to acknowledge both the pain and the views of others and then take active steps to defuse aggression by focusing on sound processes and jointly held goals. They should seek opportunities to bring people together, openly and respectfully discuss differences, commit to finding mutual goals, and celebrate when those goals are met.*

The last point is typically, uniquely New Orleans, where there's always something to celebrate if you're willing to join in the party.

IT'S GRADUATION DAY, MAY 2006, and we're having a star-studded ceremony. Celebrities are almost expected here now—in recent months, we've been visited by Cokie Roberts and Harry Connick Jr., New Orleans natives; Brian Williams, who's become a friend; Brad Pitt, Wendell Pierce and the *Treme* crew, Michael Lewis and Walter Isaacson, who all want to come and help. But today is extra special, with speeches from former presidents George H. W. Bush and Bill Clinton, who have been working together on a Katrina Fund that's raised $130 million, and music by clarinetist Michael White. Ellen DeGeneres shows up in a bathrobe ("They told me everybody would

**Image 3** Ray Nagin

Mayor Ray Nagin in a horse-drawn carriage, greeting constituents on the streets of New Orleans. On Martin Luther King Day, January 16, 2006, Nagin delivered his controversial Chocolate City speech, calling for an African American city, "the way God wants it to be." The speech came at a moment when the city was struggling with the difficult question of whether to rebuild in the low-lying, predominantly African American, neighborhoods.

*(Photo credit: Paula Burch-Celentano, Tulane University)*

be wearing robes") and offers sage advice to the graduating class ("Hydrate, exfoliate, moisturize...").

A special moment comes right at the beginning, when Irvin Mayfield, the young trumpeter, performs the national anthem. At age 28, he's a creative force. Named the cultural ambassador of New Orleans, he's also director of NOJO, the New Orleans Jazz Orchestra, which was in residence at Dillard until the campus sank under ten feet of water. This semester he brought the organization to Tulane. He's on the board of everything, the BNOB

Commission, Tulane's School of Architecture, and he's bringing his music into the public schools of New Orleans. The son of an army veteran and a schoolteacher, he had a scholarship to Juilliard but went to the University of New Orleans instead because Ellis Marsalis, who was head of the jazz program there, asked him to.

His trumpet sounds like a human voice, throbbing, soaring. You can almost hear tears in the "Star-Spangled Banner," the way he plays it, and I think of what we're trying to do in the city—how we're trying to revive the dream of opportunity that defines our nation. And I think what it means that Irvin Mayfield is playing at graduation. His father drowned in the flooding after Katrina; his body was found several months after the storm, on a street named Elysian Fields. The corpses of the city make for a wrenching, heart-breaking story: decomposed bodies identifiable only by DNA and dental records; the horror of not knowing, followed by the horror of knowing.

And still we try to heal. Graduation is a glittering event, a thrilling moment; twirling handkerchiefs, snowstorms of confetti, pulsating music, feet tapping and bodies on the move. It's one of those public rituals meaningful in every detail, from the student in her graduation robes raising up a sign in block letters, TULANE LIVES, to Irvin Mayfield, who lost everything in the storm, transmuting sorrow into joy, despair into hope.

## Chapter Three

# THE CITY THAT CARE FORGOT

## MARSHAL FACTS

MARGIE AND I ARE AT BREAKFAST; I CHECK MY IPAD FOR THE day's appointments, then click over to nola.com, the online version of the *Times-Picayune*, for news. It ain't good, this October morning: three murders in the last week, which means 2012's homicide rate is likely to be as bad as 2011's. One of the reports catches my eye: Joshua Short, 25, of Dumaine Street. In a city full of sad stories, this one stops me. I know the name—his twin brother, Jonathan, is a student at Tulane. Josh's story is filled with ironies: He was outside the home of a teen he mentored when he got shot; he'd just attended a Night Out Against Crime rally; he died on Dumaine Street, the street where he grew up.

Here was a young man who looked like he'd make it. He'd been adrift, with no family support, when he got involved in the documentary *Left Behind: The Story of the New Orleans Public Schools*, both as an assistant filmmaker and as one of its subjects. The movie described the rough lives the twins had had, surviving three years of high school with both parents completely absent. Inspired by his experience making the movie, Josh enrolled in Delgado Community College's film production program. He joined the Fyre Youth Squad and the One World Foundation, traveling to India to talk to underserved youth, then coming back to New Orleans to work with the kids of his hometown. In the article, Jonathan says, "My brother had a heart of gold. He didn't really believe too much in adults. But he knew kids were the future."

The irony is complete: Josh himself has no future.

A story like this makes me want to do something. How many more Joshes will this city have to lose before we change? Josh's death is sadly similar to many of New Orleans's homicides, up to 200 of them a year: a young black male shot in the head, assailant unknown, motive unknown. Mayor Landrieu has made the point that, in a six-month period, a student attending a school in a high-crime neighborhood in New Orleans had a greater risk of dying than a combat soldier in Afghanistan.[1]

Most of these victims, like the murderers, are poor and black. The inner city has become a war zone.[2] One of the epithets for New Orleans is "The City that Care Forgot." It's a phrase with a double resonance: the place you go to forget your cares—the land of Mardi Gras and hurricane parties, of Bourbon Street and jazz, of gumbo and muffulettas—but also the city no one cares about. Garland Robinette, a radio personality in New Orleans, said that the government abandoned the city after Katrina because "we're a poor city, we're a black city, we're a city without political power."[3] And we're a city with too much crime, too much violence, too much death.

It should be said that New Orleans is hardly alone in such grim circumstances. Many cities in the United States, from Boston to Oakland, from Chicago to Atlanta, have troubling rates of homicide and violent crime. The symptoms vary somewhat from one locale to another—more aggravated assaults and fewer murders, or vice versa—but the immediate causes are much the same everywhere: easy access to guns, gang warfare, and the drug trade. These issues regularly require emergency interventions by police departments and city officials. But the deeper causes, rooted in a city's particular history—those powerful forces that produce generational cycles of poverty and despair and promote a culture of violence—cannot be overcome without the mobilization of whole communities, working in concert.

In a sense, Josh is as much the victim of these subterranean forces as he is of the gunman who took his life. I look at the picture online—Josh and Jonathan, heads close together, guarded expressions; the sort of expression you wear after two decades on the streets. There's an expression: "Tell me your zip code, and I'll tell you your chances in life." Dumaine Street is a bad zip code; since Katrina, six murders on the 2600 block of that street. Still, why Josh? Probably he was just a bystander, in the wrong place at the wrong time, but it would be good to know for sure. How can you change something if you don't have a clear grasp of the facts? A basic principle of leadership is to know what you're talking about—which is not as obvious or easy as it sounds. Trying to grasp a subject as complex as crime is a little like a blind person feeling an elephant. Groping for a sense of the contours almost inevitably yields false impressions. And the elephant is not only a complicated animal but an enormous one, just as crime is a big topic whose roots encompass a host of other subjects like education, employment, class, and race. Changing the homicide rate will never be a simple fix.

Let's put aside the blind person and the elephant and think instead of a road map through complicated terrain—a view of the main arteries and the secondary roads with a clearly marked destination. The best place to begin is with solid data and a substantial knowledge base.

*Leaders address the world as it is, without illusions. As Nehru, the Prime Minister of India, put it, "Facts are facts, and will not disappear on account of your likes." Leaders make principled decisions based not on what they hope, want, or believe they can get but on hard realities and informed judgment. And when I say facts, I mean all of them. Be inclusive in your fact finding, consider contrarian views, and understand both the root causes of problems and the range of possible solutions. Be open to novel ideas if based on reliable evidence, and build a consensus of possibilities for community assessment and debate.*

You can amass heaps of information about crimes and murders from a myriad of sources, among them the New Orleans Police Department (NOPD); the Metropolitan Crime Commission; the Bureau of Justice Assistance (BJA), a federal oversight agency; the City of New Orleans' Homicide Reduction Initiatives report; programs like NOLA for Life and Silence Is Violence, devoted to reducing violent crime in the city; academic researchers at Tulane, Louisiana State University, and other local colleges; and print and news media, ranging from the *Times-Picayune* to CNN.

The facts that emerge from all these sources are daunting. Pre-Katrina there were, on average, 50 murders per 100,000 people. In 2012, over 53 out of 100,000—the equivalent, per capita, of roughly 4,400 murders in New York City. Though analysts come up with slightly different numbers, largely because no one is sure of the population of New Orleans since the storm, it's clear that the city is a contender for the title "homicide capital of the U.S."[4] Worse, some people take a perverse pride in this distinction—we're the baddest. Perhaps the only perk is that it fuels attention and action from all over, especially the federal government. In 2010 the BJA, an arm of the Justice Department, came to town to assess and then, in 2012, overhaul the NOPD.

Historically, certain fluctuations in the murder rate seem traceable to specific events. For example, white flight to the suburbs after the schools were desegregated (*Brown v. the Board of Education*, 1954) left the city's core poorer, blacker, and more vulnerable to violence. The infusion of crack cocaine in the 1980s caused another spike in homicides. The year 1994 was an epidemic one: 424 deaths, with no one clear cause. The year 1999 saw a steep reduction—161 murders—a decline that Tulane criminologist Peter Sharf attributes to a new data system, COMPSTAT, which supplied the NOPD with crucial information for locating and prosecuting violent offenders.[5] In 2005, after Katrina, many of the worst criminals in New Orleans—a list of 112 compiled by the Federal Bureau of Investigation—scattered with the rest of the evacuees, and there was actually a dip in crime, with spikes in some of the destinations where these hardcore characters landed. Now they've come back, bringing with them new contacts from drug trafficking centers like Houston, reconstituting their gangs and redefining their turfs, stockpiling weapons and murdering potential rivals and witnesses. The people who've suffered most since their return are, once again, working-class African Americans, whose neighborhoods border the most dangerous areas of the city and who are most likely to be in the wrong place at the wrong time.[6]

These are the facts, but what do they mean? Some even dispute the accuracy of this basic account, like bloggers who point out that gangs are far less important here than in other cities; there are no Crips and Bloods in New Orleans, just loose associations by street or vicinity.[7] Most murders occur in neighborhoods, right in front of people's houses, and often in broad daylight. David Kennedy, a criminologist and an advisor to NOLA for Life, thinks that the street code of honor and revenge is a more significant factor than formal gang affiliations or drug rivalries. If he is right, the question becomes whether the street code has become the de facto law due to the inadequacy of the NOPD.

Never known as a model of integrity or efficiency, the NOPD was involved in outright criminal activities after Katrina—not just mishandling of evidence but assaults, murders, and cover-ups. One notorious instance is the case of Henry Glover, a young man shot near an Algiers strip mall where looting was going on. His brother, a friend, and a good Samaritan who offered his car brought him to an elementary school where the police had set up an outpost in the days after the storm. The cops assaulted the three young men, leaving Glover to bleed to death in the backseat of the car, and then commandeered the car. Later it was discovered burned and abandoned at a nearby levee, with Glover's body, reduced to bones and ashes, still in it. Through the investigative journalism of A. C. Thompson of *The Nation*, the body was ultimately identified, and federal investigators ascertained the shooter, a police officer named David Warren[8]; Warren was convicted, as were several other policemen involved in an extensive cover-up. The Danziger Bridge shootings we talked about in chapter 2—police firing on unarmed African American pedestrians, wounding four and killing two—also resulted in convictions of the offending officers, though not until the case went to federal court after mistrials at the city and state levels.

The sentencing in these cases seemed like a triumph of justice, but in 2012, some of the convictions in the Glover case were under investigation by the district court of appeals because of procedural questions. In 2013 a U.S. District Court Judge overturned the convictions of the five NOPD officers convicted in the Danziger shootings on the grounds of government misconduct. In response to the ruling, the mother of the 17-year-old boy killed on the bridge said, "What's going to happen to the crimes they committed? Are they just going to sweep that under the carpet and forget it?"[9] In December 2013, David Warren, the officer who shot Henry Glover, was exonerated in a retrial after three and a half years in prison; Glover's sister broke into anguished cries when she heard the verdict and had to be helped from the courtroom.[10]

These events and others like them have left the African American community mistrustful of the police, and that mistrust may have encouraged vigilante justice on the streets. Here's where immediate interventions have made a difference. The first step in solving the epidemic of murder—a step almost everyone could agree on, based on evidence emerging since the storm—was to mitigate the mistrust by cleaning up the police department. Rehabilitating the NOPD has been the focus of the BJA, which studied the department extensively and, under a federal decree of consent issued in 2012, was granted the power to enforce its recommendations. In its report, the BJA noted the deep-seated distrust between law enforcement and African American residents, making a number of suggestions about community engagement. Ultimately the department developed a 65-point plan to address weaknesses in law enforcement, including the creation of a new staff position, community coordinating sergeant (CCS), dedicated to improving relationships with citizens. The CCSs lead outreach efforts in neighborhoods—marches, flyers, door-to-door introductions—and encourage witnesses to use the Crimestoppers anonymous tip line; they are trying to make friends on the street.

Their other recommendations include more effective use of personnel to handle the overload of cases, both past and present; and deploying manpower more effectively by mapping hot spots, targeting repeat offenders, and prioritizing homicide over lesser crimes. To achieve these ends, the NOPD increased the number of homicide detectives and switched to DDACTS—Data Driven Approaches to Crime and Traffic Safety, expanding the COMPSTAT system of the 1990s to include newer programs, including Omega Crime View, Coplink, and Corona Solutions. The department also has instituted guidelines for hiring, training, and mentoring of police officers according to BJA recommendations. Together with the district attorneys, NOPD has worked to pursue long sentences for violent offenders, identifying cynical and corrupt judges who set low bail or let perpetrators walk.[11]

Still, as an answer to the complex problem of crime in the city, all the initiatives at NOPD are at most a finger in the dyke. What about the deeper roots of crime in the community, where poverty, lack of education, and racism affect neighborhood norms and expectations and create fertile ground for violence? The answer lies at the roots.

WHAT IS IT LIKE, REALLY, OUT ON THE STREET? I'm going to give some snapshots of homicides in 2012 that offer qualitative data—the who, what, when, where, how—of life in the high-crime neighborhoods of the city.

Some of the homicides in New Orleans in 2012—a year in which 195 murders occurred[12]:

*March 2012:* Wendell Allen, a high school basketball star, 20, unarmed, killed by a policeman in a drug raid on the house where he was staying with a number of relatives, including young children. He was shirtless, wearing pants, and lifted his hands to show he had no weapon. (In 2013 the police officer pleaded guilty to manslaughter and was sentenced to four years in prison.)

Ricky Summers, 16 years old, a student at the Knowledge Is Power Program (KIPP), a nationwide college prep charter network with nine schools in New Orleans. There were two other KIPP student deaths in 2012.

*May 2012:* Briana Allen, five, killed by a stray bullet at a birthday party for her cousin, aged ten. (A 33-year-old mother, driving through the neighborhood on her way to return a rental car, was killed by a bullet in the same incident.)

*June 2012:* Marc Canty III, 18 years old. He was dialing 911 as he was being pursued by his killer, whom he named before dying. His mother said it was a gang initiation killing.

*October 2012:* Josh Short, the film student at Delgado Community College profiled at the beginning of this chapter, and Valan May, student at the University of New Orleans. Similarities: unknown motive; both shot in head; both aspiring filmmakers.[13]

The Adams toddlers—Kendall, three (shot) and Kelsey, four (drowned in bathtub). Killed by their mother, Chelsea Thornton, who had a diagnosis of schizophrenia and days before the murders said she needed to go back to the psychiatric hospital.[14]

*January 2013:* Antonio Llovet, 28, Latino, shot on his couch in the condo he rented across the street from his parents in Gentilly—a robbery. Apparently he'd Facebooked a photo of $100 bills spread out on his coffee table, and his sister said he'd been burglarized several times before.

What can we learn from these wrenching stories about the root causes of homicide in New Orleans? Wendell Allen's killing suggests that, even with new regulations and procedures in place, the police are still capable of hair-trigger responses in ambiguous situations. Every person on the list except Kelsey Adams, the four-year-old girl who was drowned, was killed by a gun.[15] Many of the killings—Briana, the young mother, possibly the KIPP students, and Josh Short—seem to have been accidental. Some may have been retaliatory—the street code of justice and honor, grudge and revenge—but we'll likely never know, since this is not information people tend to share with the police. One murder, Antonio Llovet, was clearly a robbery; Valan May, killed execution style while sitting in his car, may have been murdered for his cell phone and the contents of his wallet; Marc Canty's murder may have been gang related. Chelsea Thornton's murder of her children is different from all the rest, a case of untreated psychosis with serious implications for the future, given recent cutbacks in mental health services.

Apart from mental illness, which is at least a potentially treatable condition, there's something, it seems, in the very fabric of poor neighborhoods that promotes violence. You can list the familiar litany of "bad influences" that the wider culture tends to blame—video games, movie mayhem, rap lyrics, and the glorification of guns—and still not get to the heart of the matter. The education activist Geoffrey Canada, in his landmark memoir *Fist Stick Knife Gun*, talks about customs that are learned, local, tribal. "If you wonder how a fourteen-year-old can shoot another child his own age in the head, or how boys can do 'drive-by shootings' and then go home to dinner, you need to know you don't get there in a day, or week, or month. It takes years of preparation to be willing to commit murder.... Many of the children of America are conditioned early to kill and, more frighteningly, to die for what to an outsider might seem a trivial cause."[16]

Kids on the street, mostly boys and many of them without any fathers to speak of, try to learn from their older peers how to survive; in the process they become inured to death, seeing murder as manly, honorable, and, in the end, inevitable. Where and how do you intervene in this generational cycle? To change the social code, you must reach deep into the life of the community—using resources that already exist and also seeking points of contact, to bring help where it's needed.

HERE THEY COME ON A WARM WINTER'S DAY, strutting down the middle of the street, men and women wearing T-shirts that say BREAK THE CODE OF SILENCE, bright-colored parasols over their heads, and the Stooges Brass Band providing the beat. It's January 28, 2012, and the Prince of Wales Social Aid and Pleasure Club is kicking off the New Year with a Silence Is Violence second-line parade, starting at Lyons Park where, four hours from now, it will end with a picnic. They march down Louisiana Avenue, down Tchoupitoulas Street, past the landmark Rock Bottom Lounge, past a car plastered with photos of a high school student killed in 2008, past street shrines with teddy bears and balloons marking the site of other deaths. It's part of a Strike Against Crime week; firefighters, police, and members of the Faubourg Delachaise Neighborhood Association are part of the parade, as are bystanders who join in along the way.[17] The mood is typical New Orleans, a mix of seriousness and play. As the online ad for the parade says: "**Respect**

yourself and your culture. Leave your guns, dogs, and troubles at home."
No reason you can't have fun when you're stamping out crime. No reason
you can't laugh and cry at the same time.

As it turned out, 2012 was another bloody year in New Orleans, but the
beginning, at least, was marked by the high hopes of the Silence Is Violence
street parade. Geoffrey Canada says that to change the environment, you
can't stay at a distance—you have to take it to the streets. When he started
his first community center at a school in Harlem, New York, he had a theater
company perform outdoors to bring people out of their houses and get them
talking to each other. In New Orleans, the parades and festivals all year long
are like Canada's street theater, bringing everyone, even the cops, together
and creating zones of security out of doors.

Second-line parades like this one are powerful expressions of communal will—a sacred piece of the neighborhood fabric.[18] The power of
social cohesion is documented in a recent book by Robert Sampson, *Great
American City: Chicago and the Enduring Neighborhood Effect*, which
describes a long-term study, the Project on Human Development in Chicago
Neighborhoods. Looking at 15 years' worth of data as well as qualitative
field reports, Sampson found that neighborhoods tend to remain stable,
with persistent cultural and economic profiles, despite historical shifts and
global events. Countering an earlier emphasis in sociology on individual
choice as the most important determinant of life events, Sampson makes
the case that context—specifically, the ethos and expectations of a particular neighborhood—has powerful effects on social outcomes. He finds that
places with a rich organizational life create shared values and expectations,
promote trust, and produce positive social effects. Taken together, his find-
ings suggest that a policy of community interventions and actions may be
more effective than discrete efforts targeting individuals.[19]

New Orleans before Katrina was predominantly a city of neighborhoods, each with its own character and texture; since the storm, repairing
that fabric has been a major factor in bringing the city back from chaos, a
process exemplified by the resurgence of second lines and the social aid and
pleasure clubs. These clubs—the Prince of Wales is one of the oldest, but

there are many, most dating back to the nineteenth century—were originally founded by African Americans to create a social network that supplied medical help, family supports, funeral expenses, and other needed services in the pre–civil rights era. Like the performances of the Mardi Gras Indian tribes, the public rituals of the clubs generate a feeling of exuberant solidarity and continuity that strengthens the neighborhood effect, making the city both livelier and safer.

The clubs continue to be a robust presence in the post-Katrina years and a positive force even in the worst neighborhoods. Second lines, while sometimes marred by violent incidents, remain important as a show of communal unity and spirit. The churches also have a role, providing not only communal rites but programs and activities for young people. In addition, the city has numerous social programs directly addressing violence and murder—such as Silence Is Violence and NOLA for Life—and others that focus on education and support for at-risk youth, like Café Reconcile, Grow Dat Youth Farm, APEX Youth Center, and many more. All these initiatives are signs of New Orleans' drive and determination in the post-Katrina era. No problem too big, no setback too daunting.

THE CITY'S CULTURE IS LIKE A WOVEN PATCHWORK, varied and vibrant, but from a leadership perspective, it's a jumble: There are 73 neighborhoods in Orleans Parish, each with its own clubs, associations, projects, and programs. How do you coordinate activities? How do you measure outcomes? A business dictum, known to everyone who studies organizational strategy, states that "if what gets measured is what gets managed, then what gets managed is what gets done."[20] It's the mantra of organizational logic. But is there any logic here?

To address the problem of disorganized and fragmented initiatives, Geoffrey Canada created a unique model program, the Harlem Children's Zone (HCZ)—a hundred-block area in Harlem providing parental supports, preschool programs, charter schools, after-school programs, mentoring, tutoring, enrichment, college placements, and job training. In an attempt to make things measurable, scalable, and sustainable, the HCZ is a total cradle-to-career environment that reaches more children than Canada's early piecemeal efforts ever could. It's a remarkable experiment aimed at bringing the children of HCZ out of poverty and into the middle class by means of education, which means tests, scores, graduation rates, degrees, jobs, and professions, as well as an array of social and mental health supports. President Obama has called for its replication in cities across the United States.

It's a signal accomplishment but one that's difficult to emulate. One of the problems is that you need many Geoffrey Canadas, leaders who are charismatic, pragmatic, and, whenever possible, homegrown, with street cred; a rare commodity. Model wraparound programs also cost a lot of money, and getting city government to fund a single project at the expense of other worthy programs is always an uphill battle. Finally, even for the most effective programs, the success is still confined to a single zone.

In recent years a new model has been proposed for cities trying to solve intractable social problems: the "collective impact" model, which coordinates the efforts of community collaboratives and existing programs, bringing many stakeholders to the table, defining common goals and distributing tasks, collecting baseline data and establishing metrics for success, and measuring outcomes. In its emphasis on data, analysis, and evidence-based practices, the collective impact model is very much in line with the leadership vision of this chapter. But as the term *collective impact* implies, to lead effectively, you have to go beyond quantifiable facts to deep-rooted causes, and then, with this knowledge in place, you have to act pragmatically by partnering with others and leveraging existing resources. The ultimate aim is to bring together many organizations and programs to solve large, complex social problems, with the aim of reaching vast numbers of people in cities all across the country.

BUT NATIONAL AIMS BEGIN WITH LOCAL EFFORTS. How does the community collaborative approach work in practice? Take Central City, population 11,000, 1.4 square miles in area, and one of the poorest and most crime-ridden neighborhoods in New Orleans. Central City has an immediate response team to focus on violence: A group called Solutions Not Shootings laid the groundwork for CeaseFire New Orleans, a branch of the national program of street "interrupters" who talk people down from violence in crisis situations.[21] CeaseFire uses conflict resolution and time-outs to reduce the retaliatory killings that follow quickly on the heels of a prior murder. Dedicated primarily to prevention, the initiative has "sustainability," because the conversations that the crisis team starts with kids on the street can evolve into a model for anger management and also into relationships that help with the ongoing problem of joblessness and the chronic temptations of gangs, drugs, and guns. It's a model that looks more like medicine than criminal justice: You reduce the "spread" by treating the disease instead of punishing it.[22]

But beyond crisis intervention, Central City has become a laboratory for a collaborative approach to the deep-rooted causes of crime. It's a beehive of projects, programs, nonprofits—precisely those community organizations that, according to Robert Sampson, create enduring neighborhood effects and reinforce norms, values, and expectations. The Central City Renaissance Alliance, Harmony Neighborhood Development, the Neighborhood Development Foundation, the Ashe Cultural Arts Center, and Churches Supporting Churches have partnered in the work of transforming an entire neighborhood. A Community Benefits Coalition negotiates with developers for beneficial terms on new construction, an early childhood center and a KIPP charter school have opened their doors, and community leaders have advocated for locating the Louisiana Civil Rights Museum in Central City. Important youth projects are located here as well, including Café Reconcile, a nonprofit restaurant and job training enterprise that teaches at-risk youth skills in the food and hospitality industries, and the Youth Empowerment Project, providing wraparound educational support to young people, some of them ex-offenders, who are out of school and unemployed. Project Sprout, originating at Tulane City Center in the School of Architecture, has a pilot program in the neighborhood for revitalizing marginal properties through the planting of bioenergy gardens to prepare land for redevelopment, urban farming, or green space. On a stretch along O. C. Haley Boulevard are a row of organizations devoted to the work of recovery and revitalization: Central City Renaissance Alliance, the Louisiana Association of Nonprofit Organizations, and Good Work Network—the kind of clustered nonprofits associated with a positive neighborhood effect. Finally, the New Orleans Redevelopment Authority, Harmony Neighborhood Development, and Jericho Road are collectively working against urban blight, buying up decaying and vacant properties to transform the neighborhood, one block at a time.

CENTRAL CITY IS LOOKING LIKE A SUCCESSFUL community experiment—a milestone on the road to bringing New Orleans back—but we're forging ahead in neighborhoods all across the city. Here's what Tulane has done.[23] Through the City Center at the School of Architecture, the university has contributed to neighborhood revitalization by focusing on urban design, creating modular homes, community centers, and green spaces across the city. Many of these projects are in partnership with other like-minded organizations; for example, Tulane's urban gardens involve collaboration with the New Orleans Food and Farm Network. The Tulane School of Medicine has also spearheaded a network of community health centers in the poorest parts of town. Recently I've been in talks with the School of Social Work about building a center, if not moving the whole school, to an inner city neighborhood. Bringing academic institutions to blighted areas—taking services and amenities to where people live rather than maintaining an ivory tower distance—sends the message that "We Believe,"

But the message of conviction and hope is broadcast most strongly through the work of Tulane undergraduates, who are doing frontline, hands-on work in the neighborhoods of New Orleans through the Center for Public Service. These college students are seeking new points of contact, bringing their idealism and high spirits where they're needed—yet another route to easing the conditions that lead to violence.

IT'S AUGUST 2010, THE FIFTH ANNIVERSARY OF KATRINA, and I decide I should go to the community service day event in Iberville, part of Outreach Tulane, and see for myself how the students are doing. A contingent has gone there to provide some kid-oriented activities. The Iberville

Projects survived Katrina intact as well as the poststorm razing of public housing projects that so enraged the African American community.[24] Built on the site of historic Storyville, the red-light district of old New Orleans, the Iberville Projects are home to some 1,300 people. The Housing Authority of New Orleans has plans to replace some of the buildings with mixed-income housing so that only a third of units will be for those living below the poverty line. Where will everyone else go? Plenty of residents have asked, but no one seems to know the answer.

On this August day it's raining lightly, and the scene—garbage-strewn lots, cracked sidewalks, boarded-up windows, vivid scrawls of paint on walls and fences—is slightly softened by the fine mist. In the middle of a court-yard that's mostly dust and weeds, the students have set up a pink Slip 'n Slide, and they're jumping and sliding right beside the little kids who have all come out to play. Squeals and laughter echo in the courtyard. A small child, four or five, shoots down the cascade of plastic, her pigtails flying. It looks like fun.

I approach a man leaning against a chain-link fence, swaying back and forth. I wonder if he's on drugs, or a dealer, or maybe he's just passing the time. I introduce myself and he nods. We look at the kids slippin' and slidin'.

I clear my throat; may as well ask him. "Are my kids safe here?" I send students into the city all the time, sometimes to high-crime districts. I'm responsible.

The man sways. Is that a yes?

"They're okay," he says. "They come down here to do good. Nobody gonna touch 'em."

He sounds like he knows. I'm reassured.

Then, suddenly, music is in the air: Four guys over on the next corner, brass instruments gleaming in the mist, are improvising a jazz riff that floats over the courtyard. It's really something: the mist, the pink Slip 'n Slide, the laughter, the swaying man, the live soundtrack. Pure New Orleans.

OF COURSE, SLIP 'N SLIDES WON'T, BY THEMSELVES, end violence in the inner city—and ending violence won't be enough to correct the deep-rooted problems of racism and poverty that afflict New Orleans. In a way, beginning with crime is going at it backward, looking at the effect rather than the cause. But we need a zone of safety for children of the inner city if the other initiatives and programs are to have a chance at changing their lives. The traumatic effects of random death are hugely destructive: Children in urban environments suffer from the same kind of posttraumatic stress that combat veterans experience.[25] In New Orleans, this effect has been compounded by a swollen cohort of "disconnected youth" or, as they've been rechristened, "opportunity youth": young people, ages 16 to 24, not working and not in school, many of whom are coping with homelessness, mental or physical illness, and, all too frequently, the criminal justice system. The name *opportunity youth* underscores the potential they represent, if they can be reconnected to possibility and hope. Many of these young adults were eight or nine when Katrina hit, and with the collapse of social institutions and the obliteration of stable neighborhoods, they are even more disconnected than their peers in similar environments.[26]

Tulane is going after this specific group of at-risk kids—the same ones the police are often after—but we aim for prevention, education, rehabilitation, and hope.[27] Given that the problem of violence is complex and multidetermined, targeting a high-risk group makes pragmatic sense; and beginning with basics—that is, marshaling the facts—grounds the mission firmly in reality. Reconnecting Opportunity Youth, organized by the Cowen Institute for Public Education Initiatives, depends, first, on hard data. We "marshaled the facts," collecting a mass of information about youth 16 to 24 to establish a baseline and define which interventions to try. Our guide to the initiative, focusing on the New Orleans metropolitan area, is filled with graphics that lay out the issue, the impact, and the risk factors, all framed statistically: numbers of opportunity youth (approximately 14,000); burden on taxpayers, from lost tax revenues and increased costs for social services (lifetime, between $3.1 and $4.1 *billion*); crime statistics (1,000 juvenile cases against students in the Recovery School District in 2009; 46 percent of Louisiana teen homicide victims residents of New Orleans); dropout rate (1,170 dropouts from the class of 2010 and a cohort graduation rate of 49.7 percent). One of the purposes of doing portraiture by the numbers is to make a case for the urgency of the problem by vividly conveying the costs of doing nothing.[28]

Once you make the case by amassing the facts, then what? At Reconnecting Opportunity Youth, we're launching a pilot program with small cohorts to provide the education and technical training that lead to living-wage jobs in industries that promise upward mobility. We're also partnering with other organizations in the city to build an ecosystem of prevention and intervention on the model of outstanding community collaboratives around the country. Some successful models: the Strive Partnership in Cincinnati and northern Kentucky, a multisector consortium offering supports inside and outside of school using a common agenda and evaluation process, intelligent use of existing resources, and data-informed decision making; and Project U Turn in Philadelphia, led by the Philadelphia Youth Network, another collaborative coordinating city government, the school system, philanthropies, service organizations, and young people to turn around the dropout rate in city schools. A feature of these collaboratives is cost effectiveness; one of their mantras is "doing better without spending more."

In New Orleans, the Partnership for Youth Development, one of Tulane's local associates, is currently building a collective impact model to provide young people with enhanced opportunities for learning and work. It's also trying to reform the fractured community infrastructure by convening a broad spectrum of stakeholders, from nonprofits, to the education sector, to economic development groups. One of the chief participating nonprofit organizations is the Youth Empowerment Project started by Melissa Sawyer in 2004.

Melissa originally joined Teach For America, where she discovered she preferred out-of-school relationships with the kids to classroom teaching. After a two-year stint in New Orleans, she decided to get a graduate degree in education at Harvard, promising the students she'd met at the Booker T. Washington High School that she'd come back to them. During her time away she called one of the students she was close to—she kept in good touch with calls and postcards—and in the course of the conversation asked about another of her favorites, Peewee: It turned out that he was in jail on a felony charge. This set her thinking about the "deadend hand" that so many of these kids had been dealt, and when she came back to New Orleans, she started working at the Juvenile Justice Project of Louisiana, fighting for the release of incarcerated young people. During the space of several months, she went to six funerals of kids she knew. In a public radio interview, she described "funeral arm," a numb, tingling sensation she'd get on the way to yet another burial; she'd embraced so many weeping mothers and leaned over so many open caskets, she'd developed a physical symptom. She saw that the options were untenable: Even if someone got out of jail, the risk of eventually going back or being killed was enormous.

She decided she had to do something different with her life, or go crazy. The "different" was the first program at the Youth Empowerment Project (YEP), and the first-of-its-kind juvenile reentry program in Louisiana: a staff of five worked with 25 juvenile offenders to help with reentry into their communities. The success of this endeavor led to others, including New Orleans Providing Literacy to All Youth (NOPLAY), an intensive program that offers tutoring for general equivalency diplomas, college preparation, and job placements; the Village, another education program that in addition to academics provides psychological counseling and instruction in life skills; a summer camp; and an after-school enrichment program—a full menu of experiences to help launch kids into adult life. Nine years after its inception, YEP serves over a thousand kids annually and has a $2.6 million budget, funded in part by state and city agencies.[29]

In a question-and-answer session, Melissa described the YEP program this way: "We have a relationship-based model that is very individualized. We provide *wrap-around* services. As you can envision, by wrapping around, we're providing someone with all the emotional and psychological support they are going to need to grow into a successful person."[30]

More than anything, the YEP offers consistent, anchoring relationships that strengthen young people who have had disrupted and disconnected lives. It's less an intervention than an all-encompassing milieu; though more limited in scope than Geoffrey Canada's HCZ, YEP also takes kids where they are and adds rich nutrients for growth.

The success of YEP attests to the power of filling in the gaps and offering opportunities out of the dead end of poverty. What keeps poor people poor? Paul Tough, who wrote *Whatever It Takes: Geoffrey Canada's Quest to Change Harlem and America*, on the HCZ, and *How Children Succeed: Grit, Curiosity, and the Hidden Power of Character*, reports on research suggesting that poverty itself disrupts brain chemistry and produces profound cultural disadvantage.[31] But other research points to the capacity of the brain to grow and change across the life cycle. Even though "disconnected youth" interventions arrive late on the conveyor belt of child development, they can redirect and, sometimes literally, save a life. The aim is to achieve what Geoffrey Canada calls "escape velocity": to provide the critical nourishment and support that allows someone to break free of the constraints he's born into.[32]

AT THE BEGINNING OF THIS CHAPTER, I referred to a road map— a set of directions that can be a template for solving the intractable problem of violence that plagues our cities. As is often the case in this book, a first leadership principle leads to all the others, because solutions require synchrony and synergy: everything working at once. In the case of violence, the gathering of facts is inextricably related to a search for causes, which is deeply entwined with the effort to define a rational approach, find consensus, and propose effective solutions.

*How can leaders address the deep-rooted problem of crime in the inner city? Leaders begin by facing the facts: gathering information in an inclusive way that takes into account different, sometimes conflicting, sets of data. But they go beyond the raw data to search out root causes, interpreting statistics in order to develop innovative approaches that are based both on the evidence and on a sense of a problem's deep origins. They use these evidence-based approaches to propose reasonable possibilities for the larger community to evaluate and debate.*

To mitigate violence and its deeper roots in poverty and despair, we in leadership positions need to begin with hard data and marshal the facts. But we need to end by saving lives. Here is Deshawn Robinson, Grow Dat staff

**Image 4**   Deshawn Robinson

Deshawn Robinson, a young man with a drug-addicted mother who died, an absent father, and murdered relatives and friends, who was living on the streets before he was eleven. His life changed when he came to Grow Dat Youth Farm, a youth development program that offers social support and educational opportunity through the meaning-ful work of growing food.

(*Photo credit: Will Widmer*)

member, telling what life has been like for him, in an essay titled "From Pain to Success":

> No one can ask to be born in poverty. That's your hand, no shuf-fling. It's something that can make you better or much worse. I ignored the truth and never kept it 100% with myself. Other people's opinions would not get through to me....

My family was below the poverty line when I was born. There were plenty nights I didn't have food, family, or even a warm blanket to cuddle with. Many nights I slept in Harrell Park on the slides, hoping nobody would see me. And that was before age 11.

Just when you thought it couldn't get any worse, it did. In October 2001, a month after my birthday, I saw my mother lying long ways across the sidewalk. Her head was leaning off the curb with a little crack in both eyes, and I knew she was gone forever. At that moment I was numb. I was no longer a child and had no father figure to look up to for advice.

Hustling brought me wealth at age 15. And then I started thinking, "I don't want this for the rest of my life." My rap sheet was growing and getting a job was harder than electing Obama all over again. I just hated being broke, and not having a job made me really think that there was no way out.

One day I was chilling on the block and the next thing you know a guy in a car pulled up to another guy on the block. He said he wanted a dime. The guy on the street brought me a $10 bill and made it seem like he wanted the sack. He then brought the product to the car. I came to find out I had served a detective. Next thing you know I was sentenced to two years and two months in a juvenile detention center.

Getting out of jail was the best feeling I ever had. The day I came to Grow Dat Youth Farm and met all the cool people on the farm, my life was not the same. It changed me and showed me the better things in life such as camping, canoeing, and peaceful nature walks. All the funny games we play expand your mind in the easiest ways possible.

Grow Dat found me at the right time and made me a calm, wise gentleman. I improved in public speaking, leadership skills, growing food, and cooking. Today I honor Grow Dat for everything they did for me, as well as giving me a new start.

I'm happy I changed my life.[33]

# Chapter 4

# THE PROBLEM WE ALL LIVE WITH

## UNDERSTAND REALITY

I'M AT LA PETITE GROCERY, A LANDMARK SPOT THAT DATES back to the nineteenth century when it was, in fact, a grocery store specializing in coffee, tea, and butter. The original burned down, but it was rebuilt as a fine foods emporium, later becoming a flower shop; in 2004 it morphed into a restaurant and went on to survive Katrina. The outside of the building—low-slung with clapboard siding—looks like a corner store. Inside, it's a classy eatery, with polished wood floors, white tablecloths, glowing sconces, and an amazing menu—grilled shrimp and grits, chicken-fried pork loin with mustard greens, panéed rabbit, lobster beignets, bibb salad with quail egg: a mix of comfort food and haute cuisine.

I'm having lunch with Ruby Bridges, one of the heroes of the civil rights movement. My chief of staff is with me, and Ruby has brought along a young man who works at her foundation, but for most of the conversation, I feel like it's just Ruby and me. Ruby is wearing a suit and a strand of pearls, and she has business on her mind: she wants me to help her charter William Frantz Elementary as the Ruby Bridges School of Community Service & Social Justice, with a curriculum focusing on history, civil rights, and civic engagement.[1] "You know what I learned in the first grade? Not just my ABCs." She waves her fork *no*. "What Miss Henry taught me is that you have to get to know people. Then it doesn't matter what their skin color is."

Ruby has a lovely voice, with a faintly Boston accent that she says she picked up from Barbara Henry, the young white woman who agreed to teach her that whole first-grade year, the two of them alone in an empty classroom after the white parents had pulled out their children. Ruby and Barbara used to do jumping jacks together at recess because it wasn't safe for Ruby to go out with children in the other grades. One little boy told her, "I can't play with you. My mama said not to because you're a nigger."

In 1960 she was one of four New Orleans children—all girls, because they were thought to be less threatening than boys in the eyes of white parents—to integrate the public school system after the *Brown v. Board of Education* ruling in 1954.[2] Norman Rockwell painted an iconic picture entitled "The Problem We All Live With": Ruby at age six, white dress, pigtails, surrounded by the legs of U.S. marshals, the wall behind her scrawled with the N-word and splattered with a thrown tomato. She is marching, eyes straight ahead, chin up, to school; one of the marshals described her as "a little soldier." The school was William Frantz Elementary in the Upper Ninth Ward, which was, at the time, a neighborhood segregated by block.

Ruby still has the erect posture and squared shoulders of that little girl in pigtails; she also has an innate resilience, a willingness to frame things in the best light possible. "You know," she says, "I thought all that yelling and arm waving was Mardi Gras. It was my only point of comparison. When I figured it out, I did what Mama said and prayed for them."

I tell her I'm impressed she's not angrier about it.

"I was lonely that year. But I had Miss Henry. You know we're back in touch? We do readings and talks together. The point is, Miss Henry was

**Image 5**   Young Ruby Bridges

Ruby Bridges, age six, being escorted from William Frantz Elementary School in the Upper Ninth Ward by U.S. marshals. In 1960, she was one of four New Orleans school-girls who were the first in the South to integrate the public schools. A hero of the civil rights movement, she continues to champion diversity in the inner city schools of New Orleans, which have undergone a major transformation since the storm.

(*Associated Press*)

white. And the woman who was yelling she was going to poison me, and the one who brought a black doll in a coffin to the picket line—they were white. How could I be angry at 'white people'? That didn't make sense to me. And then after that year, in second grade, I was in a regular class, white and black children, and I never thought about it much after that."

She leans in. "But I'm thinking about it now."

Ruby wasn't always famous. Over the years, people wanted to know who the girl in the painting was, and Robert Coles, the child psychiatrist—he visited her once a week that first-grade year, for emotional support—wrote a children's book about her; gradually she was "discovered." But in between she went to college, became a travel agent, got married, had four sons. She experienced the "mundane" violence of New Orleans: Her oldest son was murdered, her brother was murdered. She took over the care of her nieces, raising, in total, eight children. She started the Ruby Bridges Foundation and began talking in the schools. She thinks that racism is an adult disease and that adults use children to spread it. The way to stop the spread? Let children get to know each other.

I'm beginning this chapter with Ruby and her vision of integrated schooling because her story contains both the problem and, ideally, the solution. Some studies suggest that integrated schooling is better for both African American and white children.[3] One of the problems of our inner cities, if not *the* problem, is demographic: Since the desegregation of schools in 1954, white flight to the suburbs has left most urban centers predominantly, if not wholly, African American. Trying to solve "the problem we all live with" will get nowhere without an acknowledgment of the facts.

But the leadership principle featured in this chapter—"Understand reality"—goes beyond a catalog of discrete facts. What distinguishes leadership from simple management is vision and hope—the freedom to imagine and the courage to aim high. At the same time, management, or what I would call flexible pragmatism, is necessary to temper ideal visions and accommodate to the reality in which you're living. Without a clear strategy for change, a steady focus on outcomes and accountability, and an ability to forge consensus, even the most fervent belief in transformative possibilities will remain just that: a belief.

*Before you can begin a journey, you have to know where you are. The best leaders have the ability to understand the reality of situations they face, to define desired outcomes, and to plan accordingly. The first, necessary step in solving problems and implementing change is an accurate and complete articulation of the situation. This assessment is based on identifying the true causes of the problem, gathering input from those affected, and clear-headed, creative thinking about how to address the problem, with a broad reach of possible solutions.*

WHAT, IN FACT, IS POSSIBLE? Can we achieve an equitable, and first-class, education for all the children of our country? And, if so, how can we achieve it?

Here's what we've done toward that end in New Orleans.

FACTS FIRST: NEW ORLEANS HAS A DEMOGRAPHIC that is roughly 60 percent African American and 30 percent white, with the remaining 10 percent Hispanic, Asian, and mixed. Most of the public schools in New Orleans are close to 100 percent African American. Before Katrina, the New Orleans education system was, as one report puts it, "a poster child for dysfunction and corruption," with enrollment declining as wealthy parents left town or signed their children up at private schools. On Louisiana's high school exit exams in 2004, 96 percent of New Orleans public school students fell below basic proficiency in English and 94 percent in math.[4] Many high schools were chaotic, and the elementary schools were uninspired. To address this "academic wasteland," Leslie Jacobs, a businesswoman serving on the state Board of Elementary and Secondary Education, urged a state amendment that would create a statewide recovery school district (RSD), modeled on a chapter 11 bankruptcy ruling. (Though "district" sounds geographic, it is actually an administrative entity, allowing a single agency to govern all the failing schools in the state.) The RSD was given the authority to take over failing schools and was empowered to hire and fire, control curriculum, and clean up finances. The takeover process started in 2004–2005. By the start of the 2005–2006 school year, five RSD charter schools were operating in New Orleans.

In response to Katrina, the Orleans Parish School Board (OPSB) made an emergency decision to approve 20 charters of its own, but the state didn't believe the local board could handle the crisis brewing after the hurricane, with most buildings damaged and destroyed, 65,000 schoolchildren in exile across the country, and the entire system in disarray. Leslie Jacobs's assertive leadership helped convince Governor Kathleen Blanco, a Democrat, to go against her political base and, in a single bold stroke, institute something entirely new. Act 35 of the state legislature, passed in November 2005, broadened the definition of "failing" so that 112 of New Orleans' 128 schools fell under the control of the state RSD, leaving only 16 relatively well-working schools controlled by the local OPSB.

The resulting arrangement is complicated and messy. Every place has its particular history, usually including factions with passionate, and opposed, agendas. In New Orleans, this history is the simmering antagonism between the state agency (the RSD) and the local administrative body (the OPSB), and the patched-together bureaucracy that accommodates both bodies. If you look at a chart of school governance in the city, it's a bewildering checkerboard of colors: RSD traditional district-run schools, RSD charter schools, OPSB district-run schools, OPSB charter schools. The existence of two administrative systems, plus the fact that the majority of schools within each system are charters, each with its own board and financial accounting,[5] has led to a confusing array of competing authorities. With so many schools coming and going, it is far from clear that "parental choice" will sort them out, as the market theory posits.[6] Still, the RSD and the state have been consistently tough in weeding out low performers and problem schools, which has led to year-by-year progress and hope.

ONE WAY TO LOOK AT KATRINA IS THAT the storm created a clean slate for the radical reinvention of the schools. It's not entirely true, because the RSD and OPSB have remained fixtures of the landscape and still run traditional district-run schools. But it is true that federal money for rebuilding flowed into the city, and talent immediately began to arrive in droves: educators from across the country, fresh-scrubbed Teach For America teachers, charter entrepreneurs, the successful Knowledge Is Power Program (KIPP) organization, all came to town to help the city in its moment of crisis. A crisis (to repeat a theme of this book) is also, crucially, an opportunity.

What the legislature had accomplished with the RSD, and what the arrival of reformers promised, was a new era in education. But what we didn't yet have was a plan. At that moment in October 2005, when the city was still half drowned, you'll recall that the Bring New Orleans Back (BNOB) Commission organized committees to plan a new, better city.[7] As chair of the Education Committee, my aims at that key juncture were to bring order and structure to the tangled system of governance as it then stood; to incorporate community feedback as much as possible, given the diaspora of half the city's population, including most of its schoolchildren; and to come up with a new approach that would address the problems of the corrupt and unwieldy central administration model that had allowed New Orleans' schools to become the lowest rated in Louisiana, itself rated forty-ninth out of 50 states in education. The goal was to articulate a vision for the future but, more important, to generate a plan that would work.

In terms of "understanding reality," we on the Education Committee grappled with the actual situation in front of us. We approached the problem from five directions:

1. We pursued input from students, parents, principals, and teachers on shared objectives.
2. We brought in experts to help define "best practices."
3. We aligned the various schools into networks according to their governing entities, allowing for shared resources within networks.
4. We emphasized the concepts of accountability, transparency, and choice.
5. We made room for diverse individual schools (a "portfolio of schools," rather than the standard cookie-cutter model).

Basically, we had a vision for a better school system, but we needed to fit it within existing structures and a community with hopes of its own.

In practice, the committee's recommendations encouraged the growth of autonomous schools (which took the form of charter schools) by endorsing decentralized control and trusting the ingenuity and innovation of charter operators and capable educators to address the city's abysmal achievement gap. Still, the Education Committee's report was in no way a manifesto: space was devoted to the cons as well as the pros of the charter model, and the main thrust of the plan was to move from a chaotic and dysfunctional arrangement to a more coherent system of school networks.[8] The plan outlined ten principles of transformation to guide the creation of a sounder, more rational organization: superior standards, empowered schools, accountability, aligned governance, equitable options, quality talent, aligned resources, community and parent engagement, effective and efficient services, and safe learner-centered environments.

The plan attracted both supporters and detractors, reflecting the larger debate about public education that is ongoing in our country right now. Those who defend a centrally administered public school system claim it's more equitable, uniform, and democratic than a charter system, which they see as inevitably two tier, with widely variable quality and a bottom-line mentality that subverts the aims of educating the most vulnerable, least advantaged children. On the other side, charter school advocates are impatient with the deadwood, business-as-usual, protectionist tendencies of the public schools, which in many places have only decades of falling scores and failing students to show for their efforts.

The argument is also about selecting the right people (boards, principals, teachers, technical staff) and giving them the autonomy to do their jobs and be held accountable for the results. Who is the best principal, who is the best teacher? A Teach For America recruit with strong content knowledge who is eager and energetic but also usually white and privileged? A veteran teacher, savvy and experienced, who knows the community but is less focused on raising test scores? And then there's the question of the best methodology: Do caring and personal relationships translate into learning and character-building experiences, albeit ones that are hard to measure? Does "teaching to the test" work (and have No Child Left Behind and Race to the Top, with the best of intentions, turned too many of our schools into test-taking factories)? Is "accountability" a mirage, with students fated to fail for many reasons beyond a failing school or a poorly prepared teacher?

The job of leadership is to consider all the arguments—that is, to understand the reality of competing views—but avoid being waylaid by them. For us in New Orleans, the job was to acknowledge points of view while moving toward the original vision: that is, the best possible education for all children. As the school system evolved in the years after Katrina, my role shifted from a facilitator, as head of the Education Committee, to founder of a new organization at Tulane, the Cowen Institute for Public Education Initiatives, which opened its doors in March 2007. Frontline educators like State Superintendent Paul Pastorek and head of the RSD Paul Vallas (and, more recently, John White and Patrick Dobard, who replaced them) have overseen the decisions on school openings and closings and charters given and withdrawn. Meanwhile, the Cowen Institute has devoted itself to research and policy recommendations—organic extensions of our original vision, articulated in the report of the BNOB Education Committee.[9]

Some recent postings on the institute website include these:

- A survey of parents in New Orleans about school choice, showing remarkable levels of public support for the reforms being put in place
- A paper by Nelson Smith from the Thomas B. Fordham Institute, an independent think tank, proposing that many of Louisiana's aggressive educational reforms be adopted by the state of Ohio
- A report issued annually, "The State of Public Education in New Orleans," assessing school performance and analyzing developments at the state and city levels
- NOLA by the Numbers, a report presenting test scores and other measures of progress or decline
- Descriptions of the work of the annual Cowen Scholars, mainly Tulane graduate students in law and public policy, who participate in AdvanceNOLA, a program of college prep and expanded Advanced Placement offerings in New Orleans high schools

I want to zero in on the State of Public Education report of 2012 because the data collected here gives us the means to understand reality and, ultimately, to change that reality for the better. The report gives each of the post-Katrina 88 public schools in New Orleans a letter grade, the School Performance Score (SPS), based on standardized test scores plus, to a lesser degree, attendance, dropout, and graduation rates. A quick look at the grades reveals some clear trends. Most A and A+ schools have a higher percentage of white students than others in New Orleans, a fact that makes Warren Easton Charter High School, 97 percent African American and also A+, of particular interest. Of the six KIPP schools—KIPP is a well-regarded charter franchise—two earned B+s and one, a B−. Sci Academy's C rating reflects a significant dropout rate, but the school posted top gains in 2012 reading and math scores, as well as a nearly 100 percent senior graduation rate.

In general, the data shows that in New Orleans, where 80 percent of students now attend a charter school, charters outperform direct-run schools.[10] High schools generally score lower letter grades than elementary and middle schools because students often enter secondary school several grades behind in reading and math, meaning lower test scores and more dropouts. American College Test (ACT) scores, soon to be mandatory in all public high schools, may reduce school performance scores, since even kids who can pass the state's standardized tests may fail on the rigorous ACT.

In the end, what are we to make of all this? What is the "reality" we're to understand? The numbers offer an overall picture, but stories add nuance and detail, which is why I'm going to tell you about a few particular schools. No two cases are exactly alike; the "portfolio management" approach means a set of differentiated schools, each with a unique culture and a distinctive story to tell.

I'll begin with Warren Easton Charter High School, an OPSB charter. The school has a history that dates back to the nineteenth century, when it was a public school for boys; after mergers with other boys' schools, it later transitioned to co-ed and, in 1967, became integrated. Now it's almost completely African American, reflecting the demographic shift after *Brown v. Board of Education*. Dedicated educators refused to shut it down after Katrina virtually destroyed the school. In 2006 Warren Easton reopened as a charter school and, beginning in 2011, has achieved a 100 percent senior graduation rate and a letter grade of A.

A videotape from, of all things, the People's Choice Awards offers a peek inside Warren Easton. The actress Sandra Bullock, a New Orleans resident, received the first-ever Humanitarian Award in 2013 for her efforts on behalf of the school. The video begins with a senior administrator, who says, "The heroes are not a bunch of old men who reopened a school; the heroes are the children." What the students say is particularly moving. One young man in military dress says, "The real world is real, and either you're going to be ready for it or it's going to take you. And I believe all a hundred percent of us are ready for it." A young woman says, "Every student has their struggle. But when you walk through those doors, it doesn't matter anymore. No excuses. They tell you, we know you don't have a parent at home. What are you going to do so your children won't have to go through it like you?" Teachers speak of the culture of the school. One says, "It's a big family. A lot of places you hear that, but here we mean it." Another says, "Children know it when parents, adults, love them, and they respond in kind."[11]

Sandra Bullock, in her acceptance speech, says much the same thing: that every child at Warren Easton feels loved and cared for; that it's the kind of place where graduates come back to teach and where the principal will go to a student's house to find out why he's not at school. The school, drawing on the key practices of "High Schools That Work,"[12] offers before-school, after-school, and Saturday support sessions; field trips and cultural enrichment; a Career/Technical Education department; intensive college prep tutoring; and one-on-one faculty engagement, counseling, and follow-up. It's a program that shores up the lives of kids who have experienced trauma, poverty, neglect, and violence. Geoffrey Canada of the Harlem Children's Zone makes a distinction between "superman" efforts—actively saving at-risk youth and filling in gaps with focused supports and surrogate parenting—and the "conveyor-belt" approach, which, as practiced in the Harlem Children's Zone, means providing built-in guidance from cradle to career, starting with parenting classes and preschool, then building cognitive and emotional skills in graduated steps, year after year, in an enriched school environment.

What Warren Easton has done is to take kids who are going into the ninth grade, relatively late in the game, and help them succeed. A comment by Emily McLendon, the chair of the Career/Technical Education Department, illustrates the you-can-do-it spirit of the school. Pointing out that they can develop valuable, and marketable, skills, even before graduation, she tells students, "People who need a website don't care if you are still in school. They just want someone who can do the job." Urban kids, just like their middle-class counterparts, are notably tech savvy. I've seen this first-hand at a youth drop-in center downtown, where everyone had a cell phone and was multitasking, surfing the web, texting. I didn't ask them where they got the money for their phones—I was afraid to hear the answer—but they definitely knew how to use them. Technological competence acquired on a cell phone can be groundwork for a job, if we can teach the kids to value their own skills.

The New Orleans Charter Science and Math Academy, known as Sci Academy, is a state-administered charter school that has achieved notable success with a more than 90 percent African American population. It shares features with Warren Easton—wraparound programming, a caring but disciplined environment—but Warren Easton has had a long history in New Orleans, whereas Sci Academy is the new brainchild of a young education reformer, Ben Marcovitz, with degrees from Harvard and Yale. He founded the school in 2008, when he was 28, staffing it mainly with young Teach For America teachers, and later developed his own charter management organization, Collegiate Academies. Marcovitz focuses heavily on assessment of both students and teachers, with specified goals, frequent testing, data collection, feedback, and tutoring—a best practices approach. When he realized his incoming ninth-grade students were reading on a fifth-grade level, he changed the entire curriculum in one weekend to spend months on phonics, literacy, and fluency before returning to a full slate of academic subjects.

The school, in five years, has achieved its aims of a 100 percent senior graduation rate and a nearly 100 percent college admissions rate as well as big gains in test scores. Still, detractors point out that these figures mask its low retention rate (almost 40 percent drop out, going to other schools, getting expelled, or leaving the city) and claim that its high test scores reflect selection bias (deselecting kids with behavioral problems and disabilities and recruiting kids and families with the innate ability to make it).[13]

A solid success or a tempting illusion? Is the data-driven, test-taking approach simply rote learning, leaving kids unprepared, in a deeper sense, for college or career? Is any mention of second-tier kids—the ones from the worst neighborhoods and families, with posttraumatic stress and special needs—a wrongheaded focus when so many lives are at stake?[14] Questions like these are being asked in New Orleans and, indeed, all across the country.

The debate is, in itself, almost a distraction. "Understanding reality" involves the recognition that, as the saying goes, the perfect is the enemy of the good—that there are no benefits without costs, that unanimity is rare if not impossible, and that ideology won't save anyone, much less everyone. Leadership (to repeat) is flexible pragmatism in the service of a vision. The kind of school is less important than the goal of a quality education for each and every child.

Take Tanara Thomas. Ten years old when Katrina hit, Tanara rode out the hurricane in her grandmother's house in the Upper Ninth Ward with her mother, a family friend, and a disabled uncle; the floodwaters swallowed up the first floor, and they lived for days on crackers and little else, until a neighbor rescued them by boat. After a brief respite on the second floor of an elementary school, they started wading through waist-high water to the Superdome, got a ride to the Hilton (no water, no electricity), and finally took a bus to Grapevine, Texas. Tanara didn't return to New Orleans for two years. In the eighth grade she finally moved back, enrolling in a failing charter school with inadequate teachers.

Smart and hardworking, but very quiet, Tanara might have ended up like many other New Orleans kids, passed along through the system, hoping against hope for a slot at a community college. But then, in ninth grade, things changed. Her mother, responding to a flier, enrolled her at Ben Marcovitz's Sci Academy with the first group of freshman. The atmosphere was different the moment school staff made a home visit to lay out what the program would be and what the expectations were. Small groups, mentoring, constant class observations and assessments, long school hours and long workweeks—it was wall-to-wall immersion. But in her junior year, despite making significant progress, Tanara had to leave; her mother, who had lost the family home in the hurricane and was struggling financially, had qualified for Section 8 housing in Texas. A year later Tanara left her mother behind in Texas and went back to Sci Academy, having campaigned for a spot in the senior class.

The director of college counseling at Sci Academy, Alexander Levey, is a graduate of Wesleyan University in Middletown, Connecticut—which is where Tanara studies now. But making the transition to college successfully is still a challenge for most graduates of New Orleans's new charter schools. They need support at every step in the pipeline, and Sci Academy has hired a staff member specifically to visit graduates in college and see how they're doing. The academy began as strictly business, without a sports program or marching band, and that intense focus has bred success.[15]

Tanara's personal success, of course, has a lot to do with who she is: Though she is now more outspoken, the shy, ambitious, hardworking girl was there before Sci Academy. But her mind has been nurtured and broadened, and her horizons have expanded. "They've helped me realize I'm not just a person who's taking up space in the world. That I can actually do something with my life that can help others. That I can change the world."[16]

MARGIE AND I ARE VISITING A KIPP primary school in Central City. The KIPP charter schools are a nationwide network, started by Mike Feinberg and David Levin, two Teach For America graduates who have been at the forefront of the "no-excuses" education reform movement. The school is housed in a series of connected trailers, put up after the storm when nearly every public school building in New Orleans was so damaged by water and mold that they required months of repair, if not demolition. It has a stark, bare-bones look: white walls, fluorescent lights. We watch the kids troop in, all dressed the same in khakis, white shirts, blazers. Some look crisp, but others, wilted, with stains on their pants and shirttails untucked. Ninety-nine percent of them of are African American, with an Asian face or two from the Vietnamese enclave in New Orleans East. As they file into class, a teacher, also African American, stands by the doorway barking at them, Mr. This and Mr. That; they're all boys, and they're all called "Mr." Everyone is extremely well behaved, eyes straight ahead, no chatter, no high fives.

We stand at the back of the classroom and watch another teacher run the kids through their paces. KIPP has a system called SLANT: *s*it up, *l*isten, *a*sk questions, *n*od, and *t*rack whoever is speaking. The boys exhibit all the pre-scribed behaviors. There are occasional moments of humor and small bursts of unscripted dialogue, but mostly it's a smooth flow of operations, almost like a military exercise. You can see KIPP is trying to teach social behaviors and techniques of attention along with reading, writing, and arithmetic. KIPP graduates—so far mainly middle school students, though recently a high school has been added in New Orleans—go on to finish their schooling, including college, at four times the rate for students from low-income families nationwide. And really, who can argue with success?

My wife, for one. When we get home, she turns to me. "That really upset me."

"You have to think about their goal."

"I know. I see they're trying to give them the tools. But it really seemed like yelling to me. Like there was a cruel thread to it."

I am not as observant, or maybe not as sensitive, as Margie, but I know what she means: The environment was extremely strict, bordering on harsh. It reminded me of boot camp. "But think about the backgrounds they're coming from. They may need the structure to concentrate."

Margie says, "Remember when I read to the kindergartners?"

I do remember. A couple of times a year, we both do read-aloud sessions in the schools, and Margie came home after one of these and told me a story. She was reading the children a book about a dog, and afterward she asked if any of them had pets. One little boy bolted straight up and raised his hand. "I have a pet," he said. "Not a dog." "What is it?" Margie asked him. "It's a rat." "Really? What an interesting pet! What's his name?" It took her a minute to realize he didn't mean a furry white lab rat with a pink nose; he meant a *rat* rat—not in a cage but running loose, and probably one of many.

Margie says, "I was thinking about Henry"—he's our grandson, age two—"how he plays with his toys, and verbalizes everything, and lights up with people. How he goes to the park and the zoo and the Children's Museum. Those kids are going to have to be able to compete with Henry."

That is the point of KIPP, after all, to help these children compete—children who have rats, not pets, and who have never been to a children's museum. The problem is, many of them are missing things from early in their lives—consistency, stimulation, verbal richness, not to mention nutritious food, decent housing, basic safety—and the schools, whether charter or traditional, data driven or seat of the pants, have their work cut out for them trying to catch up.

The questions linger. Is KIPP more factory than school? Does it cherry-pick its students? Is tough love still love?

No benefit without cost.

IN THE END, KIPP DOES THE JOB: 93 percent of its students graduate, and 83 percent of students who completed the ninth grade at KIPP go on to college. Warren Easton and Sci Academy are also achieving these goals to a remarkable extent. But not all charter schools succeed. One that failed is Sojourner Truth Academy, founded by Channa Mae Cook, a young Stanford University educator who was inspired to come to New Orleans after Katrina. Cook, along with her colleague Kristin Leigh Moody, wrote a 200-page charter application, receiving help from New Schools for New Orleans, a group organized to incubate and support new charters in the post-Katrina era. Named for a former slave who became a spokesperson for emancipation and women's rights, Sojourner Truth had the twin goals of social justice and college readiness.

Despite Cook's passionate commitment, she lacked administrative competence, and the school slipped into dysfunction and chaos. The founding vision didn't translate into an effective program of education: The SPS declined from an inadequate 53.5 on a scale of 200 to an even worse 48.7 between 2010 and 2011.[17] Channa Cook herself left for the West Coast in 2011, to begin a doctorate in education at Stanford, leaving her first (and only) graduating class in the hands of a substitute principal who failed to rally the staff and impose order. Discipline deteriorated, morale suffered; the annual audit revealed "irregularities." The reasons for the failure of Sojourner Truth are complex. There are no villains in this case because everyone was well intentioned, but in the end the key questions were: Did the board of Sojourner Truth hire the right people and put appropriate controls in place? Did board members have a plan and a clear set of metrics to measure progress? Were they getting the kind of information they needed to properly govern?

The school closed its doors in May 2012, when the state revoked its charter. By that point, there was no toilet paper or soap in the bathrooms, no school supplies, no teachers in many of the classrooms. A fight that started between two girls spilled out into the street, ultimately involving parents—the mothers threw bricks at each other, and the stepfather of one girl was arrested for hitting the other girl with his truck. Her injuries were, thankfully, minor. Still, the fracas made for a sorry coda to a story that began with so much optimism.

The failure of some charter schools is another piece of the complex reality of education in New Orleans and elsewhere. Though the closing of failed charters is the logical result of accountability—no Band-Aids, no excuses—it's the students who often pay the price in lost relationships, disrupted learning, and diminished confidence. Damonika Stokes, one of the seniors in Sojourner Truth's sole graduating class, said, "It's pretty obvious we are getting cheated out of an education—even I know that." Although she won a scholarship to Bard College in New York, she worries about her lack of preparation. "When we go to college, we're not going to know any science."[18]

Clearly the RSD has trouble maintaining stability and learning in schools that are closing and addressing funding issues when start-up grants expire.[19] The RSD attempts to find other schools for displaced students and often hands off a failing charter to a new operator. But without a systematic plan for these transitions, there's a significant human toll.

Advocates for the central administration model point out other weaknesses in the charter system:

- Nationwide, charters do only slightly better than traditional district schools on performance measures.
- High-stakes accountability aimed squarely at teachers, as if teachers alone are the problem, isn't likely to attract qualified people to the profession or engender creativity in the classroom.
- In transitioning to charters, the funding of new schools diverts money that could be spent on teachers and supplies in existing schools.
- Teaching to the test, emphasized in the data-driven approach of charter

schools, fails to inculcate critical thinking or build the character and perseverance that really matter in life.

- Low test scores reflect not teacher failure but a host of social factors that exist beyond the classroom.

Author Paul Tough argues, compellingly, that we have stopped debating poverty at all in modern America and have simply merged the problem of poverty with that of poor urban schooling.[20]

THERE IS TRUTH TO ALL THESE ARGUMENTS. But, again, we must work within the inevitable calculus of costs and benefits, means and ends. A city like New Orleans, majority African American, with all the usual urban problems, needs to bring its schoolchildren the best education possible in a measurable and consistent way; it needs to create on-ramps to a better life through jobs and college degrees. Charters are only a means to these ends, not ends in themselves.

Some say the old type of public school works well if the community supports it and administrators build a culture of quality instruction. A case in point: Union City, NJ, where the tax base funds two years of preschool for every child, where parents and teachers together have created a learning environment that's lively and engaged, where both cognitive and noncognitive skills are nurtured, and where teachers are mentored and principals lead.[21] But in New Orleans, very few traditional public schools were still standing after the floodwaters receded. Beyond that, why try to rebuild a system that was clearly failing to begin with? Hadn't the community basically given up on its public schools even before the storm? The old order's top-heavy bureaucracy, frequent administrative upheavals, strict calendar mandates, and, most of all, insidious culture of failure (test scores in the basement, dropout rates through the roof) guaranteed disaster for thousands of schoolchildren. The charter school system, despite its problems, has altered that outcome through sheer will and intention. At the heart of the successful charters—Easton, Sci Academy, KIPP schools, and many others—is a fervent attitude of optimism, a rousing *Yes we can.*

"WHO WANTS TO GO TO COLLEGE?" I'm in front of a room full of kids at the City Center in Cleveland, where I've just given a talk to city officials about New Orleans' educational transformation. The speech laid out the numbers: 80 percent of public school students in Orleans Parish attend charter schools; the senior graduation rate rose from 79 in 2005 to 94 percent in 2011; the percentage of African American students who are proficient in math and English has more than doubled; the percentage of students attending failing schools has been reduced from 62 to 13 percent.

This second talk, more of a conversation really, is with a group of inner-city teenagers. When I ask about college, the response is not exactly electric. One hand goes up, a little hesitantly; then another. I wait them out, but the showing remains sparse.

"You don't believe you can do it, but you can. Don't let anyone tell you that you won't make it."

Then I tell them my story. I begin with the fact that I pretty much lucked out in the circumstances I was born into. Even so, I had a lot of trouble with school, especially reading. I tell them about my father saying I must be either stupid or lazy. I tell them about trying to be good at other things—making a lot of friends, getting on the football team, even getting to be president of the student council. But it wasn't until I went into the army and took a special exam that I found out I had some talents that don't show up on regular school tests. I could organize people, make plans, get things done. And after that I got more confident. A lot of people helped me, and in the end I went from being in the bottom reading group in the third grade to being the president of Tulane.

"So," I say, wrapping up my talk, "here come the life lessons." I write the bullet points on the chalkboard.

- You can catch up.
- You have skills you don't know you have.
- You should find people who believe in you.

I'm not sure how much of my pep talk is working. I'm also thinking about the numbers (or, as the academics put it, scalability): How many of these kids will make it without a good school to save them?

Still, a vision of the future is the first step toward creating it. I'm trying to tell them: *Yes you can.*

BELIEF AND EXPECTATION ARE IMPORTANT, but they can grow only in environments that nurture them. What, in fact, has been proven to work in educational systems? What doesn't work?

Testing is one of the points of contention. Are tests the way forward, or is our overreliance on them a bureaucratic stumbling block? It may be that the fight over testing has more to do with the inadequacies of the tests than the concept itself. An improvement would be a set of noncognitive metrics to assess those capacities that go unrecognized on standard achievement tests. These noncognitive metrics could help identify those aspects of character or personality that Paul Tough explores so eloquently in *How Children Succeed*, including, crucially, capacities to self-regulate, plan ahead, be persistent, defer gratification, seek novelty, and form relationships.

Another point of contention: How do we prepare and motivate excellent teachers? Should we opt for Teach For America or union veterans? Professional guidelines or free-ranging creativity? Everyone agrees that the single most important factor in learning success is a skilled teacher, but no one knows exactly what makes a teacher "skilled." A lot of things you think would predict a teacher's success—BA from a prestigious university, good grades, certification—don't, in fact, correlate. Bill Gates recently donated significant money to educators to explore the issue because, he said, there seemed to be some confusion about what breeds teaching mastery, and he's curious to know the answer.

Doug Lemov, a former classroom teacher who became a managing director of Uncommon Schools, a charter network, had the idea of filming master teachers and codifying their behaviors and practices. His study of the resulting videotapes, recorded over five years of travels, led him to write the book *Teach Like a Champion*, which itemizes techniques for teachers—things like "Positive Framing," using affirmation rather than criticism to make a point, and "Cold Call," with the teacher randomly picking a student to answer a question.[22] Other researchers have different pedagogic systems, with some, like Deborah Loewenberg Ball, dean of the University of Michigan's school of education, focusing on mastery of subject domain.[23] Whatever works, I say. If these programs produce results for children, I'm for them. It's possible that places like Uncommon Schools and KIPP are performing at a much higher level than other charters because of their systematic, regimented approach to teaching. The bottom line: If we have better instruction, we'll reach more children across all types of schools, and we'll begin to change the trajectory of lives in the inner city.

But you have to ask, which lives? Another issue is equity and "the problem we all live with." In New Orleans, educational reform has aimed to redress the great imbalance in our public school system, with race and class the chief predictors of success or failure, followed by the educational level of parents. And though we're making headway, inequality persists.

Take Mary Dora Coghill Accelerated Academy, formerly Mary Coghill Elementary School. Under the leadership of its principal, Aisha Jones, it has transitioned from a state-administered direct-run school to a charter, but has retained the come-one- come-all open enrollment policy that prevailed before the transition. That policy means, in practice, a disproportionate number of children with special needs, serious disabilities, and behavioral problems. The refusal of many charters to serve such children is usually framed as a budgetary issue. But the result, across the city, is a tacit two-tier system, with slots in the stronger charters going to kids whose scores are already higher.

RSD charter schools, as opposed to any other type of charter, are not allowed to set admissions requirements or deselect children with special needs; if one of the RSD charters is oversubscribed, it has to run a lottery to determine who gets in. In the recent education documentary *Waiting for Superman*, the most wrenching scenes are of charter school lotteries where desperate mothers hope their child's number will be drawn, underscoring what should be an obvious point—that chance is no way to guarantee everyone equal opportunity. The film shows how diligently urban parents work to get a good education for their children, despite widely held (and patently false) perceptions that low-income parents don't care about schooling.[24]

Open enrollment in New Orleans schools is more of an idea than a reality, with many children shuffled to particular schools by the luck of the draw or by a covert sorting process. Though parents are supposed to have the freedom to choose a school for their child, for the first years of our reform, "free choice" wasn't all that free. The decentralized model of numerous charter schools and networks has spawned a confusing tangle of options for parents, who must make time to learn about, and apply to, each school individually. Those with more skills, connections, and savvy tended to grab the best places early on, leaving some parents out in the cold.

A recent innovation, which educators hope will lead to greater equity, is the OneApp, modeled after the National Resident Matching Program for American physicians: A student fills out one application that goes to all schools participating in the OneApp system, parents rank the schools they prefer up to a total of eight, and students are assigned to schools taking into account these preferences. But given that all schools aren't equal, choices are never going to be equal. And, as Aisha Jones, principal of Mary Coghill Elementary School, has pointed out, all the city's schools, charter or district run, are failing in another way: integration. "If you look at our student population, we are almost completely African American, I mean almost completely," she says.[25]

So we're back to the problem we all live with. The achievement gap between white and African American children has widened again, after a brief period when integration seemed to be addressing the disparity. (And it was a rise in black students' test scores, not a decline in white students' performance, that narrowed the achievement gap during that time.)[26] In New Orleans, demographics and recent history work against integration, but the facts speak loudly. And Ruby Bridges speaks loudly too: Bringing diverse people together, she argues, nourishes growing minds.

As it turns out, there's a charter for that: the Morris Jeff Community school, an RSD-run charter, with a student body that is 55 percent African American and the remainder largely white, closely reflecting the demographics of New Orleans. It's too soon to judge if the experiment is a success—Morris Jeff is still a young school—but it's a sign of revived communal will, that special New Orleans ethos of "we're all in this together." It's also a sign of the strength of the new educational vision in New Orleans, where autonomous schools can create agendas that reflect a community's deepest hopes and wishes.

THE RESHAPING OF THE PUBLIC SCHOOL SYSTEM began in 2005 with the Education Report of the BNOB Commission; the basic vision of numerous diverse schools run by committed educators and organized into networks has been largely realized, and with fundamentally positive results. I take a pragmatic position: A school that works is a school that works. But I do believe that autonomous schools are the best route to the outcomes we're looking for: higher graduation rates, lower dropout rates, better scores, more college admissions and completions, more job training, more careers, and better lives.

*To sum up the principles that animated the work of the Education Committee in 2005 and that continue to shape transformative change in the schools of New Orleans: Leaders confront the situation as it exists. They pursue input from all stakeholders and consult experts on best practices. And, importantly, they are open-minded about solutions, developing diverse means to arrive at the goal.*

Taken together, these principles constitute a nuanced and flexible approach, based on a thorough understanding of multiple realities, including community vision, expert opinion, the existing power structure, and diverse educational strategies. This approach is a means to an end, a tactic in the service of a strategy. And that strategy is to return America to its position as a global leader in education, with an educated citizenry prepared to live in a complex, competitive, and changing world. With globalization has come fierce competition in all realms, and education is no exception. Take the (shocking) fact that the United States ranks twenty-fifth in math among industrialized countries—and the equally shocking fact that 71 percent of U.S. students express high confidence in their math ability.[27] The gap is stark evidence of a failure by students (along with parents, teachers, and politicians) to fully understand reality. We are a nation living in an outdated illusion that we are the first, the best, the most scientifically advanced, the most technologically innovative.

To make that vision of ourselves a reality in the twenty-first century, we have to educate our children for the twenty-first century.

MARGIE AND I ARE VISITING ARTHUR ASHE Charter School, a "turn-around" school in the FirstLine charter organization run by CEO Jay Altman.[28] The children are wearing gray pants or skirts, white shirts, and little bow ties, and they're sitting at long desks, faces lit by glowing computer screens, hands moving cursors and click-click-clicking. The teacher has gathered a small group in one corner of the room, seated around a table, where a quiet mini-class is in session: Hands shoot up, voices murmur, laughter ripples. They are talking about caribous, food, and extinction. The room hums with energy.

Arthur Ashe Charter School is one of five FirstLine charters in New Orleans, all turnaround schools: Dibert, Green, Ashe, Langston Hughes, and—toughest of all—Clark High School. Starting a charter from scratch is one thing: usually just one or two grades at the outset, adding a grade a year until you have a full school population and regular graduating classes. But to turn around a school that has been failing, taking the students as they are, where they are, and improving not just test scores but the entire culture of the place, is a steeply uphill climb.

The teacher guiding us through the school explains the computers: FirstLine has adopted an approach known as blended learning, whereby students get time each day at the computer to work at a comfortable level, setting their own pace and working toward individual goals. During this period the teacher pulls out small groups of kids who are all on the same level or works one on one with children who are struggling. The teacher says test scores have leaped enormously in the last year, because children are receiving targeted and appropriate attention instead of the everyone-lumped-together scenario of conventional classrooms.

One of the students, a little girl with her bow tie askew, tugs at the teacher's Harvard sweatshirt—college sweatshirts seemed to be favored faculty attire, sending the not-so-subtle message of "We all go to college here; you will too!" The little girl whispers something and the teacher gives her a hug, then excuses herself. She and the little girl hold hands as they go out of the room.

We wait a little, then go out into the hallway. I turn to Margie. "So?"

"Well, you'd think it was a factory with all those computers, but it doesn't feel like that. Everyone looks pretty happy, like they're playing video games."

Nothing wrong with technology in the service of learning. And I'm pleased to see a development, long awaited—ever since the days of the BNOB Commission. Arthur Ashe isn't a stand-alone experiment but part of a network of schools sharing organization, resources, ethos, and practices.

We walk through the halls, bright yellow and turquoise walls, gleaming floors, and listen to the murmuring voices in the classrooms. It feels like a well-regulated household. Or, even better, a school for the twenty-first century.

## Chapter 5

# MAKE IT RIGHT

## AIM HIGH

I'M FLYING IN LATE ON A SUNDAY NIGHT FROM PANAMA, WHERE Tulane has a strong alumni group. As the plane begins its descent and people start shifting in their seats, putting away laptops and folding up newspapers, I look out the window and, as always, think: water, water, everywhere. Below me, a wide expanse as far as the eye can see, broken only by the commuter bridge across Lake Pontchartrain, the longest of any in the world across water. It's hard to distinguish, looking down, which water is which: Somewhere below in all that boundless blue is the wide mouth of the Mississippi, with the curve of the Gulf Coast broken up by inlets, estuaries, bayous, wetlands, and swamps. As the plane banks right, New Orleans rises up, a narrow strip of land sandwiched between the snaking curves of the Mississippi and, to the north, the broad expanse of the lake.

Whenever I fly over the city, I remember that helicopter ride of September 2, 2005, surveying a sea of muddy water broken only by rooflines and treetops—80 percent of New Orleans completely submerged. But now, almost a decade later, you can see the city coming back—not just the sliver by the river, the elevated land along the Mississippi that came through relatively unscathed, but also the back of town, between the river and Lake Pontchartrain, which suffered the worst of the floods.[1] The houses and streets are more scattered, less dense, but still visibly there.

THIS CHAPTER IS ABOUT THE PHYSICAL rebuilding of a drowned city. The leadership principle, "Aim high," is almost a pun: an instruction both to build above sea level and, figuratively, to hold up a vision of urban vitality and renaissance as the ultimate goal. Or, to put it another way, "ambitiously optimize"—choose the best available options and pursue the best partnerships in a situation fraught with obstacles.

*Aiming high is about the art of setting goals. Lofty expectations, ambitious yet achievable, are the most effective way to motivate people. Successful leaders use the goal-setting process to focus people's attention and energy. They also understand that the best goal setting, though fact based, should also be guided by an intuition of what will inspire people to reach further.*

The ultimate message: Nothing is impossible. As I've mentioned elsewhere (and as I allude to in the title of this book), geographer Peirce Lewis called New Orleans "the inevitable city on the impossible site"; the drive to turn what looks impossible into something inevitable is a recurrent feature of the city's long history of devastations and resurrections. After Katrina, we set ourselves the daunting goal of remaking the city—this time almost from scratch. Given the man-made nature of the flooding, the first and most important priority was to reconstruct the flood protection system and restore the wetlands and barrier islands that are a natural defense against storm surges. Over the course of eight years, the Army Corps of Engineers repaired and rebuilt the canals, levees, drains, and pumps that ensure the basic safety of the city. It's true that the new fortifications have produced the paradoxical levee effect, encouraging people to live in high-risk zones because of the perception of safety. But the levees also represent an engineering solution to the human necessity—or at least fact—of living near the coasts. New Orleanians were going to come home, no matter what.[2] And the rebuilt levees have withstood recent tests: In August 2012, during Hurricane Isaac, a massive Category 1 storm, the city remained safe despite local street flooding.

Shortly after Katrina, I testified in Congress for timely federal help in the rebuilding effort, especially in relation to the Stafford Act, which, among other provisions, asks cities to front the money for repairs after a natural disaster for reimbursement later—an absurdity, given the dimensions of Katrina. On one occasion or another, a number of members of Congress asked me point blank why should we rebuild the flooded neighborhoods at all, given that they're below sea level and disasters were only going to happen again. I always felt fury at those moments, and gave them my standard reply:

> As I hear you, you're proposing a new standard for what the United States owes its communities. Logically, then, you don't rebuild New York City after 9/11 because it's prone to terrorist attacks. You don't rebuild San Francisco if it has an earthquake because it's prone to earthquakes. Same for tornadoes in Huntsville or Springfield: just let all these communities disappear. This is not the kind of country I think about when I think about America. I think of America as a place that values all its cities and towns, and that believes in preserving them generation after generation.[3]

I won't repeat all the details from chapter 2 about the Bring New Orleans Back (BNOB) Commission report on land use and the intense debate over "green dots" representing parkland where the Ninth Ward once was. My honest assessment of the report was that it wasn't all bad; it was a working proposition that, with some tweaking, might have bridged two extremist views—"New Orleans exactly as it was" versus a shiny new "New Orleans of the Twenty-first Century." But Mayor Ray Nagin, because of vocal opposition from the black community, basically left the question of land use open. Another urban planning process—this one initiated by the New Orleans City Council and called the Lambert plan (after the advisory firm)—focused solely on the rebuilding of flooded neighborhoods. Twenty-two months after Katrina, in June 2007, the Lambert plan was merged with yet another one, the Unified New Orleans Plan (UNOP), funded primarily by the Rockefeller Foundation and addressing all neighborhoods in the city; this final version was accepted by the Louisiana Recovery Authority and forwarded to Washington, DC, in order to receive federal monies for rebuilding.[4]

Three plans, 22 months, and, in the interim, endless dispute. One group that offered some chance of success during this chaotic period was the New Orleans Redevelopment Authority (NORA), founded in 1968 to reduce blight and prevent the spread of slums in the city and with the legal capacity to acquire and dispose of real estate. After Katrina, NORA's board was expanded—I became a member, along with other civic leaders—and the focus became comprehensive neighborhood redevelopment rather than single-property expropriations. But NORA didn't get its promised funding from Nagin in the first year after Katrina, and then it met with opposition from Ed Blakely, whom Nagin hired to lead the recovery effort in early 2007. Blakely, a professor of urban planning at the University of Sydney, Australia, had publicly remarked that what New Orleans needed was a "recovery czar," and Nagin seized on the phrase and the man, hoping for some kind of magic.

Blakely, who left the job after two years (and has written a book, *My Storm*, about what he perceives as his many accomplishments[5]), is widely disliked in New Orleans, for his inflated rhetoric ("cranes in the sky," he famously promised); his ignorance of the city's geography and history; and his dismissive remarks on its citizenry.[6] He also wanted control over NORA in order to implement his own plan involving 17 "target zones" for rebuilding.

Blakely came across as mostly bluster with little substance—not unlike Ray Nagin, especially in his second term as mayor. Basically, for almost two years after Katrina, the failure of top-down leadership led to uncertainty, chaos, and roadblocks to progress. Meanwhile, tens of thousands of New Orleanians continued to live in trailers and shelters, or in other cities and states, while the Lower Ninth Ward grew into Jungleland and other neighborhoods remained blighted. True recovery started only when nonprofits and local groups began to create a grassroots movement that cut across all segments of the community; this groundswell, from the bottom up, produced an organic and unified vision of the city that embraced, and indeed grew out of, the context of unique neighborhoods.

Nagin and Blakely talked the talk but didn't walk the walk. "Aiming high"—or "ambitiously optimizing"—is not about doing what is expedient in the moment or playing to the lowest common denominator. It's about reimagining the future while respecting the past. It's about challenging the status quo while adhering to the values and culture that make a city unique.

WHAT MAKES NEW ORLEANS UNIQUE IS ITS MUSIC, food, architecture, history—and its neighborhoods. The city, with a total area of 350 square miles, has 73 of them,[7] based on geographic boundaries and the names people give to defined and well-known areas, with populations ranging from 1,500 (in Pontchartrain Park) to 15,000 plus (in Audubon, where I live).[8] One of the first neighborhoods to rebound after Katrina—in terms of populations, services, and amenities—is Village De L'Est, the Vietnamese enclave in New Orleans East, where immigrants who arrived after the fall of Saigon in 1975 founded a thriving community. Many of the original arrivals were Catholic, and it was Archbishop Philip Hannan, visiting Vietnamese refugee centers across the country, who got in touch with New Orleans Catholic Charities and arranged for a thousand immigrants to move to Louisiana. By 1990, through "chain migration," with émigrés paving the way for friends and relatives, the community had grown to 5,000, almost equaling the number of African Americans who lived in the area.

The head of the Catholic community in Village de L'Este after Katrina was Father Vien Thé Nguyen of Mary Queen of Vietnam Church; following in the tradition of Vietnamese Catholic priests, Father Vien has served as primary leader of both religious life and the parish community in the years since Katrina.[9] Largely through the influence of the church, the Vietnamese of East New Orleans, who started out crowded into a building complex called the Versailles Arms before developing their own neighborhood in Village de L'Est, managed to preserve the tightly knit parish structure of their native land. For almost 30 years they remained unusually independent of city and state government, creating their own networks for health care and social support, with a seven-zone church organization that was further divided into hamlets—streets with their own saints and feast days. Hard hit by the hurricane and scattered across a number of states, these community members were among the first to return after the storm—600 of them by December 2005—aided by a network of communication through Father Vien.

Father Vien oversaw the cleanup and the start of construction on the decimated housing stock and in February 2006 helped organize a protest against a nearby landfill, a hated symbol of the BNOB land use plan to bulldoze the neighborhood and turn it into green space. Because of this highly effective protest, the landfill contract was not renewed. The active engagement of Vietnamese residents reflects an experience going back to the 1970s, when some of the original immigrants were boat people, refugees from the Vietnam War who escaped in fragile boats at great peril to their lives. One of these older residents said, "It is harder leaving from your culture. Hurricane is nothing. In the hurricane, you have your family with you all the time."[10]

Cultural resilience and independence characterize the Vietnamese community as a whole, including its leader, Father Vien. Sidestepping Ray Nagin's circus of dysfunction, Road Home, the private nonprofit housing assistance program often criticized for its inadequacies, and FEMA, also inadequate, Father Vien came to me early on to consult about two pressing necessities beyond houses: a health care center and a school. Acting as a facilitator, I put Father Vien in touch with the Tulane City Center (TCC) of the School of Architecture, the Tulane School of Medicine, and staff members at the fledgling Cowen Institute for Public Education Initiatives. Collaborations between the university and the Mary Queen of Vietnam Community Development Corporation, the grassroots association representing residents, have resulted in several solid accomplishments. The development group collaborated with Tulane School of Medicine to start a health clinic to serve immediate needs; also, TCC has created a new primary care center, culturally sensitive and neighborhood based, repurposing an old post office in Village de L'Est to provide a spacious and inviting environment.

As part of the systemwide transformation of schools, Abramson High School in New Orleans East, a failed school that, after a series of transitions, was being administered by the Recovery School District, was finally shut down in 2013. But the school system in New Orleans East also has had its successes, for example, Sci Academy, the innovative charter run by Ben Marcovitz. But Father Vien wanted a neighborhood school specifically devoted to helping Vietnamese children acculturate to mainstream society while at the same time preserving traditional values; he applied for, and received, a charter for the Intercultural Charter School. The school's mission was "to create an excellent school for our community with academic rigor, great pride in diverse cultures, and a passion for learning throughout life...a community-based school that will reflect the lives of the community and integrate our projects (urban farm, open market, health center, retirement center, cultural center, etc.) into the curriculum and students' daily lives."[11] The school offered instruction in Vietnamese as part of the program of study, and a website photo showed children performing a traditional dance in full native costume.

Though neighborhood-based initiatives have the benefit of being local and culturally sensitive, they sometimes fail to meet external standards. Intercultural's fate, like that of Sojourner Truth mentioned in chapter 4, is, in the end, a story of noble aspirations that miscarried. The downside of the school was its academic program: It earned a school performance score of D in 2011, based on attendance rates and test scores. In 2013, the Board of Elementary and Secondary Education approved its takeover by Einstein Charter, which received a $1 million Investing in Innovation grant from the Federal Department of Education to develop effective academic programs and boost performance scores.[12]

A less fraught project in Village de L'Est is the planning of green spaces. TCC has designed a site plan for a 29-acre parcel of land as an urban farm to replace the neighborhood's lost network of gardens, dating back to the 1970s, which provided specific produce central to Vietnamese cuisine and culture.

Other neighborhoods in New Orleans have shown a similar commitment to rebuilding their communities. Take Broadmoor, a mixed-race, mixed-income area that is at the very center of New Orleans's "bowl"—the lowest point in the whole city, flooded by ten feet of water—and, as a side note, Walter Isaacson's neighborhood. (He's a huge fan, booster, and fundraiser.) Broadmoor wrote its own redevelopment plan in 2006, the only one of the city's 73 neighborhoods to do so. In the years since, the Broadmoor Improvement Association has developed an "Education Corridor" with a new school, library, and fine arts and wellness center. Another neighborhood, Holy Cross, flooded by levee breaks along the Industrial Canal and the Mississippi River–Gulf Outlet (MR-GO), has developed a Global Green initiative—five Brad Pitt–type houses, with eco-friendly design, akin to Pitt's own Make It Right houses in the Ninth Ward (he was design jury chairman for the Global Green project), plus a planned 18-unit apartment complex and a community center. With the help of the Preservation Resource Center and its allied programs, Rebuilding Together and Operation Comeback, Holy Cross has also restored many historic shotgun houses. Basically, the community has moved on both fronts of recovery, creation, and preservation.

Speaking of shotguns: The design is pure New Orleans vernacular. Other local styles include Creole cottages, Craftsman bungalows, and European townhouses, but nothing says New Orleans like a shotgun. Usually three or four rooms ranked one behind the other, with no connecting hallways, the shotgun house supposedly got its name from the fact that someone standing at the front entrance could fire a gun straight through the house and the bullet would fly out the back door without hitting a wall. Shotguns may also reflect the influence of the river: According to this line of thinking, competition for frontage on the Mississippi led to the construction of long houses with narrow facades, set perpendicular to the river. Some say the building design was imported from Haiti. And some argue it's a tax thing: In the nineteenth century, you were taxed on the basis of the facade's dimensions rather than square footage, so the less facade the better.

And here a brief personal anecdote: In 1998, the first year Margie and I lived in New Orleans, we rented the second floor of an upscale shotgun on St. Charles Avenue while the university completed renovations of the President's Mansion.[13] There were things I loved about that apartment: the floor-to-ceiling windows opening out onto a small porch; the whir of the ceiling fans, stirring the long curtains; the foreignness of it all—the feeling that I was someplace "else," far removed from New Jersey and Cleveland, my other two homes. One night as I stood out on the balcony under the stars, listening to the clang of the streetcars beneath me, it was all I could do not to pull a Marlon Brando and yell "Stell-la" into the humid New Orleans night.

An amazing thing about the shotgun is how varied the basic type is: double shotguns, sidehalls, Eastlake detailing (turned columns, lacy decoration), Italianate types, and the variation known as the camelback, with a "hump" of a second story in the back part of the house. But one and all have a front porch. New Orleans is, by and large, a front porch culture, everyone within eye view and earshot of the neighbors, everyone sitting out in midday or after supper, voices ringing up and down the block. The "neighborhood effect" Robert Sampson talks about—social cohesion, close affiliations even when not kinship relationships, the tacit enforcement of social norms—is in part due to the way the old houses sit next to each other, cheek by jowl. Or perhaps the social cohesion was there first, in a shared background, history, and culture, and the houses express the feeling rather than create it. Cause, effect, chicken, egg; maybe it's impossible to say. But as recovery and reinvention go forward, it's an argument for building houses in clusters, with an eye to density and an ear to earshot, to truly recapture New Orleans as we knew it.

MICHAEL PICOT, OUT IN THE SIDE YARD of his Make It Right (MIR) house—an eco-designed space-age shotgun—calls for his wife, Mary, who steps onto the porch to say hello to a visiting journalist from the *Times-Picayune* who has brought along some out-of-town guests. Everyone from out of town asks to see the Brad Pitt MIR houses, which rise out of the wastes of the Lower Ninth Ward like a dream village, multicolored, multi-angled, fantastical. The group has already cruised by the boxy-looking Frank Gehry house, front half painted vivid pink and back half a glowing purple, with an exterior staircase and slatted porches that seem meant as a riff on New Orleans shutters. Whenever I visit the neighborhood I always feel like I'm at Disneyland, looking up at Technicolor houses on stilts, or like I'm on a stage set of facades without interiors.

The Picots have been living in their new house since 2009, long enough to know if it works or not. Michael likes the floor plan, which he describes as "trailer-like"—maybe it's his retirement dream, like living in a silver stream-lined recreational vehicle, or maybe he's been brainwashed by the FEMA trailers all over town in the last years. Mary says she likes being up high in the air, with breezes wafting through all the rooms, and she loves her

**Image 6** MIR Gehry house

A house designed by famed architect Frank Gehry as part of Brad Pitt's Make It Right housing development in the Lower Ninth Ward. The MIR project features eco-friendly materials and energy-conscious design, but has been criticized for neglecting the neighborhood culture of New Orleans in favor of isolated architectural statements.

*(Photo credit: Sally Asher, Tulane University)*

energy-efficient kitchen appliances and the solar panels that save so much money.

Inside the house: no modernist furniture or abstract paintings, no polished woods floors and track lighting, but overstuffed furniture, knick-knacks on every shelf, framed Super Bowl T-shirts on the walls, and a poster of Rickey Jackson of the New Orleans Saints lit, like a saint, by a looped string of leftover Christmas lights. It's incongruous yet strangely heartening. Whatever the architectural visions of Brad Pitt's dream team designers, the people living in these houses bring their authentic selves with them.[14] The MIR houses aren't simply stage sets or facades; people are living real lives here.

About Brad Pitt, a celebrity who has gone all out to bring back a part of New Orleans that suffered the worst of Katrina: He has brought aesthetic design into an abandoned place and has funded the research and cutting-edge technology to create green houses for the twenty-first century. One of the MIR consultants is William McDonough, author of the best-selling environmental design book *Cradle to Cradle*,[15] who has spoken at Tulane on the subject of eco-architecture. His design philosophy calls for self-sustaining structures made of recyclable materials; houses that imitate the beauty and efficiency of nature's own architecture—of a tree, for example. MIR offers a stirring image of future cities, living and breathing in harmony with the universe, embracing the cycle of growth and decay and using clean energy to become part of an organic whole.

Brad Pitt deserves much credit for bringing these ideas to what was, essentially, a ground zero for rebuilding. The crisis of Katrina was, again, an opportunity to remake the city. Pitt himself has been an ambassador for a worldview that combines environmental responsibility with social justice; and he's attracted media attention and money not only to "make it right" but to make it work. When Tulane tried to give him an honorary degree in recognition of his contributions, he refused, saying he didn't want the limelight or the credit.

So applause is warranted, even if Pitt isn't asking for any. Still, there are those who beg to differ. Among them is Kevin Fox Gotham, a professor in the Department of Sociology at Tulane, who has written several articles on the media circus occasioned by Katrina—what he describes as the "spectacularization" of disaster. Gotham makes the point that of all the celebrity philanthropy in play after Katrina (and many famous people have brought their star power to New Orleans in recent years), "Pitt's campaign has been the only one to build a foundation to leverage and combine corporate donations, architecture firms, and merchandising opportunities to help rebuild a major section of New Orleans."[16] But on the negative side, Gotham also notes MIR's tendency toward "commodification" and the pursuit of "merchandising opportunities and consumption-based entertainment practices."[17]

A more widespread perception in New Orleans is that Brad Pitt, in his well-intentioned focus on green innovation, has neglected some ordinary and humble necessities in the post-Katrina landscape: chiefly, the history and culture of neighborhoods in the city and the importance not just of houses as islands of energy-efficiency and modern design but of the communal life of people connected by kinship and social networks—which means, practically speaking, located near churches, schools, parks, community centers, health care centers, and other homes. Statement architecture only goes so far when the backdrop is Jungleland, a snake-infested swamp with a jack-o'-lantern pattern of clustered houses interrupted by vacant lots and marshy tracts of nothing.[18]

In fairness, MIR has also made efforts to rebuild the community—a playground with state-of-the-art equipment and a skate park in collaboration with Lil Wayne, a rapper from Hollygrove, another low-lying African American neighborhood in New Orleans. MIR has hosted an ice cream social; staged a "Pink Pavilion" event with mini-houses made of pink fabric (pink for hope) representing the MIR houses of the future; met with community leaders; and invited a new group of people, not originally from the Lower Ninth and primarily employed in public service jobs—schoolteachers, firefighters, emergency medical technicians—to apply for mortgages. No question, the 90 houses built so far represent a substantial achievement. But the ultimate vision of the MIR Foundation—new architecture for a new century—noble as it is, may not be the most practical model for bringing New Orleans back.

ANOTHER INDIVIDUAL WHO HAS AIMED HIGH, but in a different way, is Len Riggio, founder and executive chairman of Barnes & Noble, whose idea for rebuilding the city goes beyond constructing houses to the more ambitious goal of restoring neighborhoods. Riggio was born in the Bronx, the son of a cabdriver, and his wife, Louise, is the granddaughter of Italian immigrants who settled in New Orleans. Their great wealth gave them the means to make a difference, but their choice of where, what, and how grew directly from their own histories—Louise Riggio's roots in New Orleans; and Len Riggio's working-class background that gave him a real understanding of ordinary people's lives.

The Riggios' response to the horror of Katrina was to found Project Home Again, personally funding the effort with $20 million from their charitable foundation. Len Riggio came to me after meetings with Ray Nagin had failed to produce a response, and I suggested he go to NORA, which by 2008 was actively involved in restoring neighborhoods and properties.[19] Partnering with NORA, Project Home Again built 101 houses in Gentilly, another neighborhood that suffered huge flood damage when the levees broke, with a target date of 2014 for another 100 houses. Project Home Again chose Gentilly for development in part because it was a stable, racially integrated, close-knit, working-class neighborhood and in part because a large parcel of vacant land was available there. Riggio says that the second round of houses "is about making neighborhoods whole again. We need to encourage continued development and repopulation. While individual homes are the centers of family life, communities are the centers of civic life."[20]

Every aspect of Project Home Again reflects an understanding of, and respect for, the history and culture of the neighborhood. The two-, three-, and four-bedroom designs in the Gentilly development adhere to a modified Craftsman style, the most common architectural type of the washed-away neighborhood, with deep eaves, front porches, and columns. Though equipped with energy-efficient heating and air-conditioning, the houses still

**Image 7** Project Home Again
A house in the Project Home Again development in Gentilly. Created by Len Riggio, founder, former CEO, and current board chair of Barnes & Noble, Project Home Again has built more than 100 houses, with another 100 scheduled for completion by 2014. The houses, clustered into neighborhoods, feature a traditional modest design, energy-efficient heating, and subsidized mortgages that make them affordable to the working class people Riggio calls "the backbone of this city."
(*Photo credit: Ryan Rivet, Tulane University*)

feel like home because of their traditional modest design. And the Riggios pay for all home furnishings, selected by homeowners and reflecting who they are—their tastes, idiosyncrasies, and values.

The financial structure also reflects a grasp of people's real lives. The process begins with a house swap—what Carey Shea, the executive director of Project Home Again, calls "Cash for Clunkers": A homeowner trades in a damaged house and pays any difference between the paid-up mortgage and the cost of the new house (the Riggios cover all overhead) through a loan that is forgiven over a five-year period. The loan is subsidized in part by NORA's Neighborhood Stabilization Program grant funds and New Orleans' Soft Seconds Mortgage Program.[21] The bottom line is that poor and low-income New Orleanians can shed worthless property and move to a part of the city where there are lights on at night in other houses when the sun sets.

At the same time, the plan embraces the whole of the city. Project Home Again looks at a blighted property, tears down the damaged house, and does a thorough cleanup. Then, if it's a buildable lot with enough of a setback to meet modern housing codes, and if there are enough other occupied houses on the block—at least 40 percent—it builds. If the lot is unbuildable, it is traded to NORA to be used for side yards for existing homes and, in exchange, Project Home Again receives a lot for the new development under way in the St. Anthony neighborhood of Gentilly.

These details may seem dry, but they're important: This is how a city comes back, lot by lot, house by house, but chiefly neighborhood by neighborhood. Density matters—sufficient population to generate communal and commercial activity; and zoning matters—how are houses taxed, what are the setbacks, where are the parks and schools and business zones. Project Home Again houses may look more modest on the outside than a Frank Gehry MIR wonder, but the logic and care of the planning have achieved what Len Riggio hoped for at the beginning: the revival of a solid working-class neighborhood where houses had been passed down in families, so that the cycle can go forward and generational wealth can accumulate once again. Riggio says, "We thought working-class people were the fabric and the culture and the backbone of this city."[22] And that's where he chose to invest.

PITT, RIGGIO, AND THE ARCHITECTS AND PLANNERS at TCC have all provided vision and produced tangible results. But some of the rebuilding of New Orleans has been done by New Orleanians themselves, through the intensified engagement and activism sparked by the storm. One project that represents an intersection of individual philanthropy with community activism is the Musicians' Village in the Upper Ninth Ward, built by volunteers for Habitat for Humanity as a residential area for musicians displaced by Katrina. Founded by Harry Connick Jr. and Branford Marsalis, the village consists of 72 homes (so far) for singers, jazz musicians, guitarists, and songwriters, with a music center and performance space named for Ellis Marsalis—jazz pianist, father of Wynton and Branford, and, as head of the jazz studies program at the University of New Orleans, mentor to many famous performers.

One of the residents of the village is Cherice Nelson-Harrison, daughter of Mardi Gras big chief Donald Harrison; she oversaw a ritual ceremony when she moved in—water for washing the steps, tambourines, and drums of the Guardians of the Flame Mardi Gras Indian tribe, and a priest's blessing. Al Johnson, best known for his "Carnival Time" Mardi Gras anthem, also lives here, as do performers ranging from Michael Harris, a singer-songwriter and jazz bassist, to Kathleen Westfall, an operatic soprano. The village is not just housing but a space for cross-fertilization; musicians sit on their front porches, trade ideas and riffs, jam together.[23] The moral is that rebuilding means not just a "place" but quality of life and creative opportunity. In addition, the Musicians' Village realizes one of the visions put forward in the BNOB Commission report on culture: that the distinctive music of New Orleans be preserved and honored not only in the French Quarter or Treme but in venues all across the city, including the neighborhoods where musicians live.

ONE LEADER IN THE PHYSICAL RECONSTRUCTION of New Orleans was, and is, Tulane's School of Architecture; as an anchor institution, the university has been able to help revitalize the cityscape by pulling together resources, collaborating with communities, and developing a citywide vision that embraces both preservation and innovation.[24] The TCC has taken on all of New Orleans, from its blighted properties to its food deserts,[25] from its housing collapse to its damaged schools, as well as the complex domain of flood control and the environment.

Among the projects that TCC has already completed are the Hollygrove Growers Market and Farm along with the Hollygrove Growers Pavilion and Shade Units—an urban farm with plots for growing fresh produce in one of the heavily flooded inner-city neighborhoods. The farm features a storefront facility that sells foodstuffs, slanted roofs that collect rainwater for use in irrigation, and shaded structures that provide shelter for lectures and training workshops. As is typical of most TCC projects, the Hollygrove initiative is a collaborative effort, involving the Carrollton-Hollygrove Community Development Corporation and the New Orleans Food & Farm Network.

TCC has also designed plans for urban farms associated with Covenant House, a homeless shelter for teens; these farms, planned for some of the 30,000 blighted lots across the city, will be both a source of fresh produce and a job training program for disconnected youth, resurrecting the Victory Garden concept as part of a recovery model.

The center has also created individual structures that will serve as prototypes when funds for more building becomes available. For example, a streetcar shelter has been constructed on Carrolton Avenue at the beginning of the St. Charles streetcar line, with a steeply pitched roof providing protection from the elements and Y-shaped columns that echo the shape of the trolley wire supports apparent along the streetcar route. Prototypical homes have also been built at the rate of one a year. Each house is distinctive in look and layout—for example, one prototype is a modernist rendering of the traditional camelback design, and another has sliding panels on its outer deck to provide hurricane-proofing, privacy, and shade—but the houses share certain features, too. All are constructed using eco-friendly building materials and prefabricated components that can be reconfigured in a number of ways; all address the need for affordable housing and fulfill the requirements of post-Katrina building codes; and all have a front porch to promote classic New Orleans socializing. (One of these homes is on Dumaine Street, where Josh Short, the young filmmaker described in chapter 3, was raised, and killed.) TCC has designed and constructed a building to house Mardi Gras Indian costumes (the House of Dance and Feathers) and is assisting with research and preparing a brochure for a museum in historic Treme honoring Tootie Montana, the most revered of the big chiefs, which will display artifacts from African American culture in New Orleans from its origins as an early eighteenth century settlement.

And there's more: TCC has planned community greens where people relocated to new housing complexes can create gardens and rebuild a sense of community. It's begun an initiative called CityBuild, a consortium of ten universities partnering with local organizations to build or rehabilitate urban structures, and a project called Dutch Dialogues, with plans being developed for an urban park on Mirabeau Avenue in Gentilly—a 25-acre parcel owned by the Sisters of St. Joseph, with sandy soil that provides good drainage. This park, modeled on urban parks in the Netherlands, embraces floodwater rather than tries to keep it out, with a storage tank for rainwater, purification of urban runoff, a pond for swimming, and a water garden. The goal: A plot of blighted land will be turned into a place where water rises and subsides, diverted away from people's houses and harnessed for good use.

Plans are also in the works for a new skate park, to be constructed in flood-damaged City Park, one of the largest and oldest urban parks in the nation, to give teenagers a place to blow off steam rather than hanging out on the streets. TCC is also providing a facilities upgrade for an environmental education program for schoolchildren on the shores of Lake Pontchartrain, focusing on forestry. And it has authored an urban farming toolkit that provides instructions for creating kitchen gardens, food cooperatives, and community-supported agriculture, and a how-to pamphlet on hurricane-proofing. The breadth of vision, truly citywide, is made possible in part by the university itself, as a source of creative talent and a magnet for organizations and philanthropists searching for viable and innovative projects.
The physical revitalization of the city is so varied and far-reaching that it's hard to tell the whole story—but I'll end here, with the leadership principles involved in restoring the very fabric of the city.

*Leaders "aim high": They pursue ambitious and imaginative agendas, setting goals that motivate others to strive. They also aim wide, thinking holistically of the entire cityscape: of water, land, people, amenities, green spaces, and the spirit of place. They "ambitiously optimize" the resources available, working collaboratively with neighborhood associations, city agencies, federal programs, and nonprofit organizations. And they act as historians, cultural anthropologists, facilitators, and catalysts, putting the right people together and inspiring them to make something happen.*

I said it was "the end," but I can't resist one last story—because in New Orleans, there's always one more. We call it *lagniappe*, something extra.

This story is about Hollygrove, home to the Hollygrove Growers Market and Farm, mentioned earlier. A neighborhood on the opposite side of town from the Lower Ninth Ward that got so much of the media's attention in Katrina's aftermath, Hollygrove flooded too, when the hurricane breached the 17th Street Canal. The Hollygrove story has its own distinctive stamp. Predominantly African American, the neighborhood has a history that encapsulates what happened everywhere in inner cities in the second half of the twentieth century. A mixed neighborhood that became segregated after white flight in the 1950s and 1960s, Hollygrove experienced spikes in poverty and crime, particularly after crack cocaine hit the streets in the 1980s. Families and the elderly began to stay indoors, people's health deteriorated, businesses moved away, properties decayed.

Then Katrina blew in and the place was deluged with up to 12 feet of water. It was a do-or-die moment. As Kevin Brown, director of the faith-based development organization Trinity Christian Community, puts it, "The hurricane completely wiped us out. But at the same time, I knew that it was also our chance to shine."[26]

How did Hollygrove turn itself around, with more than three-quarters of its households receiving mail by 2010?

Here's what makes Hollygrove special. Of its 2,700 houses, a thousand heads of household were active members of the American Association of Retired Persons (AARP), a demographic of New Orleanians that tends to stay put in the spot where they were born, a behavior known as nativism. After AARP noticed the high membership rate in Hollygrove's zip code, Nancy McPherson, the AARP Louisiana state director, arranged a meeting with residents and partnered with Louisiana State University to conduct a Leadership Training Academy for those interested in learning the rules of community organization. The training provided people with the tools to prevent deadlocked neighborhood factions from stopping progress.

This was the beginning of a collaborative effort to rebuild Hollygrove better than it had been in many decades. In the immediate aftermath of the storm, Trinity Christian Community set up a circus tent next to the church where volunteers gathered to renovate ruined homes, ultimately leading to the rehab of 1,600 properties. A core group of homeowners, many of them in the older demographic, organized teams to address health, crime, transportation, and economic development. The health team instituted walks (and, a happy by-product, the presence of walkers scared away drug dealers); the team also saved a historic senior center, which in the 1940s had been the South's only privately owned black hospital and later became a center for civil rights activists, by transferring FEMA money originally earmarked for its demolition into a fund for rebuilding. And then there's the market and farm, mentioned earlier, providing community gardens, educational programs, and produce for the food desert left behind by the exodus of businesses in previous decades.

All of these things are remarkable accomplishments, but the most remarkable of all is the rebirth of the "neighborhood effect." Joe Sherman, in his late 60s, can testify to this. He moved to Hollygrove in 1948, when he was five. He moved away for college and became involved in the civil rights movement; and after many decades away, he came back home, at age 59, to the same house he'd grown up in. When he was a child on Edinburgh Street, he says, "Everyone was your mama." You couldn't get away with anything; with all the neighbors minding each other's business, it was a safe and nurturing place. But in 2003, the year of Sherman's return, there were local murders every other minute. Post-Katrina, there's been a citywide anticrime initiative, as noted in chapter 3, but in Hollygrove there are also neighborhood watches, volunteers fixing streetlights, citizens calling in tips. When there were three murders in 2010 in Hollygrove in the space of a month, the city, responding to neighborhood pressure, came in and tore down an abandoned house, center of the drug trafficking that had fueled the violence.

Ruth Kennedy, 75, leader of the walking club in Conrad Park, says, "People aren't as afraid now." The Community Development Corporation director, Paul Baricos, says that Hollygrove Farm "teaches local people how to grow food in vacant lots." Everyone is abroad on the streets, living the out-of-doors life that characterizes a thriving, resilient, vibrant neighborhood.

Joe Sherman, who has seen it all in his 60-something years, says that, since his days in the civil rights movement, "I have been trying to make things the way they ought to be." He's a man with a mission.[27]

In Hollygrove, it took a hurricane, but—because of community vision and will, strong partnerships with AARP and TCC, and individuals like the senior citizens of Hollygrove—things are more the way they ought to be.

# Chapter 6

# FIGHT, FIGHT, FIGHT

## STAND UP FOR YOUR BELIEFS

I'M SITTING WITH LEROY AND LAVERNE DUBOIS, A BROTHER AND sister, 60-somethings, on the front porch of their new townhouse in the Harmony Oaks development in Central City, on the spot where "the Bricks" once stood—identical low buildings, 110 of them, that made up the C. J. Peete housing project. C. J. Peete, also known as Magnolia, was one of the "big four" projects of New Orleans that housed many thousands of low-income African Americans. Cooks, waiters, shipyard workers, maids, iron-workers, Mardi Gras Indians, and street musicians as well as the elderly, disabled, and unemployed all lived in the projects. The decision to demolish the Big Four after Katrina was, its supporters argued, for the good of all New Orleans residents, including the most vulnerable. The new develop-ments would lift everyone up and integrate the poor into the fabric of the city.

On this bright spring Sunday, I've come to Harmony Oaks to see if it lives up to this promise. Leroy, Laverne, and I are having iced tea on the freshly painted porch, looking out over a neighborhood of pastel facades, each a little different. Leroy has retired from his job as dockworker and Laverne from hers as a nursing assistant; they lived in C. J. Peete for 30 years before Katrina displaced them. In the fine tradition of siblings everywhere, they disagree about a lot of things, including Harmony Oaks.

When I ask them how they like it here, the first thing Leroy does is show me his hands. They're calloused and gnarled, and the index finger on his left hand is missing. "I worked my whole life and I still couldn't make it out of the projects." He folds his arms, tucking his hands away. "Garbage, broken windows, backed-up plumbing. Rats. So many killings you lost count." He shakes his head. "No one should have to live like that. This here, now"—he pats the railing of the porch—"is something. You walk into your little house and it's your house, not 'the projects.' Everything works, the dishwasher, the lights. It's safe around here. Everything's nice."

Laverne, dressed in her church clothes, a bright yellow suit with matching hat, gives a shrug. "It's pretty enough."

I say, "You and Leroy don't agree?"

"Hell, we never agree," Leroy says.

Laverne smiles, rolls her eyes. She rocks in her chair, the brim of her hat nodding. "You know," she says, "the projects were made out of brick. Blow my house down, but not those houses. They were fine. The housing people could have fixed them up for a lot less money."

"But what Leroy said, about the conditions?"

"We had a community there," she says. "People looked out for their neighbors. We took care of each other's children and of whoever got sick and whoever had man trouble. We had a history."

I try to imagine life in a place like C. J. Peete—not how it looked from the outside but the real life, inside.

"They just took it away from us." Laverne leans in, lowers her voice. "Now, with these developers"—she underlines the word—"there are rules.

How many people allowed to sit on the porch, you can't plant your own garden, no water for the kiddie pool." She looks out from the porch at the pale townhouses lining the street in either direction. "We have a lot of new people from all over. The C. J. Peete people, I'd say only 70 or so families from before." She rocks back and forth. "You got to ask, what about everyone else? Where are they?"

There's a moment's silence, then Leroy stands up. "Come on, I'll show you the house." We walk through bright rooms with finished ceilings and walls, hardwood floors, new appliances—the works. It's a showplace, all right. At the end of the tour, we all shake hands.

On the way home, I think about how pretty Harmony Oaks is, as pretty as its name. But I can't stop thinking about Laverne's question: *Where are they?*

THIS CHAPTER IS ABOUT FIERCE BATTLES over urban institutions that define the modern city: public housing for the poor, health care for the uninsured, and a newspaper serving the entire community—battles fought against the backdrop of not only of Katrina but, starting in 2008, the Great Recession. The leadership principle "Stand up for your beliefs" is at the heart of all ethical decision making, but here the emphasis is not on the morality but on the fight itself, the "standing up." Part of moving things forward is accessing the necessary will, resolve, and sometimes even aggression to oppose the forces of stagnation, indifference, greed, and corruption. Even if the outcome is less than perfect—the usual complicated tangle of costs and benefits—the battle is worth it. Without a fight, no good can emerge, and no progress can be made.

*One of the most important attributes of leaders is integrity: Do they have principles, can they be trusted, and do they hold to what they believe no matter the consequences? People will follow those who stand for something they respect, who adhere to a code of ethics, and who are consistent in their thoughts and actions. A leader who lacks a moral compass, compassion, and a willingness to fight for his or her beliefs is not worth following.*

Fighting may come naturally to Louisiana. The populist strain in the region—a tendency to take up causes and fight for the little guy—dates back to Huey Long, who in four years as governor, 1928 to 1932, transformed the state. Long was a self-styled man of the people, bypassing the press and politicians, speaking directly to the rural population, whom he called the "hicks," on the radio, through flyers, and in the fiery stump speeches he gave all over the state. Much of what he achieved was admirable: enfranchisement of the poor, including African Americans, by ending the poll tax; extending medical care and public education to all and halting abuse of the mentally ill and disabled; building the entire modern infrastructure of roads, bridges, schools, and hospitals. His phrases were resonant: *Every Man a King, Share the Wealth.* To this day, Long remains a contested figure: Was he a hero or a demagogue? A reformer or a fomenter of class warfare? But the best part of his legacy, a passionate commitment to "the people" regardless of race or creed, survives in today's populist movements for political and institutional fairness.

People in Louisiana get involved. They don't back down. They relish the fight. You could describe the residents of the state as a "third sector," separate from government and business and committed to collective action around shared interests and values.[1] In New Orleans, citizens lead the charge in public debates and, in so doing, empower others to stand up and fight.

The people's campaigns for fairness heated up in the aftermath of Katrina, further stoked by the economic downturn and the struggle for resources. Battle lines were drawn from the beginning; immediately after Katrina, furious conflicts broke out, the most powerful, as we've seen, about land use. The solution that prevailed was basically laissez-faire: The rebuilding of neighborhoods proceeded in tacit defiance of the original land use recommendations. A related fight was the housing projects, but there has been nothing laissez-faire about that struggle; as we'll see, it led to one of the only episodes of public violence in the post-Katrina period and garnered the attention of the United Nations Human Rights Council. In the end, the people living in the projects lost their battle, and the advocates of razing the Big Four won.

But perhaps the language of combat, with its winners and losers, is too absolute for these civic struggles. Battle imagery denies real-world compromise, the realm of partial victories, incremental improvements, and surprising compensations. Still, there's something valuable in the all-in, this-is-what's-right stance. By standing up for what's right, leaders, both official and ad hoc, ensure that some good will emerge from the arena of conflict and that solutions will continue to be discussed and pursued. The first fight begets a second and often a third and a fourth, until a more just outcome is achieved.

TO GO BACK TO THE HOUSING PROJECTS: the Big Four—B. W. Cooper, C. J. Peete, St. Bernard, and Lafitte—represented an earlier era of urban planning, the 1940s and New Deal social optimism. Sturdy brick

**Image 8** CJ Peete

The C.J. Peete housing project, one of the "Big Four" projects in New Orleans, represented the New Deal era of urban planning and social optimism in the 1940s. After Katrina, four of the largest housing projects in the city were demolished, despite having come through the storm relatively unscathed; the loss of public housing meant that many who had fled the city could not afford to return, occasioning major protests in the African American community.

(*Courtesy of Francine Stock*)

barrack-style housing was built all across American cities, funded by the federal government with the aim of helping and supporting the underclass. As the decades rolled by, these enclaves came to exemplify the opposite of progress: Segregating their residents by architecture, geography, and demographics from the surrounding urban landscape, they signaled stagnation, a dead end rather than a new beginning.

In New Orleans, years before Katrina hit, the viability of the projects was already in question. When I first came to Tulane in 1998, I inherited oversight of the Housing Authority of New Orleans (HANO) as part of my job as president. The U.S. Department of Housing and Urban Development (HUD), seeking better management and more focused attention on the projects than HANO had provided, handed Tulane the task of "fixer" for a brief period. I visited all of the Big Four and other projects in the city; over and over I saw the deep-rooted problems of drugs, violence, prostitution, teenage pregnancy, HIV/AIDS, abuse; plus deplorable living conditions, which seemed to be inseparable from all the social ailments. In 2002, HUD once again took over the projects with new plans to improve them. Three years later, even though the Big Four came through the storm unscathed except for some minor flooding—"the Bricks," as Laverne DuBois pointed out, were hard to blow down—officials seized the moment as an opportunity to get rid of them. Why bother to renovate when you could demolish?

That's not the way many residents felt. Handed Section 8 vouchers that wouldn't cover the cost of new, higher rents in the proposed mixed-use developments, they wanted renovation[2] or, barring that, a binding guarantee of one-for-one replacement of the 3,000 occupied housing units (out of a total of 4,500) of the old Big Four. This fight was even more painful than the one about rebuilding houses in the submerged neighborhoods, because it affected the poorest of the poor—not homeowners but renters, and renters who relied on government subsidies for the roofs over their heads.

The contentiousness grew over the course of two years while many thousands of poor African Americans remained displaced, priced out of the housing market. Estimates vary about how many have been unable to return, but one figure suggests the dimensions of the problem: of some

29,000 applications on a waiting list for rental vouchers from HANO in 2009, 20,000 households—over 83 percent of total applicants—reported income 30 percent or below area median income.[3]

After Katrina, the Big Four projects, which for nearly half a century had provided housing to the poor, were fenced off with chain link and barbed wire, preventing residents from cleaning up their apartments or retrieving their possessions. Meanwhile, the 23,000 FEMA trailers that had provided temporary housing to people were withdrawn in June 2007. Since then, the homeless population of New Orleans has doubled from 6,000 to 12,000.[4] There have been reports of families with children living out of cars and people squatting in some of the 65,000 abandoned properties in the city. A protest march organized by St. Bernard residents led to a clash with security guards and the building of a tent encampment, "Survivors' Village," on the median strip—the "neutral ground"—outside of the project.

Things came to a head in December 2007 at a city council hearing, with activists claiming that the demolition plan had been instituted without city permits. Only a month before, a city council had been elected that for the first time ever was majority white, largely because the diaspora of poor African Americans were unable to return to New Orleans and cast their votes. While project residents trying to break through iron gates and a cordon of police-men into City Hall were tasered, pepper-sprayed, and handcuffed, inside City Hall the council voted unanimously to raze the Big Four.[5]

On the heels of this decision, developers were brought in as partners to create the new housing, and government monies—largely community development block grants and Gulf Opportunity Zone tax credits for invest-ing in "difficult development areas"—helped to defray construction costs. Alphonso Jackson, HUD secretary under Bush, resigned in 2008 amid a federal criminal investigation over cronyism in awarding HUD contracts. Reports in the *National Journal* and elsewhere aired allegations that Jackson had financial ties to the St. Bernard redevelopment group, and his wife to one of the C. J. Peete developers.[6]

The net result, eight years (and counting) after Katrina: four new mixed-use developments, with what are described as "affordable" units, "low income" units, and "fair market" rentals. However you describe them, only about 10 percent of the units are occupied by former projects residents, and, as mentioned, 20,000 very low-income households have applied for subsidized housing. But even if vouchers came through for these many thousands, a Brookings Institution article points out that the subsidies (Low Income Housing Tax Credit and Small Rental Property Program) are, in fact, too low to help most former projects residents afford rentals in a market where rents have gone up 45 percent since Katrina devastated the housing stock.[7]

So the answer to Laverne DuBois's pointed question, "Where are they?" is grim: everywhere and nowhere.

A huge proportion of displaced residents has had to scramble for housing both within and outside of New Orleans, which is shameful. Still—and I say this in sorrowful recognition of the price paid—I have always believed that, on balance, the projects had to go. People cannot live well without a decent environment; they can't aspire if they're never given basic dignity— something the Big Four couldn't provide. The fact is, the older model of public housing came from a period when America was still a segregated society. The time has come for a more integrated, organic vision that offers the poor a way into the mainstream.

Among the good things that have emerged from the battle over housing is an intensified community engagement, like that occurring in Central City, where resident leaders at Harmony Oaks have put pressure on the development corporation to provide services and programs. Central City Partners has agreed to provide job-training programs and to allow residents to manage the community center; case managers help residents find schools, day care, and adult education classes; social aid and pleasure clubs—the Exquisite Beauties, for one, a youth group involved in community service— have sprung up as people have begun to associate and congregate.[8] What's happening at Harmony Oaks may be a glimpse of a better future: a "project" transformed into a neighborhood.

An even more promising model of housing has taken shape in the Bayou District, where the old St. Bernard housing project once stood. The

Image 9: Harmony Oaks

The new mixed income development that replaced the C.J. Peete housing project, with apartments described as "affordable," "low income," and "market rate." The new development provides modern amenities and community services, but with only 10% of units occupied by former C.J. Peete residents, controversy continues about the fate of people displaced by Katrina.

(Courtesy of McCormack Baron Salazar)

new development, Columbia Parc, is a "purpose-built community," constructed as a unified urban neighborhood from its very inception. Modeled on East Lake, a community in Atlanta developed by Tim Cousins, Columbia Parc looks like a dream come true: beautiful apartments, fitness center, three playgrounds, swimming pool, NFL playing field, movie theater, and a soon-to-be-developed community health center, food market, and K–8 school. Perhaps most important of all, Columbia Parc envisions offering a cradle-to-career educational pipeline located in the heart of the neighborhood: Educare's brand-new early childhood center (ages 0–5) is already open. Eventually, the community will have a new K–8 school and easy access to McDonogh 35 (grades 9–12) currently under construction a few blocks away. The neighboring golf courses of New Orleans' City Park will provide youth development programs and job opportunities as well as ongoing revenue streams for school operating costs.

Yet the question of what has happened to the poorest of the poor still lingers. Another consequence of the fight over the projects is a new wave of advocacy for those still without housing. Community groups have arisen, partly spurred by the UN's special report on adequate housing[9]—groups like the Fight Back Center near the site of the old St. Bernard and national organizations like the Campaign to Restore National Housing Rights. The Greater New Orleans Foundation's housing initiative, which allocates money from private donors, is focused on meeting the needs of those still searching for a place to live. Since 2007 the foundation has awarded 63 grants totaling over $20 million to over 50 organizations, intended to result in the rehabilitation and creation of affordable housing for 9,000 families in Orleans Parish.[10]

As Sam Jackson, a community organizer from the old B. W. Cooper project, puts it, "This is a new fight. We done been through the old fight. That was about demolition and right of return, and then one-for-one replacement. This is something new here. It's about housing as a human right."[11]

One possible outcome of a lost battle is a new battle. It ain't over till it's over.

I'M DRIVING ON THE I-10, THE BIG interstate that slices through New Orleans and looking at a skyline dotted with cranes, like brontosauruses towering over the city. Here they are at last, those "cranes in the sky" that Ed Blakely, the recovery czar, promised back in 2007.

Six years later, the future seems to have arrived. At this huge construction site in Mid-City, across the highway from the old Charity Hospital, a sprawling Biosciences District is under way, anchored by the new University Medical Center (UMC). The UMC hospital will be high end, with a full complement of subspecialists, state-of-the-art technology, and cutting-edge research labs: the works. The hospital has been leased to Louisiana Children's Medical Center (LCMC), an effective hospital system, thereby improving its chances of success; but several challenges still remain, particularly its financial viability. Add to the price tag the demolition of still vibrant historic neighborhoods in a 37-acre footprint in the heart of downtown.

How did we get here? And what, exactly, have we wrought? Those cranes do look a lot like dinosaurs. Maybe we aren't going forward but sliding back.

THE FIGHT OVER HEALTH CARE IN NEW ORLEANS began immediately after Katrina, when the point of contention was whether to renovate the old Charity Hospital or redirect FEMA dollars for construction of a brand-new medical center. Charity, which first opened its doors to the indigent in 1736, is the second oldest continuing public hospital in the United States. (The oldest is Bellevue in New York, which also opened in 1736, a month before Charity.) Over the years, cataclysmic events—fires, hurricanes, epidemics—led to renovations, relocations, and new construction. The current Charity was completed in 1939 by the Public Works Administration; a handsome art deco building, it was, as it had always been, an open-admission hospital specifically dedicated to the poor. It was also a centralized locus for state-of-the-art care (including a level 1 trauma center) and a teaching hospital for physicians in training drawn from both Tulane Medical School and Louisiana State University (LSU) Medical School.

LSU Medical was started by Huey Long; he situated it down the street from Tulane School of Medicine as a thrown gauntlet. The story goes that he was furious with some now-forgotten criticism of him from a Tulane professor, an insult he perceived as typical of Tulane's elitism[12]; he answered with a populist flair—a state institution, backed by state money, that would be solely for natives of Louisiana. But house staff from both medical schools continued to serve at Charity, and many older doctors in New Orleans still recall their training there as one of a kind: a magnificent introduction to medicine in all its variety and a great proving ground. Here was a place where you saw everything—not just mainstream disease but strange tropical parasites and "fascinomas"; and where you saw every*one*—people of every ethnicity and social class.

Flash forward 65 years. What once looked modern and progressive was, according to some, now outmoded. By 2005, many people thought of Charity as a relic, one of the last surviving hospitals in the old two-tier system of big state-run public hospitals for the poor and private hospitals for those who could afford them. It was also a "big box" model, a large facility in the heart of the city to which people had to travel, sometimes from considerable distances. Despite the dedication of doctors and residents, Charity also had significant problems: The physical environment was dilapidated, outcomes tended to be poor, and care was expensive. A single emergency room visit—the way most of the uninsured, which meant most Charity patients, got care—cost an average of $1,000.

When Katrina flooded the city's hospitals, Charity got out with less damage than others, and military personnel scrubbed it down and judged it "medical ready" within weeks after the storm. The fight began exactly then: LSU said that Charity was unsalvageable and that the FEMA money marked for its renovation should go to a new facility that it would build north of the I-10. A lot of people agreed that this was our best chance to get rid of a "fossil" and create a hospital center for the twenty-first century—a familiar refrain in the post-Katrina landscape. On the other side were physicians and community leaders who thought Charity should be rehabbed, because it was the quickest, most cost-effective way to meet the widespread and urgent medical needs of the African American population after the storm. The Committee to Reopen Charity Hospital was formed to oppose the LSU plan and remains in existence as a rallying point for those who believe in the value of the traditional model of medical care.

At Tulane, there was skepticism about the LSU plan, even though, after LSU, Tulane has the longest-standing relationship with Charity, and the largest number of its medical residents would rotate at the new facility (i.e., UMC). Tulane and others were concerned with how FEMA and state money would flow, especially to LSU, and whether LSU might use this situation to diminish Tulane's role in the state hospital. But my own chief objection to a new hospital at the time was that the financial model made no sense. As mentioned, we already had too many hospital beds in the city before Katrina, and the UMC was going to add more than 200 new ones[13]—beds that weren't going to be filled by people flying in from elsewhere for specialty care, given that Houston and Birmingham, both major medical meccas, are nearby. The estimated cost to fully renovate Charity was a fraction of what it would cost to build UMC—approximately $1.2 billion and counting, much of that amount still unfunded as of the groundbreaking.

Despite these objections, the question "Should we build another big box?" was answered with a yes, largely through the influence of LSU, and FEMA money ($475 million) was redirected to new construction. Many state and local officials at the groundbreaking ceremony hailed the coming medical center as an economic engine that would generate many thousands of high-level jobs and, by attracting top physicians and researchers, make it competitive with regional centers. We all talk about the knowledge economy and the ultimate profit associated with being a "brain magnet."[14] Nevertheless, we're worrying about UMC becoming an unsustainable financial drain on the state.

It's the usual tangled story of rivalries and money, but the main cost has been borne by the poor and working-class neighborhoods of Mid-City. Heavy equipment moved in and crushed rows of historic shotguns and bungalows, hundreds of them, many dating to the nineteenth century. Some of the people who lived in those houses had restored them with Road Home money after Katrina.[15] Some who were still living in exile didn't know that their homes had been "expropriated"—the Louisiana term for eminent domain—and crunched to rubble.

Some homes were moved to empty lots, without permission of owners who were still in exile, to await an assessment at some uncertain date as to whether they were salvageable. Preservationists raised an outcry. Brad Ott, a Mid-City neighborhood activist, said, "They did this swap deal where they took people's houses, their land, for pennies on the dollar." Many lacked the financial resources to relocate with their houses to new sites. As Sandra Stokes, a board member of the Foundation for Historical Louisiana, explained of the houses supposedly salvaged, "There is still no salvation for these houses. They were decapitated—cut into 'convenient' sections—put on trailers and corralled into this holding area. But unless they are secured, they won't survive."[16]

Was all this demolition and removal even legal? The state's expropriations of people's property might be permissible only if those expropriations
were for a public project, and UMC, as mentioned, has been leased to a private
entity, the Louisiana Children's Medical Center (LCMC) Corporation[17]—
Governor Jindal's solution to the hospital services problem he was handed
by Kathleen Blanco when he took office.

There's little doubt that the new medical complex will be focused on
financial sustainability, which may mean private beds and the exclusion of
the poor and uninsured. UMC will not be another Charity. Add to that the
destruction of poor and working-class neighborhoods and you have gentri-
fication in a nutshell—the emergence of a whiter, richer demographic. The
pattern is familiar: Look at the housing projects or, 50 years ago, old African
American neighborhoods like Treme, half destroyed by urban planning and
the construction of the interstate. Charity itself, an architectural landmark,
was in imminent danger of the wrecking ball for many years after Katrina,
despite its potential for repurposing.

Many chapters of the post-Katrina transformation of New Orleans feature lost causes. The painful obliteration of people's lives and hopes—of
their health and future prospects—is still part of the story all these years
after the storm; and the fate of Charity Hospital—basically, unsurprisingly, a
fight about money and real estate—stands as a symbol of what the new New
Orleans might look like if those with financial means and political muscle
control the entire scenario.

So where is the victory in this fight? The good news, such that it is:
Privatization is probably the only way out of the looming fiscal disaster. LSU
will get out of the business of managing a hospital, something for which it's
ill-suited anyway, and the LCMC Corporation will step in, with a good chance
of success: Its Children's Hospital is successful, respected, well managed, and
profitable. Statewide privatization—long-term leases to private groups—will
lead to consolidation in the marketplace and a reduction in the number of
surplus hospital beds currently plaguing the city's administration.

Another sideways victory: On the margins, the real story of health care
reform has been unfolding, a story that went largely unnoticed by those

promoting the Bioscience District and UMC. We have to loop back to what happened in New Orleans immediately after Katrina to see how health care in the city took a surprising turn. In August 2005, after the levees broke, the city's medical system virtually collapsed, not only because of the flooding but because of power outages that rendered computers and equipment useless. Of the sixteen hospitals in the metropolitan area, only three were functioning, all of them in the suburbs outside of New Orleans. In the city hospitals, dead bodies were floating in the basements, and nurses and doctors struggled heroically to get the sickest patients out: Helicopters landed on the roofs and staff members formed human chains in the stairwells to carry intensive-care patients to safety.[18] Beyond the hospitals, many of the people crammed into the Superdome and Convention Center, or standing on the overpasses and on the roofs of their houses, were sick—suffering not only from heat exhaustion, hunger, and dehydration but from serious chronic illnesses.

It was only days after the storm that Dr. Karen DeSalvo called me up. She was then an associate professor of internal medicine and geriatrics at Tulane Medical School, with a master's in public health and a specialty in epidemiology; since that time, she's become a full professor, vice dean of the medical school, and, for the calendar year 2012, health commissioner of the city of New Orleans. Back in August 2005, what she wanted to know was whether she could set up a treatment center on the street to bring immediate care to people stranded in the city and whether she could use Tulane's resources to do it.

One thing I'm good at is saying yes to a good idea. So Karen set up her clinic on a sidewalk—a scene you may remember from chapter 1, when I recounted the immediate aftermath of Katrina. The "clinic," you'll recall, was basically a card table, a cardboard sign with TULANE COMMUNITY HEALTH CENTER written in marker, an ice chest with vaccines and drugs, and a staff consisting of medical interns and residents. Crowds of people, mainly African American, mainly poor, lined up around an entire city block. But Karen knew there were many more she wasn't reaching, so she found money for mobile units that went into the flooded neighborhoods to provide urgent care. Others joined the effort, setting up tents and borrowing buildings, with volunteers stepping up to provide care wherever there was space, often without power, water, or sewage disposal.

This ad hoc disaster response became the foundation of a network of community health care centers, operated by a range of academic, government, and faith-based organizations. Some of these centers have become federally qualified health centers (FQHCs) and free clinics. Out of a crisis, an opportunity—New Orleans, with a decentralized model of care that is neighborhood based, open access, and focused on health and prevention—has become the leading edge of the nation's health care reform.[19]

Karen has been instrumental in shaping the policy, especially in terms of funding. Pulling together federal monies and philanthropic contributions from sources like Johnson & Johnson and Qatar, a sovereign Arab state, she has expanded the community health model all over the city. There are now eight Tulane health centers staffed by faculty physicians, residents, interns, and medical students, including the Ruth U. Fertel/Tulane Community Health Center, housed in the old Ruth's Chris Steak House, donated to Tulane by the family and offering expanded services. There's also, as noted earlier, a Tulane clinic in New Orleans East to provide health care for the Vietnamese community. All 93 of the community health centers, though run by various entities, have the shared mission of delivering care to everyone regardless of ability to pay. They are also redefining themselves in the new model of the medical home that offers open access, drop-in appointments, and an array of services that increase wellness in addition to treating illness.[20] Some clinics, the Ruth U. Fertel Center among them, offer exercise, nutrition, literacy, and computer classes; support groups and mental health services; and legal aid and transportation. Centers are forming collaboratives to integrate care and reduce redundancy and are replacing paper with electronic medical records to reduce error. The community health centers are also receiving workforce development funds as training programs for primary care doctors, who are in short supply, given the expected influx of people seeking medical treatment under the Affordable Care Act. Finally, compared to a $1,000 emergency room visit at the old Charity, care for the average person for an entire year costs $223, a savings of $12 million a year when multiplied by the total number of patients.[21]

Karen DeSalvo is the powerhouse behind this progressive model of community health care. If ever anyone was willing to stand up and fight for her beliefs, it's Karen, who is the kind of leader who sees what has to be done and just goes ahead and does it. As is often the case with people who fight successful battles and achieve innovative results, the source of Karen's motivation is personal. Growing up in Texas with a single mother who developed cancer, she saw firsthand her mother's futile efforts to get care from a system that routinely neglects the poor. She herself felt what it was like to sit forever in the limbo of a waiting room and then see her mother receive paint-by-numbers care from indifferent doctors. This experience fueled Karen's desire to become a better kind of doctor—though she'll tell you she was going to be a ballerina originally—and then to fight for institutional change.

How does this story of individual initiative fit within the larger fight over health care in the city? In a way, it's a case of the margin displacing the center. While the big guns were battling for big money for a big box hospital, a new model was emerging that looks a lot more like the probable future of medical care in this country. When Karen DeSalvo talked to administrators at LSU and others in the state, raising the point that the community health centers could have an impact on the big box model under way in the Bioscience District, they seemed not to hear her. But if the rise of community medicine couldn't deter the backers of a mega-complex, it did profoundly change the picture of health care in New Orleans. Some victories come without bloodshed.

I'M AT ANNE MILLING'S HOUSE, A GRACIOUS uptown manor house in the same Audubon Park neighborhood as Tulane—it's one of those imposing piles with three-story pillars, wide flagstone porches, and gabled roofs. Anne is a major presence in the civic life of New Orleans. Founder of Women of the Storm, an advocacy group that has worked to bring Congress members to post-Katrina New Orleans in order to encourage government funding of everything from coastal restoration to infrastructure needs, she's also on the advisory board of the *Times-Picayune*, our daily newspaper. Today we're all up in arms, Anne included, because of yesterday's announcement from the Newhouse family, the *Times-Pic*'s owner, that they're cutting back the paper to three days a week. The region's populist fervor extends to all of us in the room, though we're not technically "the people" of Huey Long's fan base. We're ten or so uptowners—civic leaders, you could call us—with addresses in the right part of town and the material comfort of significant income.[22] But the outrage is also palpable in the barbershops and coffeehouses and convenience stores. In New Orleans, the spirit of community, of we're all in this together, extends up and down the social scale and is particularly evident in regard to the newspaper, which belongs to all of us.

Anne starts the meeting: What are we going to do, in what order? First thing, talk to the Newhouses and persuade them that New Orleans shouldn't be the guinea pig in the downsizing of print journalism. If the Newhouses go through with this, New Orleans will be the largest metropolitan area in the United States without a daily print newspaper. Advance Publications, the corporation run by the family, owns some 30 newspapers, and has downsized smaller papers, including those in Birmingham and Huntsville, Alabama, and in smaller northern cities too. Syracuse, New York, three times a week? Okay, maybe. New Orleans? No way.

Our gang of ten also composes a letter to members of the Newhouse family:

> It is painful to report that right now it is nearly impossible to find a kind word in these parts about your family or your plan to take away our daily newspaper.... If your family does not believe in the future of this great city and its capacity to support a daily newspaper, it is only fair to allow us to find someone who does. If you have ever valued the friendship you have shared with our city and your loyal readers, we ask that you sell *The Times-Picayune*.[23]

And our third prong of attack: Join forces with the city's other outraged citizens, including some very famous people, and make a racket that can't be ignored. You don't mess with New Orleans. David Carr, the *New York Times* columnist who broke the story about the Newhouses' plans for the paper back in May 2012, before anyone in town knew of it, himself wondered why the newspaper clan chose New Orleans for their experiment: "I never got an answer from Mr. Newhouse. They own a lot of newspapers. Why pick a town where they knew it was going to make a ruckus?"[24]

THE *TIMES-PICAYUNE*—ANOTHER INSTITUTION emblematic of the city's identity—has a colorful 175-year history in New Orleans going back to 1837. Then called the *Picayune*, it sold for the price of a picayune, a small Spanish coin worth about six cents. Through the nineteenth century into the twentieth, a succession of different publishers and editors ran the newspaper, including a woman publisher, Eliza Jane Nicholson, who inherited the paper in 1876 when her husband died and introduced innovations including society reporting, children's pages, and a women's advice column written by social reformer Dorothy Dix. The paper was renamed the *Times-Picayune* after its merger with the *Times-Democrat* in 1914.

The paper's storied past includes some very famous correspondents: William Faulkner, O. Henry, and Edgar Allan Poe all wrote copy for the *Times-Pic*. In a more recent example, Chris Rose's evocative columns in the paper post-Katrina became the basis for his book *1 Dead in Attic*, one of the most vivid narratives to come out of the storm. Despite many other news sources around the city (*Gambit*, *Uptown Messenger*, and others), the *Times-Picayune* has been the glue of the community, the one source shared by everyone, rich and poor, uptown and downtown. A political consultant living in New Orleans, Cheron Brylski, describes the paper as "a lifeline for the Southern, working-class city, providing government announcements, obituaries, Carnival and scoops on local corruption."[25] The point about corruption is important: In a city where cronyism, patronage, and graft are practically tradition, the watchdog function of a widely read newspaper needs preserving.

Finally, the role of the *Times-Picayune* in helping the city through the trauma of Katrina cannot be overestimated: The paper operated online when power failures prevented the manufacture of the print edition for three days after the storm, and then it covered the ongoing crisis with searing photographs and frontline reporting—day by day telling the story of what was happening, and why. The paper won two Pulitzers in 2006, one for breaking news and the other for public service.

Preserve the *Times-Picayune*, or give way to the realities of the modern digital age, with declining print subscriptions and anemic ad revenue? Even in a bad time, the New Orleans market for print was atypically robust: Pre-Katrina, the city boasted some 260,000 paid subscriptions, with the decline to about half that amount due mainly to the loss of more than 100,000 residents after the storm.[26] But forget the numbers: New Orleanians were not about to let their paper go without making some noise.[27] The racket grew all through 2012, as hopes rose and setbacks followed. A petition, Save the *Times-Picayune*, attracted 9,440 signatures. The petition read, in part, as follows: "Few believe a three-day-a-week newspaper, reduced staff and a mediocre website are acceptable alternatives to today's *Times-Picayune*.... Please join with New Orleans residents, community activists, newspaper lovers and others—" and then a drumroll, with names including James Carville, Garry Trudeau, Cokie Roberts, Ed Asner, Michael Lewis, Garrison Keillor, Anne Rice, Branford Marsalis, and Roy Blount studding the long list of luminaries in support of a daily paper.

A rally at the Rock 'n' Bowl parking lot in early summer 2012 attracted many hundreds of participants, some wearing hats with the *Times-Picayune* masthead, others carrying placards ("7 DAYS A WEEK! OR FIND A BUYER!"). Anne Milling was there, and her words were quoted on the evening news: "You have to try to reach for the stars and you might get a moon. Maybe they'll find out New Orleans is different from the other markets they're talking about." Dalton Savwoir, of the Gentilly Civic Improvement Association, said, "Many people in Gentilly are elderly people. It would be a disadvantage [for them] to go online or to go the library to look for the paper every day."[28] Allen Toussaint played the piano, Kermit Ruffins showed up. A typical New Orleans gathering: public outcry and a little music on the side.[29]

The setbacks looked pretty definitive: The Newhouses were going to cut back to three days a week, period; and the paper wasn't for sale, period. Their reasoning was the usual: Readers should head to the web, where print media was going, given the decline in readership and profits. But the principle of fight, fight, fight—don't give up: change tactics (or "swerve") but never lose sight of the goal—pertains here too. The swerve here involved Baton Rouge—specifically, the Manship family, who for nearly 90 years had been the continuous publishers of that city's *Advocate*. David Manship intervened in September 2012, just as the *Times-Picayune* was closing out its seven-day-a-week operations, announcing the *Advocate*'s launch of a daily New Orleans edition (an announcement that took place at the Rock 'n' Bowl, with music by the Lagniappe Brass Band).[30] Within the first few days, 10,000 subscribers signed up, and since then the paper has developed a strong following throughout the city.[31]

And that's still not the end of the story: In April 2013, another scion of another old Louisiana family, New Orleanian John Georges (a neighbor of mine at Audubon Place), bought the *Advocate* from the Manships. To great fanfare, Georges announced that there would be a continuation of the New Orleans daily edition of the *Advocate*, separate from the Baton Rouge paper, with an expanded staff of reporters and photographers and two veteran editors from the *Times-Picayune*, Dan Shea and Peter Kovacs, acting as general manager and editor respectively. Asked if it wasn't crazy to invest in newspapers at a time like this, Georges said, "Warren Buffett and the Koch brothers are getting into it. I don't know who says it's crazy."[32]

Georges sounded feisty in interviews, vowing to give the *Times-Picayune*, with its Wednesday, Friday, and Sunday print editions and its website, nola.com, a run for its money. The very same week, the *Times-Picayune* announced a "tabloid" edition of the paper on all those missing days to be called *TPStreet*, not delivered to subscribers but available in stores and newspaper boxes on the street. A typical jaundiced comment on the nola.com blog, from someone with the alias BeignetBob: "C'mon guys, just admit it: The grand digital experiment is a big bust. We tried to tell you, but would you listen? Noooooooooo. Next time, listen to the readers."[33]

That's the point: The will of the people will find a way. And in the case of the *Times-Picayune*, the events as they've unfolded have a particular regional feel, from the music in the parking lot of the Rock 'n' Bowl to the handshake that brought a daily paper back to town—that close-knit, traditional, idiosyncratic way of doing business. Georges himself noted the in-house, our-house quality of the deal: "They [the Manship family] could have sold to bigger-name people than me. They're a legacy family—how often does a newspaper change hands? Once every hundred years?—and I want to honor that. Like them, I run a nearly-100-year-old family business. The paper was not sold to a national chain. I'm a Louisiana boy."[34]

FIGHT, FIGHT, FIGHT—THE PHRASE IS FROM Tulane's fight song (no surprise there), but its applicability to contests off the football field, in crucial areas of urban life like housing, health care, and the daily news, should (I hope) be evident by now. The leadership principle "Stand up for your beliefs" extends to all kinds of leaders, from a Sam Jackson or a Karen DeSalvo or an Anne Milling to the ordinary citizen—the one who lives in Harmony Oaks, goes to Covenant House for a hot meal, and picks up an *Advocate* from a newspaper box. Any vision of public life that leaves out communal will and engagement is likely to fail, and models that embrace the whole community—even if imperfectly, even via compromise—are the road to a more vibrant city in the future. So here are my how-to suggestions—which I say with tongue in cheek, because they are less how-to and more an existential posture, a sequence of options, a map with alternative routes that still get you to the ultimate goal:

*Leaders stick to their guns. They stand up for their beliefs against opposing forces of stagnation, corruption, greed. Faced with a setback, they adhere to first principles, and carry on the battle in a second (or third, or fourth) phase. Confronted with an ultimate defeat, they remain consistent in their vision while being willing to swerve in the implementation—to innovate, invent, and partner, in order to find a new pathway.*

It's Super Sunday in New Orleans, the Sunday closest to St. Joseph's Day, with the usual parades and music and food and drink.[35] But here there are also Mardi Gras Indians. The tribes have gathered at A. L. Davis Park, formerly known as Shakespeare Park, opposite the old Magnolia/C. J. Peete housing project, now known as Harmony Oaks. Everything in New Orleans has at least two or three names, reflecting layers that go back in time. Every street corner, every event, is archaeological.

Today the tribes have arrived in the park to give their Mardi Gras outfits a final airing before they're put away for the year. A little girl decked out in a yellow beaded outfit, with a slipping-down high-crowned beaded hat, is waving a feathered scepter. A man who looks like a tree in motion, all green foliage and swaying fronds, shouts out a rhyme. A woman resplendent in white plumage with medallions of black beads, shaking her arms, tossing her braided hair, sings a rap, "Celebration...resurrection...incarnation...Washington nation." I'm never sure of the words, but it doesn't seem to matter—the songs and rhymes come across as shouts of joy and pride. The tambourines and drums beat out a rhythm that sounds straight out of Africa.

Every time I see the tribes out in force, I'm mesmerized. It's like being in the presence of some kind of time-lapse history, African, Native American, and Caribbean influences all present at once—today's reenactment performed on the doorstep of the projects, where African Americans have had another displacement and another resurrection. After the fighting, after the urban renewal, which is also, in a sense, an urban loss, the community finds its own way to swerve, taking its performance to the new mixed-use development. The community doesn't abandon its values; it persists, with its traditions and rituals intact.

Okay, it's not that simple. But there is something about this latest cycle of resurgence after Katrina that affirms the continuity of the past, that makes a space, in the old Shakespeare Park, for another dazzling display of New Orleans' self-expression.

# Chapter 7

# GROW DAT

## MAKE CONTACT

IT'S A BEAUTIFUL MILD DAY IN MAY, WITHOUT THE USUAL humidity and high heat that signal the onset of a New Orleans summer. I'm standing in the middle of a green landscape, with crops—lettuce, kale, collard greens, cucumbers, tomatoes, peppers—growing in neat furrows, tall stakes planted at rhythmic intervals. A breeze ripples across the field, bringing a smell of aromatic herbs and freshly turned earth.

In the field with me are Johanna Gilligan and Leo Gorman, cofounders of Grow Dat Youth Farm, located on four acres in the middle of City Park, one of the oldest urban parks in the nation. Johanna is in rolled-up jeans and Grow Dat T-shirt, Leo's in overalls. They are both 30-something, athletic, cheerful, and they are enthusiastically pointing out the latest improvements. Leo is particularly thrilled about the composting in the toilets, where solid waste is mixed with sawdust. Recycling at its most local.

We walk across the muddy ground that separates us from the outbuild-ings, handsome open structures with concrete floors, pale green walls of corrugated metal, and porchlike areas with wooden slats like blinds. We stand in the new prep-and-demonstration kitchen, where produce is readied for distribution. I ask what they would think about an open-air market on McAllister Avenue on the Tulane campus, where Grow Dat could sell pro-duce and introduce undergraduates to the program.

Leo thinks it's a good idea. "The kids like fresh stuff because they can't get off campus to the grocery stores. Knowing Tulane students, we should probably get some cookies too."

Johanna says, "It could bring in community people too. Plus, it could be good for *these* kids"—she nods toward the teenagers, all in Grow Dat T-shirts, who are bopping into the shed on this Saturday morning—"to see *those* kids." Not so that they can see how the other half lives, but to see how they themselves might live.

We discuss the expansion of the farm, which will be incorporating another three acres this summer, two of which are arable. It's not just the space that's growing but the program: This year's graduating class is 25, but we're aiming for numbers like those of the Food Project, a 20-year-old urban agriculture program in Boston that has graduated thousands of kids.

A young man comes up to say good morning, flashing a megawatt smile.

"You're up early," Johanna says.

He nods. "Yep, early." He turns to me. "Just like the real farmers."

We introduce ourselves, Scott, Quion; Quion, Scott. We shake hands, and Quion heads out to the fields. We watch him go.

Johanna says, "Now there's a story. His brother was murdered last year, and he was coming apart at school. So we get him over here and for a long time he never looks at anyone, hardly speaks. Then Josh, one of our counselors, sits down with him—the topic is nutrition—and Quion just starts telling his whole story. After that, the smile comes out, a little bit at a time, and things get better at school." She is watching the youth crew with their hoes and buckets, standing in the furrows. "A lot of these kids, they can't do regular psychotherapy. It's really unimaginable, the trauma they're dealing with. Not just Katrina—the ones we have now were nine, ten, when the storm happened—but things that happen every day. They need a safe place, a rhythm. Then the feelings come out. And they stand a chance."

GIVING KIDS A CHANCE IS CHANGING New Orleans. Grow Dat Farm is one example—a particularly sterling one—of a wave of social innovation that has developed in the city in the years since Katrina. In response to the urgent needs of the community, the desire—indeed, the necessity—to find new ways to address social problems emerged both at Tulane and in New Orleans at large. We were facing the reality that it wasn't enough to rely on the government; the private sector would need to contribute novel solutions

**Image 10** Grow Dat

Ire Sterling, a crew member at Grow Dat Youth Farm, out in the fields. Grow Dat is one of a wave of socially innovative programs that are rebuilding New Orleans by focusing on its young people, redirecting lives derailed by poverty and trauma through education, job training, mentoring, and psychosocial support.

(*Courtesy of Johanna Gilligan*)

to intractable urban problems like public education, health care, and disconnected youth in order to build a healthy, vital city.

Grow Dat and other similar efforts illustrate a cultural change from a bureaucratic, top-down approach to the bottom-up activism of community leaders and civic institutions like Tulane. On the national level, the White House Council for Community Solutions exemplifies the shift to an emphasis on social innovation, which holds great promise for our country's enactment of positive and enduring changes in the social fabric.

How do leaders stimulate, promote, and sustain socially innovative endeavors? The leadership principle of this chapter, "Make contact," sounds almost too obvious: Of course change can happen only when people get together one on one and experience differences and commonalities firsthand. But accomplishing this kind of direct interaction is not as simple as it sounds. You need to develop the machinery to bring ideas into the community across social, institutional, racial, and class barriers, and you need to fight the psychological forces that pull the other way, toward disengagement and distance, conceptual thinking and empty rhetoric. And those forces are especially powerful in emergencies, when the impulse is to issue commands, act in controlling ways, and simply skip the process of engaging the community.

*As the saying goes, leadership is a contact sport. Leaders actively engage with others who can help them comprehend and address issues fundamental to the future of their organizations or communities. Making contact is a two-way street, with both sides learning from and influencing the other. Such engagement breeds the trust, understanding, and camaraderie so critical to solving problems through collaborative efforts and, ultimately, achieving collective impact on a national scale.*

To return to Grow Dat: The program, like many others devoted to social innovation, actively engages with youth from diverse backgrounds, applies sociological concepts to real-world problems, and reminds us that the status quo always can be changed, bit by bit. The farm has figured out how to operationalize its mission of youth development, creating a place and structure for life-changing experiences.

For Tulane, which has been an engine of programs like these, it all goes back to that moment when the future of the university hung in the balance, and we had to ask ourselves the hard questions: What if the school doesn't come back? How can we justify its existence? What, in fact, is the ultimate meaning and value of a university? In chapter 1 I sketched the history of higher education in this country, going back to the land grant schools meant to produce an educated and engaged citizenry. But over the years, the primary aims of higher education became learning and research, with civic engagement lagging behind. After Katrina, forced and inspired by tragedy, Tulane reinvented itself as an anchor institution with a powerful role to play in the larger world. It committed itself to public service and experiential learning—a two-way street in which the community benefited and the students broadened their reach. Moving beyond the ivory tower, the undergraduates became not just thinkers but doers.

Tulane's Center for Public Service and a host of programs originating in the various schools of the university were matched by a tremendous proliferation of 501(c)3's—nonprofits aimed at alleviating the human misery produced by Katrina and rebuilding the city. Funding followed, from the government, from foundations and corporations, from private donors, and from countries as far away as Qatar. The money for Grow Dat started with a matching fund—I kicked in half of the seed money personally and made a call to a friend for the other half. Since those early days, the farm has won national recognition and attracted other sources of revenue. In 2013 it produced 8,500 pounds of food, selling 60 percent at farmer's markets and restaurants (with earnings of $17,000) and donating 40 percent (3,400 pounds) as "Shared Harvest" to partner organizations, youth and their families, and hunger relief agencies.

How does a program like Grow Dat develop? The background, in New Orleans, was a disaster that elicited an outpouring of help and money; in the foreground, the spark has come from individuals with bright ideas and the energy to implement them. I tend to invest in a person even more than a project itself—someone I can believe in—and for Grow Dat, that person was Johanna Gilligan. A Tulane graduate, she spent time as a high school college-prep teacher in several open admission public schools, plus a magnet school for high achievers. She began to notice that the magnet students were thinner, healthier, and better rested than the public school kids, who often dragged into school after working night jobs in fast-food restaurants and who suffered from all kinds of stress. She also admits she wasn't the world's greatest tutor: A kid would begin to tell her about a traumatic event and she would have to say "Not now, you've got to learn these fractions or you're going to flunk the test." (And she kept having this underlying feeling: Why hadn't they learned fractions when they were supposed to? She felt her help was too little, and too late, to fill in the gaps.)

Putting together her thoughts about nutrition, fast food, health, and achievement, Johanna developed the idea of an urban farm, drawing on models like the Edible Schoolyard, a school-based gardening program, and the aforementioned Food Project, with its long history of success in urban agriculture. She then took jobs at the Brooklyn Botanical Garden and, post-Katrina, at the New Orleans Food & Farm Network in order to gain the expertise and experience she would need to bring her idea to fruition. As an Urban Innovation fellow in Tulane's Social Entrepreneurship Program, she developed a successful pilot program. Tulane City Center (TCC) was enlisted to design and build farm buildings, expanding on its architectural designs for Hollygrove Market and Farm, the community garden and market described in chapter 5.

Leo Gorman, also a Tulane alum, came to the project after some serious persuasion from Johanna and the TCC. A teacher at Warren Easton Charter High School—one of the most effective public schools in the city as well as one of the oldest—Leo was happy teaching but began to see how farming offered opportunities for kids to integrate cognitive, emotional, and social learning in ways that went beyond the classroom and helped them transition into adult life—a transition that is precarious for a lot of kids, even the ones who manage to graduate from high school.

Since that time, around 2008, the program has grown from an initial 11 graduates to incrementally larger cohorts in succeeding years. Johanna told me, "You think it should be easy, support 20 young adults in a program for growing fresh food, but it isn't that easy. What really makes it all work is Tulane." At this point, my chest puffs out a little. I love hearing that the university has made a difference. "Just the architecture alone, created with such attention to quality and beauty—it sends a message to the kids, 'You have value. We take you seriously. We expect things of you, and we're going to take care of you.' "[1]

But it's not only the architecture; Tulane's stamp is all over Grow Dat, in myriad ways. Right now, the farm has an intern from Tulane's School of Social Work who provides case management for the kids—everything from eyeglasses to transportation. Another intern from the School of Public Health teaches nutrition and community health and helps run cooking classes. The farm has volunteers and visitors from the Schools of Medicine, Business, Science and Engineering, and Liberal Arts as well as undergraduates fulfilling their community service requirement. The Cowen Institute has helped pair the farm with high schools: De La Salle, Warren Easton, the NET, Sci High, and Clark.

The farm attracts people for different reasons: Some are in it for the environment and the organic composting; some come because of an interest in nutrition and health; some are studying public architecture and its social meanings. A socially innovative program like Grow Dat achieves a lot at once: By integrating an array of organizations, objectives, interests, and ideals, the farm has achieved a kind of critical mass—a confluence of factors that dramatically redirects, even saves, lives. The central, continuing focus of the farm, as of so many groundbreaking initiatives in New Orleans post-Katrina, is youth development. The participants are still in school, some struggling, some not. For the at-risk kids, it's a preventive measure, helping them find a foothold so that they don't drift into the category of disconnected youth—that 16- to 24-year-old cohort of late adolescents and young adults who are in danger of permanently falling into the abyss. For those who are doing well, the farm is a leadership development program, helping them hone the skills to lead in other settings. Grow Dat's ambitions are matched only by its determination: Through the meaningful work of growing food, it aims to heal trauma, rebuild trust, cultivate confidence, strengthen character, and incubate leaders for the next generation.

What I love about Grow Dat is that it offers a solution to two urgent problems at once: the threatened loss of human potential that disconnected youth represent and the hunger in urban centers. Like many other cities in the United States, New Orleans is basically a food desert, where the predominance of fast food and packaged food is fueling an epidemic of obesity and diabetes among the poor—a phenomenon made worse by the aftereffects of Katrina and the patchwork nature of neighborhood redevelopment. After 2005, the number of grocery stores in New Orleans Parish dwindled from 30 to 21, with most of those stores in wealthy white areas; the nearest fresh food in the Lower Ninth Ward is up to three miles away from any house. Given that only about half of African Americans living in poverty in New Orleans have access to cars, many people in the large section of the city below sea level rely on corner convenience stores, which have eggs, milk, and processed meat on the shelves but no fruits and vegetables. Most Grow Dat crew members, according to an in-house survey, have reported coming to work hungry. But they can eat as many fruits and vegetables as they want at the farm and take produce home to their families. The point is, nourishment and nurture are interconnected: The youth at the farm begin to have a sense of being cared for, loved, nourished—some for the first time in their lives.

MANY METRICS CONFIRM GROW DAT'S ACHIEVEMENTS: volume of food produced, number of enrollees, number of permanent job placements. But the best measure of the farm's success is the qualitative data—the stories of kids who've gone through the program. Here is "Muffin," aka Franchel Stevenson, talking about what Grow Dat means to her.

> At the Farm, you can't give it your half, you have to give it your whole. Coming here is a stress relief. It feels like home to me.
>
> You have to want it to be here. You have to want to be a better person and do the job.

They have a thing here called Real Talk and we have deltas. A delta means a change, and you give advice to someone about how to make it better. First you say what they are good at and then the things they can improve on. Like for me, my delta was to speak up. It used to be I was afraid to be wrong and now I'm not. Now I'm like, "I got this."

The people here, they make my thoughts bounce. They make you think more than you used to think.[2]

Torrey is another kind of success story, though at first glance you might not think so: He left Grow Dat eight weeks into the five-month program (two after-school days and a Saturday during the school year, expanding to four full days in the summer). But the departure, for him, was a part of his growth curve. The farm's program incorporates social learning—rules and regulations that apply to any workplace—as well mini-lectures and ad hoc seminars on agriculture, nutrition, and the environment. It describes itself as a "value-based" community, founded on ideas of gratitude, trust, compassion, and, not least, responsibility. Grow Dat's expectations—no sleeping late, no fooling around, no skipping days—awoke Torrey to the fact that he needed to study harder at school to get where he wanted to go: to meet expectations academically and to take himself seriously.

Not everyone makes it all the way; some derail after graduating because of ingrained social inequities, or the relentless temptations of the street, or simply bad luck. Take Deshawn Robinson, the Grow Dat graduate whose essay "From Pain to Success" ended chapter 3. He credited the farm with giving him a new start and changing his life as he went from being a crew member to an intern; he then continued to visit the farm for help from the social worker with school support and job applications.

But shortly thereafter, Deshawn was arrested on charges of burglary and possessing stolen goods, though, in his words, he was only giving a ride to a friend who wanted to "pick up" some garden tools. His guardian couldn't afford the nonrefundable bail of $2,400, so Deshawn missed the end of the academic year and didn't graduate with his high school class. Johanna spoke to the public defender and found him a lawyer (a friend of a friend) who got bail reduced to $200 and arranged probation for him: no jail time if he drug tested clean every week and finished high school in the summer. Even though Deshawn may not have been entirely blameless, the consequences of a conviction would have been devastating: Without expert legal help, he would never have been able to get a high school diploma and would have ended up a felon, essentially marked for life.[3]

There's a tweet going around, a line from the movie *The Best Exotic Marigold Hotel*, that goes: "In the end, everything will be all right. If it's not all right, it's not the end." An existential uncertainty hovers over kids like Deshawn, who came to Grow Dat disconnected in the extreme, with a drug-addicted mother who died, an absent father, murdered relatives and friends; he was living on his own, in the streets, at age 11. Still, it's not the end. A place like Grow Dat, and people like Johanna and Leo, persist against the odds. They offer second, even third chances. They believe in people so that they can begin believing in themselves. And they are changing the world, one person at a time.

LEO IS OUT IN THE FIELD WITH HIS CREW, where they've been down in the dirt weeding between the furrows. "Why do we weed?" he asks. Muffin says, "Because we don't use chemicals." Muffin admits she doesn't like to get her fingernails dirty, but she likes growing things, and "That's the price you pay." The kids will go home tonight with tomatoes and cucumbers.

"Okay," Leo says, standing and stretching. It's time for the group cooldown session after a long day of work. "Clap it up!" he says, and starts a rhythm, slapping his shoulders, thighs, knees. The rhythm runs through the group; everyone is clapping and slapping, a drum circle of sorts. The energy is palpable, and so is the hope.

IT'S TULANE'S WAVE OF GREEN DAY of service, and a group of two dozen faculty and staff has gathered at Café Reconcile in Central City. I've dropped in to take a look, the first of several sites I'll visit in the course of the day. Chef Joe greets everyone at the door, ushering them into the stainless steel kitchen and organizing them into teams for the tasks ahead. They'll be preparing food—roast chicken and slow-cooked brisket, smothered okra, red rice and beans—for 20 families in the area. Trainees in the Reconcile program, mainly teenagers, help the Tulane contingent find their way to the prep stations and coach them on techniques of slicing and dicing, steaming and sautéing.

Chef Joe keeps up a patter of instructions and suggestions. Someone asks him how much salt should go into the okra and he says, "It's called soul food 'cause you don't measure it, you just gotta feel it." He lifts the lid off a pot roast and delivers a parable directed to his teenage crew: "The real world's gonna judge you like they look at this here roast. See how it looks all burnt up and crusty? But"—he slices open the charred brisket with a graceful stroke of his carving knife—"take a look in here. It's pink, it's tender, it's delicious. You have to be like that inside yourself."[4]

Café Reconcile isn't just a kitchen; it's the kitchen of life. Its mission: to train disconnected young people, with traumatic histories behind them and treacherous terrain in front of them, in the social behaviors and job skills that may literally save their lives. Predating Katrina by nearly ten years, the café began its existence because Craig Cuccia, back from a mission in Jamaica to a tent village of 5,000 living in abject poverty, decided he had to do something for his home city. The name "Reconcile" is drawn from a passage in Corinthians that speaks of God's request that we be ambassadors of reconciliation in the world: "Whoever is in Christ is a new creation: The old things have passed away; Behold, new things have come. And all this is from God."

Craig jokes that he still doesn't know how to spell *entrepreneur*[5]—the café was more like a calling than a business, and it grew out of his Catholic faith, his close association with homeless advocate Reverend Harry Tompson, help from his brother-in-law Tim Falcon, and affiliations with other denominations and faith-based organizations.[6] A spiritual quality animates the entire place. As Chef Joe says, he's not just there to cook dinner; he's there to save souls.

But it's not a charity either. (Craig quotes the old saw about ending hunger: "Don't give a man a fish, teach him how to fish.") A practical aim of the program is to prepare kids for the hospitality industry, which dominates the city's employment landscape. By providing training and practice, Reconcile produces graduates who perfectly fit the jobs available, saving employers the time and effort required to train a new worker and preventing turnover. For example, there's a dishwashing system called AutoChlor that Reconcile trainees learn thoroughly. They can earn $9.50 an hour rather than $8.00 in their first job because they have that skill, and they can keep the job, gaining the stability and income that open more doors. So in one sense, the café is a workforce development initiative.

In another, it's a community revitalization effort that makes contact at ground level, in the heart of a tough neighborhood. Craig remembers back in 1996, when he bought the five-story brick building on Oretha Castle Haley Boulevard, that Central City was "murder capital of the murder capital," full of drug dealers and prostitutes and guns. He made it his business to make friends with people on the street so that they wouldn't burn down the building he'd just purchased. Beginning with a bake shop called Sweet T after Tyrone Hall, the flamboyant character who ran the place decked out in a red bow tie, the café slowly took shape. First there were once-a-week community dinners, then cooking lessons for kids, and then a small lunch counter with a tiny menu. Finally, in 2000, the full-fledged restaurant opened, with excellent food—locally sourced ingredients, soul food, healthy vegetarian choices, five-star dishes, a prize-winning bread pudding. As Glen Armantrout, the newly appointed chief executive officer, puts it, they've designed it so everyone can come to the table.[7] And it's been a resounding success for a long time. Back in 2003, the café started to take on aspects of a community center, given the numbers of kids drawn to the program, because they realized here was a place they could get help.[8]

But Katrina meant a do-over. Though the café came through it better than most in other parts of the city, with only a couple of broken plate-glass windows and some rain damage, its customers were dispersed all over the map, and the city itself was under siege. Craig says that seven days after the storm, he decided that "we have to go get it open." Then some staff started showing up, and some of the kids, and he put them to work. Five weeks later, Reconcile served its first meal since the storm, one of only 12 functioning restaurants in all of New Orleans. Everyone rolled up their sleeves and just did it, even though the streetlights didn't come back on for months.

National recognition, including nods from the White House Council for Community Solutions, National Public Radio (NPR), and many other media outlets, plus new funding from corporate donors, gave Cuccia the leeway to retool the basic concept.[9] Once a catering salesperson at a big hotel, he understood the importance of revenue, and he envisioned a catering hall on the second floor to bring in more money. Glen Armantrout has been in charge of a $5.9 million reconstruction and expansion, including the catering operations, the development of a separate area for case managers to meet with youth in the program, and a renovation of the restaurant itself. The café has brought in an outside group to provide parenting classes, tutoring and GED preparation, and classes on financial literacy and healthy living. A construction training program, affiliated with the café and employing disconnected youth to build low-cost homes for Central City residents, was also in operation for several years; Chef Joe was the very first to buy one of the new houses.

Another job training initiative in the food industry was started by the celebrity chef John Besh, a Louisiana native; his Chefs Move scholarship for aspiring chefs from minority backgrounds brings the best and brightest to New York to train at the International Culinary Institute and apprentice at fine Manhattan restaurants. Besh wants to see young African Americans move up from being dishwashers and line cooks to higher levels of the hospitality industry. Interviewed on NPR with Reconcile graduate Chris Okorie, who won a Chefs Move scholarship, Besh says that the tradition of black cooking has been carried on mostly by "the grandmothers"; it wasn't something young black men learned. Poverty also means poor-quality foods, if not hunger. But he thinks Reconcile could be a springboard for real social advancement, and real earning power, in the culinary world. As Besh puts it: "What happens to those with the smarts, the drive and the tenacity to move on into management levels? And ultimately, what I would like to see done is that they, you know, allow that entrepreneurial spirit to take over and start opening their restaurants, their businesses, really putting their indelible mark or imprint on the culture of New Orleans. I think that would really change things and I think offer so much potential to young inner-city people across the country."[10]

All of this may sound a little rah-rah, but it's hard to talk about the social innovations in New Orleans since Katrina without sounding like a member of the chamber of commerce. At the heart of all these enterprises—Grow Dat and Café Reconcile, but also the Youth Empowerment Project, the Tulane Drop-in Center, APEX, the Juvenile Justice Project of Louisiana, and a hundred others I could name—is a passion to connect and do good. Johanna Gilligan and Leo Gorman, Craig Cuccia and John Besh, and countless others have found personal resolve and a sense of mission in the city that care forgot and are part of an army of individuals who, stirred to action, are creatively reshaping the urban landscape and opening the door to new possibilities for cities across the nation.

Craig, speaking to the New Jersey Summit on Social Entrepreneurship in 2011, refers over and over again to certain guiding principles. His language is simple, direct, and resonant: *rub elbows, go into the neighborhoods, gain trust, create a world, tap passion, go back to core values, gather people to the cause, be present, branch out, build relationships.* In short: make contact.

But principles, however stirring, are abstractions only. What matters is their application in real-life circumstances. And the circumstances are typically grim, even hopeless. Take Ryan Dalton, born into poverty in the Eighth Ward, the sixth of 11 children in a fatherless household, a high school dropout, a teenage father, a user and seller of drugs, shot three times in gang wars, his older brother and a cousin murdered.

But—and it's a huge "but"—something changed. Here is Ryan's current resume, from the Café Reconcile website under "Our Staff":

In December 2009, Ryan completed Café Reconcile's program and earned a job at the New Orleans School of Cooking, where he worked for seven months. Ryan currently serves as Café Reconcile's floor trainer, supervising and training all students working in the front of the house. He plans to continue working full time and attend college at night, where he will study social work and management. Ryan has been selected and currently works as an ambassador for the Youth Leadership Institute for which he recently attended a Youth Summit for Community Solutions at the White House. He is also currently working to launch his own non-profit, the "Perseverance Understanding Success and Healing" or P.U.S.H. project. Ryan also currently holds a position as a council member with the National Council of Young Leaders through the Gates Foundation. Ryan is also on the advisory committee for the "Chefs Move!" scholarship hosted by the John Besh Foundation.[11]

The P.U.S.H. initiative is a wonderful spinoff of the socially innovative spirit of Café Reconcile. Ryan sees idleness as one of the root causes of teen drug use and violence, and his project—the winner of a Spark Opportunity Challenge, a crowdsourcing contest for youth initiatives in education—is designed to create camps and after-school programs during the summer, using underutilized city parks, in order to "keep the education flowing" and "create job opportunities for counselors and coaches."[12]

The journey from there to here is one that the social innovators of New Orleans hope to see repeated over and over, for hundreds, then thousands, then tens of thousands of disconnected youth suffering from neglect, abuse, and the daily trauma that poverty inflicts. The aim, over time: a critical mass of young people who are connected, focused, and productive and who will be the leading edge of generational, enduring change.

GROW DAT AND CAFÉ RECONCILE are both rooted in the food culture, in the very soil of New Orleans; they're homegrown in every way. And they are both devoted, in different ways, to youth development, vocational guidance, and leadership training. But there are many other kinds of initiatives going on in the city. For instance, Tulane's Disaster Resilience Leadership Academy (DRLA), another instance of social innovation, has global reach. Drawing on the university's expertise in emergency response after Katrina, DRLA brings together a number of graduate schools—architecture, business, law, public health and tropical medicine, social work—and undergraduate programs like sociology and mathematics to study leadership and decision making, collect data and analyze disastrous events as they occur, develop methods to mitigate physical damage and human suffering, and train effective leaders.

The need for a systematic approach to operations, risk reduction, humanitarian relief, and, above all, effective leadership has become urgent: In the last 30 years, there has been a fourfold increase in the occurrence of natural disasters, nine out of ten them climate related. The United Nations reports that five times more people are affected by disasters than a generation ago, with nearly 93 million people displaced globally by war, violence, and urbanization as well as natural disasters. Though hurricanes, earthquakes, war, and industrialization may all be inevitable, the man-made component of disasters—misinformation, misuse of resources, collateral trauma—is within our control.

DRLA, by focusing on leadership and partnering with universities in the developing world to train local leaders, aims to strengthen sustainable disaster risk reduction through smart planning and intelligent mitigation. Fact finding and analysis is one of the pillars of its work, and one of DRLA's early projects, a report titled "Haiti Humanitarian Aid Evaluation Structured Analysis," focusing on the 2010 earthquake in Haiti, marshals the facts. Introducing a conceptual framework—social, economic, infrastructure, and environmental—the report offers statistics, maps, and bar graphs, exploring the welter of discrete facts in order to see exactly where money, volunteers, and humanitarian aid groups went, and to understand which interventions promoted resilience in the population.[13]

Comments on current events (a note on the increasing difficulty of data acquisition due to postelection political unrest and the cholera epidemic) acknowledge that a disaster has a long and complex aftermath. Comments about "unintended consequences" are also important in evaluating how aid works, or doesn't, in disaster response scenarios. One such consequence is the "substitution effect" of the humanitarian response, "in effect taking on the role of the government in many domains" and driving out local professionals and private organizations. The overwhelming focus of aid on directly affected areas also has an unexpected negative consequence, "leaving poor host communities in other parts of the country burdened by the displaced and other effects without humanitarian assistance."[14]

The Haiti report essentially uses the earthquake as a laboratory and class-room, with lessons about how to operationalize contact, pinpointing where and how support should be delivered to the people who need it. Domestic disasters have received similar scrutiny: The DRLA has produced reports on the Deepwater Horizon (BP) oil spill, analyzing affected communities in coastal Louisiana, and, in a collaboration with Yale, an "emergency support function" analysis of Hurricane Sandy issued in the days after the storm, tracking events in real time, analyzing hot spots, and recommending how to deploy resources.[15] At the same time, DRLA is conducting interviews with established leaders in disaster management like Randolph Kent, director of the Humanitarian Futures Program at King's College, London, and Gisli Olafsson, disaster management technical advisor at Microsoft Corporation, to investigate those skills and traits that promote effective action. Such ana-lytic efforts are designed to improve management of critical emergencies, when leaders are often prone to extremes of impulsivity or disengagement, as when President Bush handed off to "Heck of a job" Brownie or looked down on the devastation of Katrina from Air Force One.

In catastrophic circumstances, the poor and marginalized usually bear the brunt of adversity, with gender, race, and class significantly affecting individual outcomes. In the DRLA report on the oil spill, maps pinpoint zip codes most affected by the spill, and, within those communities, the popula-tion subsets most vulnerable to negative consequences: families in poverty, those over the age of 65, female heads of households with children, rented-occupied households, and Native American and Asian populations. Maps also portray race, employment, and income distribution patterns in the affected areas. The report is ongoing as researchers try to achieve "granular-ity" of data in groups that are difficult to assess statistically—for example, the Vietnamese fishing population, which conducts much of its business in cash, doesn't always keep accurate records, and is linguistically insular.

The DRLA reports, despite their statistical bent and numerous graphs, are more than academic. The numbers tell an eloquent story about vulnerability and are the groundwork for delivery of services in order to enhance resilience. Posttraumatic stress disorder is not only an individual pathology; it can be like a contagion, undermining whole communities if appropriate support is lacking. As we've seen over and over, Katrina produced traumatic consequences for the entire city but most grievously for those without resources.[16] Examples include the Danziger Bridge shootings and other episodes of police violence against African Americans; the razing of the projects that produced tens of thousands of "internally displaced persons"; and increasing numbers of disconnected youth, without family supports or job training, and often without high school diplomas. The crisis may be global or local, but, as noted many times before, a crisis is always, in part, an opportunity to respond creatively, innovatively, humanely—which means facing up to painful realities and engaging on a personal level; translating numbers into individuals, making contact, and grappling at ground level.

"MAKE CONTACT" SOUNDS MUCH easier than it is. In fact, it's often easier not to make contact. In a crisis, spending time consulting with "the community" seems inefficient at best, foolhardy at worst. Meanwhile, the very business of leading and administering produces barriers to personal engagement. When much of the day is spent in an office or a boardroom, discussing people who are not there, it's easy to forget that enduring change requires a process, not just a top-down decision. The isolation of authority can lead to missteps and misreadings of all kinds, resulting in decisions that are wrongheaded or ineffectual. Though social innovations posing new approaches to old (often age-old) problems often begin far away from the community in a university or office building, to achieve success you have to come down into the streets. After the idea comes the work of actualizing and realizing—which may involve physical labor, like hammering nails, or desk work, like phoning donors, but always requires the building of relationships. There really is no substitute for listening, for looking into someone's eyes and feeling what his or her experience must be like.

*How do leaders "make contact" in personal, visceral ways that enhance social innovation and change? They build real and enduring relationships. They are open and available, engage in a process, and not only seek to influence others but allow themselves to be influenced. They have the humility, the curiosity, and the willingness to experience, up close, another person's point of view and imagine what it's like to be that person.*

I've come home from campus, a five-minute walk, on a day when Margie is having one of her famous women's luncheons at the president's house—her way of bringing the larger community into contact with Tulane. It's a salon in the classic sense, a gathering where important public issues are discussed by experts in their fields. I'm not on the guest list; it's women only. My role has always been to suggest the speaker, and today it's Charles Figley, distinguished professor at the School of Social Work, head of the Traumatology Institute, and graduate academic director of the DRLA..

As I head toward my upstairs study, I can't resist a moment of eavesdropping. Figley is behind the lectern in one of our large reception rooms with their slightly faded elegance—leaded windows, Persian rugs—facing rows of women united by their New Orleans roots and their tendency to dress to the nines for occasions like this. Figley moves out in front of the lectern in line with the projector, words from a PowerPoint slide wavering across his three-piece suit. He's describing "Trauma Opportunities" that people in New Orleans found in response to Katrina. I catch a few phrases: *cognitive disorganization in response to adversity; impaired decision-making; adaptation to the "new normal"; recognition and management of uncertainty; trauma memory management; integration and resilience...*

His voice is earnest. You can tell, despite the PowerPoint and the faintly academic language, that he's speaking from the heart. Figley is a Vietnam veteran whose early work on trauma related to combat soldiers; two decades ago, he was in the group that first defined posttraumatic stress disorder. His study of resilience in individuals and families in response to war, violence, and disaster investigates a key question: How do people come back from horror and loss? Figley's answer stems from a systems approach that sees an individual in the context of family and culture. According to Figley, to overcome traumatic experience, whether in the tent cities of Port-au-Prince or the projects of New Orleans, the community needs to have a say and participate in its own healing.

I pause on the landing. Figley's voice floats up the stairs: "This whole city has been traumatized, but it's also incredibly resilient. People have learned to turn away from the pain, or go past it, or use it as a spur to action, and we're taking the lesson about coping and survival to Haiti, to Rwanda, to Peru."

And we're taking the message to Central City, New Orleans. As I continue up the stairs, I'm remembering the listening session we had at Café Reconcile—I was there with Jon Bon Jovi and a bunch of kids from the café, the Youth Empowerment Project, and the Tulane Drop-in Center. Bon Jovi and I were both members of the White House Council for Community Solutions, which in 2011 organized a series of events to engage communities in problem solving. At the session at the café, I remember one young man wearing a black Tulane Drop-in Center T-shirt, hands raised, fingers spread, sketching his ideas in the air. His recommendation: Always offer food (people will show up because of hunger). Someone else said focus on jobs (because that's what saves kids). Others spoke up, too, about child care (many of them are raising younger siblings or babies of their own) and about transportation, gun control, legal aid.

I said to them at the end, "You've been great teachers today, and I hope we've been good listeners."

It's this kind of face-to-face, heart-to-heart dialogue that alters the people engaged and that fuels meaningful activism, meaningful change. How do you alleviate suffering and help people recover from pain? Make contact. Listen. Have an idea. Implement it.

And bring food.

# Chapter 8

# INFLECTION POINT

## INNOVATE

IT'S 93 DEGREES AND HUMID, NOT A GREAT TIME TO LEAVE THE air-conditioning, but here I am outside Gibson Hall, the Romanesque administration building at Tulane, wilting in the heat. I'm talking to Rob Lynch, BA from Loyola, MBA from Tulane, bicycle enthusiast, entrepreneur, and founder of Bike Taxi Unlimited. *New Orleans CityBusiness* is doing a piece on tightened budgets and enrollment competition in area universities and wants to photograph me in one of Rob's bright yellow pedicabs, which are fast becoming a fixture around town, from the French Quarter all the way to Uptown.

Rob is explaining the birth of the idea. "I was doing corporate work in St. Louis but I missed New Orleans, and my brother, who lives here, said, come on back. And then we got to talking about the hospitality industry, and what kind of gap or need I could fill, and he mentioned the pedicab boom in Charleston. I love bikes. And New Orleans is flat, no hills, which makes it perfect for a taxi tourist thing."

I ask him how he got started.

Rob says, "At the ground floor. Actually, below the ground floor. I lived in a friend's basement for two years, eating peanut butter and jelly and saving up cash. Then I worked with city council for more than a year on ordinances and setting fees, plus I trained people, put together insurance, bought equipment. There was an administrative argument about how to award the contracts, by application or a lottery. The mayor said lottery, because he felt there weren't criteria to make meaningful distinctions. I have to say I protested that—I said, reward hard work. What kind of message is that to young entrepreneurs trying to make a start? But as it turned out I was one of three companies to get a city contract." He shrugged. "Lucky, I guess. Fifteen cabs for each outfit, to start. I made back my initial investment in the first few months."[1]

After I've spent a few minutes with the reporter from *CityBusiness* talking about Tulane's budget (solid) and enrollment (up), the photographer asks me to get into the pedicab. I climb onto the cushioned seat, roomy enough for three, and Rob straddles the bicycle, which has high handlebars, a rearview mirror, and thick tires that can handle potholes. Rob looks cheery in his spandex bicycle shorts and yellow polo shirt with BIKE TAXI UNLIMITED emblazoned on the front. He also looks hot and sweaty. I don't want to know what I look like.

The photographer clicks away.

When *CityBusiness* finally leaves, I say to Rob, "Let's give her a whirl, if you're up to it." I'm feeling bad for him—I'm a big guy, and it's hot, hot, hot—but he's happy to do it. "These are great machines," he says, patting the handlebars the way you'd stroke a horse's head. "They do a lot of the work."

Off we go. It's like a rickshaw, eco-friendly, street level, open air. There's a breeze blowing, and I can see the beauties of St. Charles Avenue—live oaks, stately mansions, stone walls—without obstruction. Over his shoulder, Rob is describing the awning he uses when it's raining and the blankets for when it's cold, but rain and cold seem unimaginable on this hot, bright, breezy day.

**Image 11** Pedicab

Rob Lynch, Tulane graduate and founder of Bike Taxi Unlimited, on one of his fleet of pedicabs. His particular arena is the tourist industry, but he represents the entrepreneurial spirit typical of many young people who have flocked to New Orleans since Katrina, making the city a "brain magnet" with "start up fever."

*(Photo credit: Paula Burch-Celentano, Tulane University)*

I lean back in my chariot, banish all thoughts of bad weather, and watch the world fly by.

I'M BEGINNING WITH BIKE TAXI BECAUSE this kind of urban amenity is one instance of continuity between pre- and post-Katrina New Orleans. The New Orleans "brand" is synonymous with hospitality, beauty, pleasure, and escape, and despite all the changes this book has documented thus far, it still offers that enduring message: Come on down! Forget your cares! Let the good times roll!

Rob Lynch, with his bike tours, has found a niche in the town's well-established industry of service and entertainment. He hires young men and women who are physically fit, charming and charismatic, and well informed about the city. Applicants have to pass a drug test and federal background check and are trained intensively in the art of driving the cabs around the city's busy, narrow streets. Feedback has been enthusiastic, despite the price (set by the city) of $5 for the first six blocks, $1 per block thereafter, per passenger. Bloggers describe Bike Taxi Unlimited as a lot of bang for the buck, given the tour guide component and the do-it-yourself embellishments (including, but not limited to, boom boxes, drinks, and Mardi Gras beads). Basically, Rob understood the culture of the town, identified a need, came up with a novel idea, and made a go of it—a great American tradition.

But since Katrina, the entrepreneurial spirit of experiment and risk is burgeoning in a whole new way in New Orleans. Basically, New Orleans is changing its image from party town and charming backwater to a city for the twenty-first century. The leadership principle of this chapter, "Innovate," describes the vision and energy that fuels such a transformation: By developing, welcoming, and supporting new ideas, leaders create a fertile seedbed for products, services, and inventions that improve lives.

*Innovation is the lifeblood of high-performing organizations and initiatives. Leaders foster cultures of innovation and continuous improvement that inspire creativity in problem solving. Such cultures are laboratories for progress, yielding novel approaches that have the potential to alter the landscape of the future.*

The city's embrace of novelty and creativity has produced an inflection point—that moment when positive changes, rapidly accelerating, lead to an explosion of business opportunity and growth. The headlines announcing New Orleans' arrival are everywhere, from *Forbes*, to *Time*, to *Details*: #1 region of information technology job growth in the United States, a "brain magnet," a "Fast City" with "start-up fever."[2] *Forbes* publisher Rich Karlgaard calls New Orleans "One of the great turnarounds in American history." The website of the Greater New Orleans economic development group, GNO, Inc., shows graphs with arrows pointing up, up, up: wages, jobs, population, school reform, businesses. The arrows suggest a powerful trend: In New Orleans, we're transitioning from a culture that was resistant to change to one that embraces innovation.

This transformation would not have occurred without Katrina. Prior to the storm, economic activity, apart from the hospitality industry, was narrowly focused on the Port of New Orleans and on chemical and energy companies, and it was difficult to convince new firms to come to the city. Talented young people wanted to stay in the urban core, but jobs were not available. Beyond that, the city was lacking some of the basics, like good public schools and affordable housing, which attract young families and singles. Visitors to New Orleans loved the food, the music, the atmosphere, but thought of it as a place to escape to, not a place to call home. There was also the perception, real or imagined, that New Orleans was tradition bound and insular—unwelcoming to people not "from here." Most critically, it lacked an infrastructure to support entrepreneurship and innovation—things like incentives and tax credits, incubators and seed accelerators, and a tech community.

The storm jolted new transplants and native New Orleanians alike into recognizing that the city needed to change if it was to survive. It became a strategic goal of the entire community to make innovation a top priority and to develop all the resources necessary to support economic development. Some of those resources emerged organically from the situation we faced: After Katrina, the town received a stimulus package in the form of FEMA money, and idealistic young people flocked to the city to seek opportunity and help in the rebuilding. But other ingredients were the result of strategic planning and communal will: a city hall that modernized its administration after Mayor Landrieu was elected in 2010; a coalition of private and public institutions producing improvements in education, housing, and public safety; and numerous civic organizations—among them GNO, Inc., the incubator Idea Village, and Tulane's Social Innovation and Social Entrepreneurship program—working together to create an environment of possibility and welcome.

Now there's talk of New Orleans as Silicon Bayou, Hollywood South, Tech City, and Brain Magnet, to pick a few recent headlines. Other tech communities, like Silicon Valley or the Route 128 corridor of Boston, developed out of densely populated centers with a high concentration of young people skilled in computer science. Here it was a sudden event, an influx of the "new"—ideas, people, ventures—that reconfigured the city.

About "Hollywood South": The movie industry took root in New Orleans back in 2002, before Katrina, when the state legislature authorized tax credits for 30 percent of production costs. Even before 2002, some famous productions were filmed here, among them *Interview with the Vampire* (based on the novels of Anne Rice, a native New Orleanian steeped in the local vampire lore); a number of John Grisham–inspired movies (*The Pelican Brief, The Client, Runaway Jury*); and *All the King's Men* (from the novel by Robert Penn Warren about "Willie Stark," a thinly disguised Huey Long). In recent years, the floodgates have opened, with films ranging from *The Expendables* (action adventure), to *Twilight Saga Part Two* (vampires), to *21 Jump Street* (buddy comedy), to *Django Unchained* (a Quentin Tarantino film), to *Beasts of the Southern Wild* (Oscar-nominated indie bayou film); Katrina-specific projects include HBO's *Treme* and Spike Lee's documentaries.[3]

A fight in the legislature in 2013 about continuing those movie tax credits showcased the competing agendas of the state and the city: Louisiana loses money on most of these projects, but the hotels, restaurants, and entertainment venues of New Orleans profit from the presence of the movie industry. Putting aside the politics and the coolness factor, one strongly positive result of all the productions has been the emergence of a digital media sector, especially augmented reality, or special effects (FX), companies based in New Orleans. (Video games too: Gameloft, originating in Paris, has located one of its North American studios in New Orleans.) Digital media has also gotten tax credits and incentives from the state, and the perks have brought Bayou FX (run by Huck Wirtz, native New Orleanian) and Spectrum FX (run by Matt Kutcher, LA special effects wizard) to the city, along with their entire studios.[4]

And with those businesses have come jobs, everything from electric and grip, to technical animation, to screenwriting and directing. NOVAC, the New Orleans Video Access Center, affiliated with the Tulane Center for Public Service and many other local organizations, provides networking, workshops, and training for people entering the film industry. Expanded entrepreneurship also provides opportunities for social innovation; for example, NOVAC partnered with an independent production company, Scrub Brush, to produce *Shell Shocked*, a 2013 documentary about violence in New Orleans, with seven teenagers armed with cameras filming details of their lives.[5] The movie biz may not be the prime indicator of the business activity that has emerged since Katrina, but it shows how entrepreneurial vigor links with people's actual lives. When we talk about an inflection point, we are also talking about opportunity—specifically, an expansion of the workforce that lifts people out of poverty into stable, meaningful jobs.[6]

What are the central areas of serious investment and growth that have brought new eminence, and new possibilities, to New Orleans? GNO, Inc. lists them on its website: advanced manufacturing, energy, international trade, digital media, biosciences, and emerging environmental.[7] There's a new wind blowing and new ideas emerging from everywhere. Kenneth Purcell, native New Orleanian, founder of iSeatz, a successful software development company that bundles the booking of multiple travel reservations, describes the economic resurgence in his hometown as "a lot of bubbling petri dishes."[8]

What's in the petri dishes? What new and as-yet-unimagined things will emerge from this rich substrate of creative activity, with the potential to improve our lives?

IT'S EARLY MORNING, I'M AT THE BATHROOM sink brushing my teeth—and it's amazing. I wouldn't believe it except for the evidence of my senses, right here, right now: a burst of flavor, chocolate of all things, when you're expecting mint. My mouth tingles. This stuff tastes great, feels great.

Theodent Kids, a tube of which I've just popped open, is new to the market, and it's not just a flavor thing. Arman Sadeghpour, the inventor, has lived in New Orleans nearly his whole life and is a Tulane grad not once but four times over: BA in French, BS in psychology; MS in computer science; and PhD in bioinformatics. He grabbed me in the hall one day and started talking about this cocoa extract toothpaste that was the subject of his doctoral dissertation. Toothpaste? Chocolate? My first thought was, this is insane, but then Arman sent me a tube, the kid version, I suppose because of its wild flavor—and I'm a convert.

More important than the flavor is the science behind Theodent. Bear with me here for a moment: The product uses an extract of the cacao plant, theobromine, which is a methylxanthine that increases the crystallite size of a hydroxyapatite, a basic component of bones, including teeth. Yes, it's complicated—even I don't know what I just said—but clearly it's extremely well researched (you can read the scientific papers on the website), with implications not only for dental caries but for many bone disorders including osteoporosis and rheumatoid arthritis. Arman's dissertation, an outgrowth of earlier research at LSU, compared the effects of theobromine with those of fluoride, finding that the chocolate extract was much more effective against cavities than fluoride and not harmful if swallowed. The patent suggests that many products besides toothpaste are in the pipeline, including nutritional supplements and facial lotions to prevent bone reabsorption in aging and to strengthen skeletal mass after chemotherapy or fracture.[9]

The scientific evidence ultimately yielded a great market pitch: Better teeth! Tastes great! Children love it! Now Arman is chief executive of the company, and the product is spreading across the country, to supermarkets and pharmacies in California, on the Alabama coast, Chicago, and a Whole Foods near you.

Theodent's offices are located in the BioInnovation Center, situated between the Greater New Orleans Biosciences Economic Development District and the New Orleans Medical District. A consortium of corporate and academic institutions, including Tulane, the center is a technology business incubator devoted to bioscience entrepreneurship in the New Orleans area and is home to a number of companies that supply medical services, devices, diagnostics, therapeutics, and environmental solutions.

The roster of tenants and clients at the center is impressive.[10] The South Coast Angel Fund brings together investors and business leaders dedicated to accelerating early stage bioscience companies. The New Orleans Medical Complex is a group of universities concentrating on workforce development and the training of personnel to work in the medical sciences. A number of companies focus on personalized medicine: a diagnostic platform for predicting an individual patient's therapeutic response to a drug based on target protein structures and genetic biomarkers (Chosen Diagnostics); applications that help patients with HIV manage their drug regimens (NOLA MobileHealth) or provide a home monitoring kit for transplant patients with immunosuppression (TMS Bioscience); a vaccine against the opportunistic fungal infection *Pneumocystis pneumonia* (MiniVax). InnoGenomics is developing a program for DNA testing using the Alu gene (the "jumping" gene) that allows for accurate forensic results from fragmentary or degraded biological samples. Other groups are working with stem cells, cobiotics, intrauterine devices, influenza drugs, bioactive peptides, retinal implants, and an array of other medical therapies.

Biotech companies with an environmental emphasis include NanoFex, which uses nanotechnology derived from Louisiana cane sugar and crab and crawfish shells to break down groundwater contaminants like chlorinated solvents, arsenic, and heavy metals; and Meredian Inc., a manufacturer of biopolymers from renewable nonpetroleum sources and biodegradable products.

The sheer number of companies is significant in itself. Though the individual actors are highly specialized and distinct, there's a kind of scientific synergy operating at the BioInnovation Center—a collective wave of innovation and creative excitement. Although I've expressed my reservations about the new, expensive University Medical Center being built to replace Charity Hospital, on the positive side, the LSU and Tulane medical schools anticipate significantly higher levels of clinical research because of the new facility and its attraction to new faculty.

The BioInnovation Center supplies needed infrastructure for bioscience endeavors, including venture capital, workforce development, affordable space, and a climate of openness and support. Other places supporting the ecosystem for entrepreneurship include Tulane. Through the Freeman Business School, Social Entrepreneurship Initiatives, and a group called Propeller, the university annually hosts a contest for new social ventures called PitchNOLA, with students giving three-minute "elevator pitches" to win seed grants from seasoned businesspeople. Some recent winners: using goats to eat the vegetation in blighted parts of town, a plan to turn abandoned lots into citrus, banana, and fig groves, and an initiative by the Justice and Accountability Center of Louisiana to expunge the records of young people incarcerated for nonviolent crimes in order to help them transition back into society.[11]

The PitchNOLA projects focus exclusively on social innovations. In contrast, Idea Village, cofounded by Tim Williamson as a business incubator and accelerator, supports an eclectic range of projects. Successful enterprises that either originated at or received support from Idea Village include Cordina Frozen Cocktails; 504ward, a collaborative aimed at keeping young talent in New Orleans through social networking and events; Tierra Resources, water management and wetland restoration; Audiosocket, music licensing and curated music; and Crescent Unmanned Systems, drones for law enforcement and aerial geographic research.[12] Idea Village also hosts an entrepreneur season that runs from July to March annually, ending with an entrepreneurship week that showcases innovative ventures and helps grow the business ecosystem by extending the network of resources that guarantee sustainability and growth.

Some of the Idea Village offshoots have a distinctly New Orleans feel to them. At the iSeatz headquarters in the IP Building downtown, the décor is standard-issue modern and the travel service offered is web based and global, but one element speaks of something local and particular. A small segment of wall is exposed brick and pockmarked plaster—it looks like it could be an art installation made of found materials, but in fact it's an archaeological layer: a clear reminder of Katrina, poignant and evocative. Kenneth Purcell, the founder of iSeatz, is, as already noted, a native of New Orleans. At the heart of many of these businesses is, in fact, heart: personal passion and commitment.

An entrepreneurial domain that has particularly deep roots in the local milieu is educational technology. New Orleans is the only city in the United States that has almost completely transformed its public schools into charters, in the process creating a laboratory for educational research and trial balloons. Because the charter model is founded on the notion of accountability, school operators are keenly interested in data that will lead to improved performance; they also tend to be early adopters of innovative technology. 4.0 Schools, a laboratory for educational innovation run by Matt Candler, former chief executive officer of New Schools for New Orleans, itself an incubator of high-performing charters, has yielded some successful enterprises. One example is mSchool, founded by Elliot Sanchez, which gives local community centers preloaded tablet computers to start world-class academic programs, or microSchools, for students enrolled in their after-school programs. Using the most advanced adaptive platforms, math games are specifically tailored to a student's learning needs, and the results are substantial: Kids are learning about six months' worth of math every six weeks.[13] mSchool allows communities to swiftly replace inadequate math classes with more effective virtual instruction using public school dollars.

Then there's Kickboard, started by Jen Medbery, a former math teacher at Sci Academy, the charter in New Orleans East run by Ben Marcovitz that's dedicated to data and analytics (see chapter 5). At one point in her teaching, Jen says, she realized that what she wanted was not simply more information but *usable* information. Given her background in computer science, the situation "spoke to the engineer in me." She felt that teachers needed consistent, personalized information about each student's behavior to fine-tune appropriate interventions. So she created a "dashboard" for easy data entry, color coded and with a simple grading system. The resulting student snapshots are easily accessible not only to teachers but to social workers, special ed teachers, and administrators.

The dashboard, according to educators who use it, helps them mine the mountainous data from achievement and diagnostic tests, classroom quizzes, and homework assignments while also allowing them to record detailed observations about social skills, character traits, and an essential quality that Medbery calls "habits of mind." The aim is to locate strengths and weaknesses and match teaching approaches to a child's individual temperament.[14]

Medbery is like a poster girl for ed tech. She notes that the push for "the new" is fitting in a public school system that has recently reinvented itself: "The innovation happening in the schools is just a natural market to test the innovation happening outside the schools." The city's networks for entrepreneurship supported her progress from idea to marketplace, and an award won at IDEApitch during New Orleans Entrepreneur Week attracted the attention of investors. With the help of seed funds, she started her company at a local business incubator. Now the program is in 200 schools in 20 states.[15]

Like biomedical research and dozens of other realms, educational technology, is part of a groundswell of modernization. There's truth to the adage "More is more." The old guard that defended tradition, including traditional ways of doing business, is yielding ground to a wave of innovators who are changing New Orleans from a place where everything is reassuringly the same to a scene of risk, experiment, and possibility.

"DO YOU HAVE WHAT I NEED?"

These words aren't directly spoken, but that's essentially the question being posed by the executive across the table from me who is scouting New Orleans as a potential center for GE Capital Technology, one of only several in the nation. Michael Hecht, the chief executive officer of Greater New Orleans, Inc., the economic development group, has brought the executive (whose name escapes me—I'm notoriously bad with names) to Gibson Hall, where I spend most of my days when in the city. We're in a private conference room, and two minutes into our talk, before my secretary has even brought in coffee, it's clear that what the executive needs, first and foremost, is a pool of computer scientists. He's not exactly talking my language—many references to "IT environments," "relational data," LAN and WAN and firewalls—but I get the gist. And I can help.

What GE is proposing is to bring to New Orleans 300 jobs for "knowledge workers" in areas like data management, application architecture, and networking services—if, and only if, we can prove that we have the skilled labor force to do those jobs. Plus, we need to persuade them that the city has all the necessary amenities to make life livable and pleasant. A lot of cities are in contention to win the GE Tech Center. I'm going to have to make a good case.

I go into my elevator pitch, though it's longer than the three minutes allotted to contestants at PitchNOLA or IDEApitch. I begin with Tulane's nascent computer science program. Computer science was one of the unfortunate casualties in the downsizing of the Engineering School after Katrina, though it made perfect sense at the time—when computer programming had lost its cachet after the dot-com bust in 2000. But in 2010, recognizing the rise of technology sector jobs and the need to provide advanced training to students in search of employment, Nick Altiero, dean of the School of Science and Engineering, created a task force to develop a new Department of Computer Science. Now, several years later, the creation of the department is under way with the hiring of several new faculty and the offering of an increasing number of courses. The stated aim of the department is to emphasize the application of computer science to other areas of science, engineering, and the social and health sciences, with a core curriculum featuring the traditional topics of algorithms, programming, software engineering, and artificial intelligence.

The GE executive seems impressed. But what about his employees, and the life they would live here?

I go through my usual spiel: transformation of the public school system, ethics reform, new community health clinics and a university health center downtown, a thriving economy, plus affordable homes, green spaces, institutions of higher education, and (not least) the cultural heritage of New Orleans, from jazz funerals to the best food anywhere, ever.

Sold.

BACK WHEN I WAS GROWING UP, GE was synonymous with refrigerators and stoves (and the jingle still runs in my head: "GE: We bring good things to life"). Though it still sells appliances, the company has diversified and now deals in finance, energy management, the power grid, aviation, and health care. That the corporation chose New Orleans over many competitors speaks volumes about the city's new image. Of the many possible reasons GE came here, #1 was undoubtedly the rise of entrepreneurship in the city and the business-friendly climate. A related cause was a growing tech-savvy workforce, consisting of both transplants from other cities and homegrown Tulane grads. Other local schools, including Delgado Community College and the University of New Orleans, are expanding their programs in the biosciences and information technology (filmmaking too) in an effort to match graduates with jobs.

At the heart of the business boom is an excitement about ideas and a bursting creativity on many fronts, everything from new products like Flufirvitide, an anti-influenza drug from Autoimmune Technologies, to streamlined web-based services like The Receivables Exchange, an Internet company that auctions off accounts still outstanding to investors willing to take on risk for a stake in a company's fortunes. It's ideas—of all kinds, big and small, pragmatic and visionary—that make the world go round. More precisely, it's the link between idea and execution that keeps the world humming. As GE's website puts it: "At GE we put our ideas to work. We make things that matter, things that make life better. GE Works."

Lately, everything in New Orleans seems to be about putting ideas to work and making things that matter. But (and there is always a "but"), the business boom is not all roses, or cherries, or profits. Problems attend on any change, and the shift in New Orleans from a tradition-bound culture to a forward-looking, twenty-first-century city is not without costs. For instance, GE and the computer science program at Tulane—it's a great matchup, but it doesn't address the growing gap in the city between knowledge workers (both imported and native) and the largely homegrown, low-income service sector. Free enterprise may create jobs, but it can't single-handedly solve urban poverty without a concerted effort to educate kids for those jobs. While we are improving our charter schools and increasing our college acceptance rates, we haven't really acknowledged that not everyone can, or maybe even should, go to college.

I may be partly to blame for this problem. Our stated aim in reinventing the public school system was to give every child the opportunity to get a higher degree—a vision of equality and hope that I won't back down from. I continue to believe in the value of a humanistic, nonvocational education that prepares children to be full-fledged thinking citizens in a complex democracy. Yet the fact remains that there are jobs that don't require a knowledge of medieval French literature, or higher math, or even critical thinking. And there's the further fact that some—not all, but some—whose lives have been scarred by poverty and instability may derive more strength and purpose, in the immediate sense, from a good job than from a four-year academic curriculum. All of which suggests we need to revise our educational aims to include meaningful employment as a reasonable and respectable alternative to a bachelor's degree.

Of all the school programs in New Orleans, most of them now charters, there is clearly a dearth of vocational or technical schools. As we talk about the industries taking root in the city, we also have to think about training people to fill the required jobs, whether it's air-conditioning and electrical, computers, urban agriculture, biomedical research, environmental conservation, or tourism. As we've seen, youth development groups like Grow Dat (urban farm) and Café Reconcile (hospitality) are directly addressing this problem with their work-study initiatives, and organizations like NOVAC, the New Orleans Video Access Center, are offering workshops and seminars in industry-related skills. But it's clear that the schools should be doing it too.

Another potential problem with the emphasis on business innovation is a loss of traditional occupations and a trend toward cultural homogenization. New Orleans is not Anywhere, USA; it's an iconic city with a history that is central to its meaning, identity, and, despite recent changes, economy. As the environment shifts and new urbanism takes hold, what will the toll be on local treasures and unique institutions? Some of the pressure to throw out the old and welcome the new is in response to sweeping changes in the New South, with a rival city like Houston winning the competition in gas and oil in recent decades and Atlanta and Birmingham moving up the scale on all the relevant indices of success.

Still, New Orleans is New Orleans. As they say, "*Only* in New Orleans." In the contention between old and new, sometimes old wins. To take a single example: Circle Food Store in the Seventh Ward started out as an open market in 1919, becoming the first African American–owned food store in

New Orleans in 1938. The landmark building on the corner of St. Bernard and North Claiborne Avenues, white stucco and with a distinctive arcade of arches, housed not only a grocery store (selling everything from oxtails to ironing boards) but offices for doctors and dentists, serving a population of 12,000 local residents. Then Katrina hit, flooding the place with five feet of water. **Cynthia Hedge-Morrell,** a member of the city council representing District D, says, "That was the lowest point for me. It dawned on me that we were under water." And she had the further thought, or really just a hope: "When Circle Food Store is back, I'm going to know New Orleans is really back."[16]

Dwayne Boudreaux, the owner of Circle Food, says the floodwaters destroyed the first floor and looters took everything—computers, furniture, files—from the second floor. He would have to start over from scratch, if that were even possible. He went to the Tulane School of Architecture for building plans to present to potential investors and to the Tulane Business School for a business plan. Dwayne says, "People in the community would immediately hear about offers I was getting, but they said they didn't want a CVS or a Save-A-Lot in here, they wanted Circle Foods back." And the community got its wish: A $1 million loan from the Fresh Food Financing Initiative, which offers low-cost loans to food suppliers in poor neighborhoods, allowed Circle Food to reopen in 2013, preserving both its iconic architecture and its function as a multipurpose center, but in a more modern guise.[17] The tension between preservation and innovation persists as the city moves forward, and new isn't always better. The old New Orleans of diverse, engaged, committed neighborhoods is still alive in the era of Walmart, and the old New Orleans of the French Quarter and Jackson Square is still a highly marketable cultural brand.

None of this is to argue against the virtue and the necessity—and, indeed, the fact—of entrepreneurial vitality and innovation. We were going to permanently drown in Katrina or we were going to live again, and staging a renaissance entailed embracing a more modern ethos of free enterprise, business-friendly initiatives, and transparent negotiations. The benefits are pouring in: population growth, ethics reform, more houses and businesses, an influx of young people and new ideas, and better quality of living.

Katrina was the crisis that forced new ideas, and the leadership principle in this chapter, "Innovate," is really about putting ideas to work: about embracing novelty first and then forging practical links between someone's bright idea and a workable, sustainable organization. A leader says yes not only to an abstract concept but also to a particular individual—a Jen Medbery or Arman Sadeghpour; someone who has the vitality and intelligence and character to pull it off. And then a leader commits to building an infrastructure and support system—incubators, accelerators, angel funds, networking; all those things that allow a concept to take root and flower into something real and tangible. Among other things, leadership is a talent for pioneering relationships, seeing connections and structural affinities, and recognizing talent in others.

I'M STANDING AT THE PICTURE WINDOW that spans one entire wall of our living room in the condo at the end of Poydras Street, watching a working barge move with the powerful current under the Crescent City Connection Bridge. Our condo is an emblem of our love for the city. Knowing that we'd leave the President's Mansion on Audubon Park when I retired from the presidency of Tulane in 2014, Margie and I had no intention of leaving the city that's our home. And so, in 2013, we bought this place with a front-row seat on the Mississippi, using it as an occasional getaway for the remainder of my term as president.

The river, surprisingly, is invisible in most parts of New Orleans, hidden behind the high grassy knolls of the levee system. During Katrina, the waters never overtopped the impressive earthworks along the river; the breaches occurred in levees at the Industrial Canal, the 17th Street Canal, the London Avenue Canal, and the Mississippi River–Gulf Outlet, waterways built to carry commercial ships between the river and Lake Pontchartrain. The breaks in the levee walls, huge slabs of concrete buried in soft soil, are the fault of the Army Corps of Engineers, whose flawed calculations resulted in flawed designs. New Orleans, a city built between a major waterway and the huge expanse of Lake Pontchartrain, with bayous, inlets, and estuaries everywhere you turn, has been an engineering challenge from its beginnings in the seventeenth century. As the geographer Peirce Lewis put it, New Orleans is "the inevitable city on the impossible site."[18] But the city *is* here, not only inevitably but triumphantly; that's the story I've been telling in this book—a story of persistent striving and surprising success. Which brings me to two sectors of the economy essential to that success: energy and the environment.

To begin with energy: Louisiana is a gas and oil state through and through. The Gulf Coast produces more than a quarter of the nation's domestic oil and natural gas, and 76 percent of America's offshore energy production takes place directly off Louisiana's coast. Oil companies paid federal royalties but no money to Louisiana, despite the industry's harsh impact on coastal wetlands. Senator Mary Landrieu (sister of Mayor Mitch Landrieu—which tells you something about Louisiana politics) helped pass the Domenici-Landrieu Gulf of Mexico Energy Security Act (GOMESA) in 2006, insuring a fair share of offshore oil and gas revenues for the state. The revenue generated by GOMESA funds the state's flood protection and coastal restoration projects, which illustrates how energy and the environment are simultaneously opposed and intertwined.[19]

The Deepwater Horizon oil spill of 2010 is another case of the "drill, baby, drill" mind-set coming up against, and doing trade-offs with, environmental groups. Since the spill, Mary Landrieu has come out in favor of more deepwater drilling, expedited permits, and fewer regulations for the oil industry; at the same time, as lead sponsor of the RESTORE Act in Congress, which funnels 80 percent of Clean Water Act penalties directly to the Gulf Coast, she supports coastal restoration and renewal in recognition of the damage done not only to the environment but to the many claimants—including, especially, Vietnamese shrimpers and fishermen—whose livelihoods were destroyed by the spill.[20]

Even as big companies continue to rely on offshore deposits, natural gas extraction, and transport through the Port of New Orleans, other technologies are arising to offer alternative sources of energy and to protect and restore the environment. Some of these enterprises are small, even a touch quixotic, but at the same time intriguing and promising. Webster Pierce received a $50,000 award from the Water Challenge for his Wave Robber invention, which is a completely new approach to Louisiana's disappearing wetlands. Conventional tactics involve planting of vegetation and the construction of man-made barriers, but Pierce had a different idea. A 72-year-old native of Cut Off, Louisiana (you couldn't make this stuff up), Pierce has spent his life watching the land disappear at the rate of a football field an hour from his spot on the bayou. He says the wavelets are like piranhas nibbling at the coast: 1,900 square miles have been gobbled up since the 1930s. (And he remembers hunting deer and rabbit where now it's all water as far as the eye can see.) He had the idea not to simply stop the waves or create buffer zones but to put back the land that was being eaten away. He made kind of giant cheese grater and, to test it out, used a flywheel attached to the agitator of a rusted-out washing machine to generate sand-laden waves. The prototype diffused 80 percent of the wave's energy, trapping significant amounts of sediment in the process.

Pierce patented the device and placed a more sophisticated model down in the bayou: a contraption of 18 pipes and a series of plastic shields sticking out into the water. The Wave Robber did just what his homemade cheese grater had done—slowed the wave, spit out sand through the pipes, and, in the process, built up the shore in tiny increments to match the incremental losses of erosion. Pierce explains that inventing things is in his blood; his uncles invented Cheramie Marsh Buggies, tractors with 12-foot steel tires that could carry oil surveyors into inaccessible, unmapped marshland, and it was in his uncles' workshop that he first began tinkering. In the next few years, his Wave Robber will be planted strategically along stretches of coast to see how well it does on a large scale; one recent experiment with the device captured 30 out of 100 pounds of sand in four hours of wave operation.[21]

If Webster Pierce is fighting wind and water to reclaim the shore, others are trying to harness those elements as renewable sources of energy. Blade Dynamics, a European windmill blade manufacturer, representing 600 jobs and a $27 million investment, moved its headquarters to New Orleans in a joint venture with Dow and American Superconductor, manufacturing sophisticated turbine rotors for the wind industry.[22] Another green company is Free Flow Power of Boston, with a branch office in New Orleans, which has developed a plan for "turbine farms" along the lower Mississippi: Hydrokinetic turbines—basically, underwater windmills—will be planted in the central waterway on the floor of the river, below the level of ships and where fish seldom migrate. The idea is, flow dynamics of the river will generate a steady, reliable supply of clean energy. Because water is 800 times denser than air, the resultant payoff is that much greater: The average flow of the Mississippi is 5 miles an hour, equivalent in force to the wind blowing at 130 miles an hour. And the river's current is far more predictable than highly variable wind currents.

GNO, Inc. calls companies like Blade Dynamics and Free Flow Power "emerging environmental," because the technology isn't fully developed and their success isn't guaranteed. But these groups, as well as one-of-a-kind inventors like Webster Pierce, demonstrate a pioneer spirit of creativity, experiment, and conviction.

How do you survive in a changing climate, a threatened environment, an uncertain world? If New Orleans is the inevitable city in the impossible place, how do you reconcile the inevitable and the impossible? The history of New Orleans is a narrative of reinvention and resurrection, and we will continue on that path if we do what our forebears did: innovate.

Of course, nothing in this life is ever truly inevitable, and what looks like a predetermined outcome is always dependent on the application of human desire, will, and intention. The innovation that saved New Orleans required a conscious strategy, turning the contingencies of time and chance toward the goal of resurgence and resurrection.

*How do leaders promote progress and generate creative growth? The story of the inflection point described in this chapter is partly a series of external events: Katrina, first and foremost, and then the changing demographics, emerging technologies, and capital investment, both private and public, that followed the storm. But it is also the story of planning and intention. Once the goal was clearly established and articulated, we all worked to create the city amenities and the business ecosystem that would support enterprises, generate wealth, and sustain a cycle of growth.*

Desiring change is the first step, which involves courage, really—the courage to take a risk and try something new; to invest in possibility, put an idea to work, and help the world go round.

# Chapter 9

# LET THE GOOD TIMES ROLL

## EMBRACE EMOTION

IT'S COMMENCEMENT, MAY 19, 2013, AND TYPICALLY JOYOUS. What is particularly special about this one is the speaker: the fourteenth Dalai Lama, anointed at the age of two, 70-some years ago. He's consented to appear at the event largely because of the Tulane School of Social Work.[1] Last year, 14 students from the school spent time with the refugee community in India, working with children and young acolytes and visiting with a monk who had been in a Chinese prison camp in Tibet. For weeks, Tibetan prayer flags—white, yellow, red, green, blue—have been fluttering on storefronts and buildings all over town.

His Holiness gives an inspiring speech, short phrases, packed with meaning. "The very purpose of education is meaningful life. The meaning is to take care of others' well-being....Happiness comes from serving others....Our existence is based on hope....Hopeful always in spite of difficulties. Keep optimism, which brings inner strength and self-confidence. Then you will conduct yourself more honestly, and that brings trust....We need friends to solve the difficulties of the world. Cooperation, not only community but global level....For that, trust, friendship."[2]

In my own speech to the graduating class, I also talk about cooperation, community, and hope, particularly in a dark time: "Along with the many achievements that brought you here today, remember that you, together with your fellow students, contributed an incredible 485,000 hours of service in community outreach projects last year alone....Best of all, you kept hope alive. Hope did not die in Boston, at Newtown or during Super Storm Sandy or Hurricane Katrina and I know it will continue to flourish as you take your rightful place as tomorrow's lawyers, doctors, engineers, social workers, researchers, teachers, lawmakers, civic leaders, authors, artists, entrepreneurs, innovators and poets."[3] I may be an old hand at the rhetoric of a commencement speech, but it's never just rhetoric. It's heartfelt.

But nothing speaks directly to the heart like music. Among the honorary doctorates awarded during the ceremony, two go to beloved musical legends of New Orleans: Dr. John and Allen Toussaint. At neighboring keyboards, wearing their green academic robes, velvet hoods, and tasseled caps, they treat us to rocking renditions of Dr. John's "Right Place Wrong Time" and "Such a Night." Allen Toussaint sings "Yes We Can Can," with apt lyrics: "Now is the time for all good men / To get together with one another / Iron out the problems / And iron out the quarrels / And try to live as brothers /...I know we can make it / I know darn well we can work it out / Oh yes we can, I know we can can."

During the concert, the Dalai Lama goes over to Dr. John and Allen Toussaint to get a closer look and comes back to his seat fingering music in the air. He and I hold a fringed umbrella over our heads, inscribed in sequins with the words COMPASSION and WORLD PEACE, and second-line together over to the front of the stage. Meanwhile, the crowd is waving handkerchiefs and gesturing skyward with their own fringed parasols.

I'm thinking, This is great. This is *real*. The Dalai Lama is inspiring us to be our own best, truest, most joyous, most open selves, and Dr. John and

**Image 12**  Dalai Lama

The 14th Dalai Lama, who gave the commencement address at Tulane in May 2013. He appeared at the invitation of the Tulane School of Social Work, whose graduate students have been visiting the Tibetan community in India, working with children and young acolytes. Dressed in a green academic robe carrying a parasol inscribed with the words World Peace and Compassion, he spoke of hope, trust, and friendship, and boogied to the music of Dr. John and Allen Toussaint. Only in New Orleans.

(*Courtesy of Sabree Hill*)

Allen Toussaint are bearing the same message, with their stride arpeggios and chords. Exuberance, serenity, acceptance, peace: Buddhism meets funk. Namaste, y'all.

This chapter is about emotion. Or, more precisely, about cultural expression and historical legacy—the rituals and roots of emotion. The renaissance of the city after Katrina is often credited to New Urbanism, a wave of innovation bringing New Orleans into the twenty-first century, but the city's enduring meaning, the glue that holds everything together, is its culture and history. In the past, even before Katrina, New Orleans has experienced many losses of legacy and tradition. Among the most painful moments: Treme lost whole streets and neighborhoods in the name of urban renewal when the I-10 was constructed in the 1960s; just recently historic neighborhoods were destroyed downtown to make room for the new BioDistrict. (And many low-income communities lost their projects to new mixed-use developments, a renewal that, depending on one's point of view, could be looked at as obliteration.) There is always a tension between old and new and a continuing argument about what has to go to keep step with the times and be ready for the future.

*How does a leader show the way forward and still hold to core strengths and values? Embrace emotion. Recognize that identity and roots are central to urban vitality and to meaningful life. Understand the context and actively acknowledge a community's history, values, feelings, and forms of expression. Find ways to amplify the core strengths of a city—its heartbeat and rhythm and flavor, whatever is idiosyncratic and unique—while still making it viable as a force in a technological, modern, global world.*

This whole book is about necessary change. To effect such change without weakening core strengths, a leader must respect tradition, family, and neighborhood and honor the music, food, architecture, language, faith, and ritual that make up any culture.

For better or for worse (usually both), the stronger a city's culture and organization, the harder it is to change it. In New Orleans, the dominant mode historically has been resistance to change. Before Katrina, there may have been a latent desire to improve the education system and do something about crime, but there was no real will. We were all mired in the past and stubbornly attached to our own way of doing things. Katrina unlocked the potential for change. Where before, most people wanted neighborhood schools serving local areas, after Katrina, the goal was the best school regardless of closeness to home. Since the hurricane, residents have been making the effort to embrace the change in education yet preserve neighborhood culture through associations, community centers, events, and common spaces. It's not either/or but both/and.

It's true that there's often a tension—a pull toward the past rather than the new. Whenever a Costco, Walgreens, or Whole Foods comes to town, it's World War III; no one in New Orleans wants a homogenization of the culture. We're an iconic city, with a one-of-a-kind vibe, ethos, ambiance. Who would ever trade that in for a Walmart? And from a business perspective, New Orleans is also a brand. We're selling something you can't find anywhere else in the United States, because in a way, we *aren't* the United States—we're something more foreign, something a little wilder.

In New Orleans, music is the medium and the message.[4] The whole history of the city, dating back to its origins as a slave-trading center in the seventeenth and eighteenth centuries, is written in its music. From Congo Square and the tempos of Africa and the Caribbean to the latest jazz composition by Irvin Mayfield, Trombone Shorty, or Wynton Marsalis, the culture speaks through melody and rhythm. I'm not an expert on the roots music of New Orleans. I came here from far different musical realms: Jersey (home of Bruce Springsteen and doo-wop bands) and Ohio (home of, and I know this only through hearsay, Bone Thugs-N-Harmony, Nine Inch Nails, and the Black Keys). But even I, in my ignorance, have been drawn to and enchanted by the audio surround of the city: funk, rhythm and blues, Preservation Hall–style brass, zydeco, gospel, jazz.

No one is a better spokesman for the meaning of New Orleans music than Irvin Mayfield, who, you'll recall, played at the Tulane commencement in 2006, commemorating his father, who died in Katrina, with a composition titled "Elysian Fields." Despite a scholarship to Julliard, he chose to stay in his home city and study at the University of New Orleans with Ellis Marsalis, father of Wynton and an elder statesman of jazz. Mayfield founded the New Orleans Jazz Orchestra at the astonishingly young age of 24; he is cultural ambassador for the city; a trumpeter with a Grammy award-winning album; owner of two jazz venues in the French Quarter; member of the board of practically everything, including the Tulane School of Architecture; professor at the University of New Orleans; and arts educator in the public schools.[5]

With work that takes him in many directions—art, music, architecture, education, entrepreneurship (not to mention a cameo on the HBO series *Treme*), Mayfield is an eloquent spokesperson for arts literacy and cultural heritage. He points to the unusual role musicians have in New Orleans: "A trumpet player can call the mayor....Kermit Ruffins called a community meeting in his bar, where about 300 people showed up. That would never happen in New York or in any other city. At his bar. A trumpeter can move things in a different way in New Orleans. Jazz is to New Orleans what Italian opera is to Italy, what Fendi and Prada are to Florence."[6]

Mayfield's ability to move between worlds gives him a prominent role in the fight to respect and preserve heritage even in the midst of change. In his lectures and interviews, he often speaks of Louis Armstrong as an inspiration. At age 11, Armstrong was in the Colored Waifs' Home for Boys, in trouble with the law for shooting off a gun, when he found his way into the brass band there, starting on the tambourine and the drums, moving on to alto horn, and finally becoming the band's first-chair cornetist. A native son of New Orleans, he ultimately left because of Jim Crow indignities but never forgot the town and is still loved and remembered here. "Do you know what it means, to miss New Orleans?"

The subtext of many a cultural battle in New Orleans is racial, given that so much of its music, art, food, and language is rooted in the African American past. Mayfield, for one, is still fighting on Armstrong's behalf; he has written about the fences up around Louis Armstrong Park and the neglect of that landmark (including, at the heart of the park, Congo Square, site of the original gatherings of African slaves to dance and play instruments, a legacy that grew into American jazz)—an oversight the town only recently corrected with a reopening in 2011. The delay, according to city officials, had to do with safety: Murders had occurred in the park, the lighting was poor, the sidewalks cracked. To which activists said: Then fix it!

Mayfield's fight for Armstrong's memory includes the fierce determination to make music part of the school curriculum, not just "giving kids a triangle for the kindergarten music unit" but extensive, systematic exposure to the arts. Mayfield's New Orleans Jazz Institute developed the Saturday Music

School in 2009 to support and expand music education in New Orleans by offering students ages 8 to 17 ensemble and small-group instruction in jazz band, strings, piano, and voice as well as music history, theory, and performance. Mayfield is handing it on, one generation to the next, which is the way that culture survives.

Mayfield's plea for culture is passionate: "We must keep our eyes on the prize of creativity, and our ears to the cries of the suffering. Who will give their creative attention to people like Keira Holmes? Keira was the two-year-old who was recently shot while playing outside in the B.W. Cooper Housing Project. Who will dedicate a song to Keira? Jazz is not dead. Jazz will die when children like Keira no longer need a voice."[7] Musical expression is intimately linked to social striving, memory, healing, and hope, which is why it is so central to the life of this city.

Like Saturday Music School, the program Roots of Music also promotes cultural preservation and the handing on of musical legacies. The children of New Orleans have a natural hunger to participate in the city's musical heritage; it's all around them, and it's personal, often within their own families. They, like Louis Armstrong, want to pick up a brass horn. The brilliance of the Roots of Music program is that it uses this hunger to help the kids succeed at school, the mainstream education that will allow them opportunities and choices up ahead. The children receive musical training and can participate in brass band performance (including at Jazz Fest, the signature musical event of the year) if they keep their grades up in math and English, which they're helped to do by Tulane students who tutor in the program as part of their community service requirement.

The shuttering of cultural activities is often framed as a public safety initiative, as with Louis Armstrong Park. But something has changed since Katrina; even when dangers lurk or violence occurs, the city has committed itself to its festivals and street life. An illustration: On May 12, 2013, Mother's Day, the unthinkable occurred. During a second-line parade organized by the Original Big 7 Social Aid & Pleasure Club in honor of the day, two brothers opened fire on the crowd following along behind the club members and their brass band; 20 people were injured, including some children. There were no fatalities, but it was horrifying on such a festive, and some would say sacred, occasion. Second lines should be off limits to gunmen in a city that loves its street celebrations and prides itself on its open, welcoming public rituals.

A statement from the Original Big 7 Social Aid & Pleasure Club makes the point better than I can: "Crime and violence in New Orleans is a systemic problem and we strongly believe that safeguarding our cultural heritage helps to address the roots of violence. We are a cross-generational organization, ages 5–70. Our young people grow up in this culture, are fed by it, and feel loved, supported and connected in ways that build real security. That's crime prevention...." The statement describes the Mother's Day violence as an outrage to the Original Big 7 and secondlining generally, which is a celebration for the entire community, black, white, Latino, young and old, and families, and points out that in the group's 17 years of parading, "this is the first act of shooting violence that has occurred, and we pray that it is the last."[8]

The official response, at least, was heartening: Mayor Landrieu and Police Superintendent Ronal Serpas both condemned the violence (and rapidly caught the perpetrators—two brothers from the Frenchmen and Derbigny Gang seeking vengeance on a member of the Deslonde Boys from the Lower Ninth Ward). They also strongly supported the tradition of the clubs and of second-lining generally. When the club decided on a "re-do" (or, as we say in New Orleans, a "re-deaux") of the original parade on June 1, along the same route traveled on Mother's Day, both the mayor and the superintendent supported the event, and Chief Serpas was in attendance.

The Original Big 7 is a newer club, dating only to 1995, but it carries on the tradition of clubs a hundred years older: It's dedicated to community service and is part of the social network that keeps the neighborhoods cohesive, vibrant, and, more often than not, safe. The Original Big 7 represents the kind of racial mix that is hard to find in most other American cities: all colors and ethnicities. Leo Gorman, one of the (Caucasian) codirectors of Grow Dat, is treasurer of the organization; you can see him online in his white suit, yellow feathers, and yellow-and-white fedora at the re-do parade.

The club also maintains the powerful tradition of bringing children into the culture of second lines, brass bands, costumes, and proud display. A high schooler, Justin "Tugga" Cloud, started a children's tribe called the Red Flame Hunters, teaching them how to sew elaborate feathered and beaded costumes like those worn by the Mardi Gras Indians. At the re-do parade, many of the club's children participated, wearing yellow feathers and ribbons and sunglasses, strutting and dancing with the grownups.

The city's support for the Original Big 7 represents a huge turnaround from the period directly after Katrina, when the police, citing public safety, instituted exorbitant escort fees for social aid and pleasure club parades—a move that was widely seen as an attempt at cultural suppression, with racist overtones. Since that time (as described in chapter 3), the police and the social clubs have worked together to address the issues of violence and crime without hampering the street festivals that bind neighborhoods together and spread joy.

Councilwoman Susan Guidry, watching the fantastic costumes and listening to the (aptly named) To Be Continued Bass Brand as the re-do parade marched past, said, "We're reaffirming that these are our traditions, that this is our culture."[9]

MARGIE AND I ARE HOSTING A VISITING COUPLE at Antoine's, the classic New Orleans restaurant in the French Quarter, and have reserved a private room. Just walking in, you pass a gallery of old photographs showing the kings and queens of Mardi Gras of yore: The costumes are so fantastical they remind me of Titania and Oberon in *A Midsummer Night's Dream*. This town is full of references you wouldn't find anywhere else, a kind of make-believe, theatrical flourish where dressing up, adopting an alias, or revealing a hitherto hidden identity is all in the course of a day.

We are ushered into a private dining room, which, the maître d' informs us, is called the "Tabasco Room." The room, the size of a small parlor, is painted a sort of Tabasco color, reddish pink with a dash of orange.

A young man appears, blond, blue-eyed, formally dressed in a dark suit and white shirt, a serviette draped over his forearm. He introduces himself as Thomas, our waiter for the evening. We ask him about Tabasco and he launches into a story: Edmund McIlhenny, the founder of the company, moved from Maryland to Louisiana around 1840, becoming a highly successful banker. In 1868, he started bottling hot pepper sauce in discarded cologne bottles (to this day Tabasco bottles are in the same distinctive shape). The business has been in the McIlhenny family ever since.

I say to our guests, "There's nothing in this town that doesn't come with a story."[10]

At this juncture, Thomas volunteers his own. "I graduated from Tulane last year. Majored in English." A waiter with a BA in the humanities doesn't sound good. But I know enough about New Orleans, and Antoine's, to recognize that this is no stop-gap employment but a stable (and enviable) profession.

Thomas says, "I started on this before college. When I was 17, I used to ride my bike on the I-10 to get here at six a.m. That was six years ago."

"Six years?" Margie says.

Thomas smiles. "Long apprenticeship."

During the course of dinner, Thomas demonstrates the skills he's acquired. He advises on classic cocktails, Sazerac, brandy milk punch, gin fizz. He brings out the Oysters Foch, explaining the lumpy brownish sauce: The dish was named for the World War I French field marshal Ferdinand Foch, and the oysters, dusted in cornmeal, fried, and sauced with sherry wine, Worcestershire sauce, tomatoes, and Hollandaise, with caramel coloring to produce the muddy hue, are a nod to the battlefields of France. Two other appetizers follow: Oysters Rockefeller, created at Antoine's in 1899, featuring an intensely rich sauce and named for John D. Rockefeller (also intensely rich), and Oysters Bienville, a kind of oyster–shrimp au gratin, named for the founder of New Orleans.

Three dishes in, and as stuffed as the oysters, we move on to the main course. For dinner, Thomas suggests the soft-shelled crabs, which are in season, but the pompano straight from the gulf is also good, and there's always chateaubriand if we prefer. After we've eaten food too delicious to describe, he brings out desserts: a gateau, a mousse, and a pudding de pain. Dinner is like a movie, with captions.

A story for everything: It's what makes New Orleans so layered, intricate, endlessly fascinating. The high-end restaurants are like theaters with a performance every night; the food is never served alone but with a side dish of narrative. Maybe this whole description just sounds like "what I had for dinner," but there's a larger point here. Food in New Orleans is lovingly and lavishly prepared, with little regard for our modern obsession with calories and fat (no alfalfa and bean sprouts on these menus) and equally little regard for time (you don't come to Antoine's for fast food, as the menu points out). New Orleans cuisine exists in its own world, a world that is elaborate, creative, and dedicated to the senses. "Always for pleasure."

THERE'S ANOTHER KIND OF CULINARY HISTORY in New Orleans, different from the high-end restaurants of the French Quarter but equally distinctive. Its roots are in African American culture, with contributions from French, Spanish, Caribbean, and Native American cuisines. New Orleans gumbo and jambalaya have origins in West Africa, and étouffée, another signature dish, was the creation of an Louisiana Acadian family originally from French Canada. All three of them feature some combination of chicken, andouille sausage, and seafood, with okra for thickener, cayenne pepper sauce for heat, and the holy trinity of celery, onion, and green bell pepper for flavor. The Monday special in New Orleans is red beans and rice: Monday used to be laundry day in the poorer neighborhoods, and the dish made use of ham hocks leftover from Sunday dinner to flavor dried red beans slow-cooked and served over rice. All these foods differ from one another in consistency (gumbo's a soup, jambalaya is like paella, étouffée is a main dish of seafood in sauce, and red beans and rice is a creamy stew), and each varies depending on who cooks it. Everyone is an artist in their own kitchen.

"An artist in her own kitchen" would describe one of our most famous chefs, Leah Chase. Her restaurant Dooky Chase (founded by her in-laws-to-be in 1941 and named Dooky for her father-in-law) is soul food flavored with civil rights history. Hers was the only restaurant in New Orleans that was integrated in the Jim Crow era, and it served as a meeting place for heroes of the civil rights movement like Martin Luther King, Andrew Young, Thurgood Marshall, and Jesse Jackson. It was also the only place in town where black musicians, from Louis Armstrong, to Duke Ellington, to Sarah Vaughan, could get a first-class meal. The menu includes fried chicken, fried catfish, vegetarian jambalaya, and, the specialty of the house, gumbo z'herbes. The utilitarian décor is spiced by the African American art, one of the best collections in the South, hanging on the walls. Meanwhile, Leah Chase is still in the kitchen at age 90.

You can feel the love for Leah Chase when you eat lunch at her place. She's passionate about history, and Creole cooking, as a way of defining New Orleans. What do you hold onto, what do you change? Celebrity chefs from the city confront this problem when they take the New Orleans brand into the marketplace. One of the storylines in HBO's *Treme* follows the fortunes of the fictional Janette Desautel, played by Kim Dickens, a character modeled on the real-life Susan Spicer. Susan Spicer is a much-admired chef, owner of two restaurants, Bayona and Mondo, who uses local ingredients and combines them in inspired (but still New Orleanian) ways. Her fictional counterpart is similarly creative and gifted, but when "Janette" comes back to New Orleans after a sojourn working under some New York culinary stars, a corporate type takes her over and she becomes a slave to a single "signature" dish that attracts crowds of diners.[11] That's the rub: Mass marketing rewards a brand, but the city's chefs, musicians, and artists are idiosyncratic, wayward, funky, original. They don't play to the masses but to an inner beat. What they create is, in a sense, not for sale.

The opposition to plans for "a new Las Vegas" downtown, with conventions and gambling, after Katrina and the ongoing antagonism toward chain stores reflect the attachment to a rarefied identity and a disdain for selling out. Coming down to New Orleans has been, for many, a search for an authentic life and self that some American cities, with the numbing sameness of their strip malls and chain stores, can't accommodate. People here, both the natives and the transplants, want to keep it real, even if that means keeping it small.

MARGIE AND I HAVE BEEN HOSTING A FUNDRAISER at the President's Mansion, and finally the party's over—another big affair, 200 people. The caterers are cleaning up in the restaurant-size kitchen; we hear the clatter of dishes and ping of glassware. Margie and I peek in to say good night to Barbara, who runs the household and marshals the troops, and then take the elevator up to the second floor, where we've carved out an apartment— offices, an exercise room, a bedroom, a sitting room; and there are two lovely high-ceilinged guest rooms, each with bath. On the third floor there's a cozy kitchen, which we use to take our meals when it's just the two of us, a ballroom (!), and a rooftop solarium that looks out over Audubon Park.

It's a house on a massive scale, with its Corinthian columns, cascade of stone steps, wraparound porches, and huge interior spaces, with an outsized history to match. "If these walls could speak." They do speak, of grand ambitions and accomplishments from an older time. Chiefly, they speak of Sam Zemurray, born Schmuel Zmurri in Russia, a Jewish immigrant who, starting out in Alabama and then moving to New Orleans as a young man, bought ripe bananas cheaply from importers who customarily discarded them and sold the produce locally to grocers up and down major trafficking routes. From that beginning, he built a fortune as the Banana King, ultimately controlling the United Fruit Company and involving himself in Latin American politics in, shall we say, a hands-on way in order to keep his import business going.[12]

Sam Zemurray bought the house from William Jay, the cotton broker and lumberman who built it, and lived there until 1961, when he donated it to Tulane for use as the President's Mansion. In the last 50 years, several families have occupied it, but we're the ones—or really, Margie's the one—who repurposed it for modern times with the help of a grandson, Sam Zemurray Stone, who supplied the money for the renovation.

Much we kept the same, including the paneled mahogany, the intricate plasterwork on ceilings and moldings, the leaded windows, the wood floors. The chief changes: the creation of a third-floor kitchen and a re-do of the ballroom (where an Aeolian organ, since put into storage, had been built into the wall); living quarters on the second floor; a new reception hall and powder rooms on the first floor; university artworks on the walls, new paint, reup-holstered furniture, and the construction of a wall to close off the staircase from public access. (Margie had heard even velvet ropes didn't keep curious guests from wandering upstairs to the family bedrooms. The more public the life, the more you need a private retreat away from the wanderers.)

We're stepping into our private lives tonight after the reception. As we get off the elevator, Gibson, our golden retriever, joyfully slides across the polished wood floor and jumps up to lick our faces. When our children are in town, the grandchildren provide the patter of little feet (or the thump of sneakers) up and down the halls and staircases.

I strip off my tie, throw off my suit jacket, and head to the exercise bike, where I can look out the window at the lights shining up and down St. Charles Avenue or watch a movie while I put in my minutes. Ever since the storm, the exercise room has been the place to work out the stress and get to a calmer place.

It's a house—the President's Mansion of architectural lore and New Orleans history—but it's also home.

MARGIE ALWAYS SAYS ABOUT THE HOUSE THAT we're lucky, espe-cially in Sam Zemurray Stone; he not only gave money, he gave his blessing. We had him for dinner after the renovation and Margie was a wreck, worry-ing that he'd disapprove of changes we'd made to his childhood home. But, as it turned out, he was delighted.

All change doesn't go so smoothly, particularly in architecture. The tension between preservation and modernization exists in all cities, but New Orleans has an especially bad case. I'm beginning at home because our personal story is, in part, an architecture story. Do you live in a museum, or do you make it a home? In our experience, it's not either/or but more of a negotiation.

I'm aware, too, that most people don't have the luxury of renovating and refurbishing the past, because it's gone forever. Driving through the Lower Ninth, almost a decade after Katrina, you still see acre upon acre of Jungleland and the shells of abandoned houses awaiting demolition. One house still standing is Fats Domino's, a two-story brick with a front porch, its gables painted bright yellow, yellow stars hung along the fence, and a sign proclaiming his name. It's cheerful, assertive: a remembrance of times past in the middle of a wasteland. Fats himself, a rock-and-roll legend ("Ain't That a Shame," "Whole Lotta Lovin'," "Walking to New Orleans"), is living in a gated community, no longer able to handle home maintenance on his own, given his age, 85, and a host of illnesses. But the house is still there, and the rumor persists that he's coming back. He left the national stage and recording contracts in Nashville to come home to New Orleans decades ago, because, he says, "I like it here."[13] He loves the city, the city loves him—he has a fistful of awards and medals, and, over the years, an impressive run of sold-out performances at Jazz Fest.

From the mansion to the Lower Ninth bungalow, the city tries to hold on to the physical buildings that say New Orleans. As already mentioned, fights have occurred in many neighborhoods to preserve historic shotguns, and some have been lovingly rehabilitated, with hand-painted vines and flowers, bright colors, restored columns, and lacy cutouts. The town also sports some gems and oddities: These include the "wedding cake" mansion on St. Charles, all frosting and filigree, with whipped cream spires; the Edgar Degas House, a double gallery townhouse, now a bed-and-breakfast, that commemorates the artist's sojourn in New Orleans; and the steamboat houses in the Holy Cross neighborhood. These twin houses, from 1905 and 1913, the architectural equivalent of the steamboats going up and down the Mississippi, were built by the Doulluts, spouses who were both steamboat captains, the second one for the use of their grown son. Decks, portholes, strings of cypress balls like pearl necklaces festooning the upper gallery, and a pilot house up top with a pagoda-like roof—suggesting the influence of the Japanese Exhibit at the St. Louis World's Fair of 1904—these houses have it all.

Inside the 1913 house, the downstairs is encased in ceramic brick and tile in case of floods, with pressed tin walls and decorative woodwork upstairs, and narrow staircase and hallways (as befit a river boat). According to Emile Dumesnil, the investment banker who is the current owner, the ceramic downstairs made it easy to hose out, despite five feet of water from Katrina. He prizes the Holy Cross neighborhood over more usual upscale quarters in, say, the French Quarter: "There's something appealing about a neighborhood that's diversified but not for the sake of diversity. That's interesting to me," he said. "It's very eclectic. You've got folk singers, you've got welders and investment bankers. You've got sculptors and librarians and a mailman or two."[14]

The city is full of curiosities and backstories, but the cultural debate is bigger than any one house or one neighborhood. Charity Hospital—which, you'll remember, was abandoned after Katrina in favor of the spanking new medical center in a new BioDistrict—may get a second life as the new City Hall and Civil District Court, under a plan devised by Mayor Landrieu's administration. Charity is an art deco landmark—built by the Works Progress Administration during the Great Depression—and it survived the storm with minimal damage. Sandra Stokes, a board member of the Foundation for Historical Louisiana, though voicing regret that the hospital wasn't rehabilitated, has applauded the move to save Charity, a city icon, by converting it to new uses, and Kurt Weigle, president of the Downtown Development District, believes Charity's architectural stature and size will bring new commerce to the neighborhood.[15] Others raise objections, including bloggers who smell a rat at City Hall—cronyism, backroom deals with contractors, undue tax burdens—as well as judges from the Civil District Court who say the Charity building can't meet the special architectural and engineering requirements for courtrooms.[16]

No benefit without cost (or without skepticism). But the move to use what's there and save a historical legacy is, I think, a better way than slash-and-burn, clean-slate policies.

Cultural expression often takes the form of resistance against the leveling forces of a society fixated on efficiency and economy. The fight to preserve musical tradition and roots, to maintain street festivals, to keep cuisine local, and to protect architectural vernaculars is in every case a fight against homogenization, commercialization, and alienation. Mardi Gras—the chief cultural signifier of New Orleans to the casual observer—is not merely expressive and celebratory; it also draws on that spirit of resistance. It would seem to be (and in part is) a brand-name mega-event registering high on the

Richter scale, but it's also deeply idiosyncratic, funky, local, and encoded—hard for outsiders to truly understand. The TIDES program at Tulane—first-year seminars that use New Orleans as a laboratory to explore everything from architecture to ethnic enclaves—has courses that analyze the "hidden" Mardi Gras with its complex history and tangled anthropological roots. The religious origin, a Fat Tuesday allowing for indulgences of all kinds before the onset of Lent on Ash Wednesday, overlays an older tradition of European carnivals and folk festivals dating back to the early Middle Ages. These festivals often featured topsy-turvy inversions of the rigid social order in satirical, aggressive displays and skits.

The "white" Mardi Gras—with its kings and queens, its fancy-dress balls and debutante parties, its illustrious 150-year history going back to the original Mistick Krewe of Comus, its secret memberships, and its fantastic floats—all of it is, in a sense, an elaborate display of the city's social codes and hierarchies. Those social codes were challenged by an ordinance in the 1990s requiring Mardi Gras krewes to certify publicly that they did not discriminate on the basis of race; rather than identify its membership, Comus withdrew from parading. But in recent years Mardi Gras has become more inclusive, diverse, and socially engaged. Some floats are used for sharp political satire and commentary: Ray Nagin was a favorite target for a number of years (Satan, Nero, roasted pig, corpse), FEMA floats (with some choice epithets) emerged after Katrina, and many other public figures have come in for jabs, some good-natured and some not.

Meanwhile, the African American community has created a parallel universe, dating from the post–Civil War era of segregation when Social Aid and Pleasure Clubs were not allowed to parade on the main routes of Mardi Gras. The all-black Zulu Krewe, dressed in grass skirts and blackface, with the king wearing a lard-can crown and carrying a banana scepter, is basically a send-up of the Rex krewe and the other elite old-line krewes.[17] But the most powerful, moving, and artistic expression of cultural meaning may be the performances of the Mardi Gras Indians as the tribes perform their mock confrontations on streets in the back of town, along routes known only to members. You have to go looking, and be lucky, to see one of these amazing displays. The Wild Tchoupitoulas, Creole Wild West, Yellow Pocahontas, Wild Magnolias, and others—38 tribes in all—mask in elaborate bead-and-feather costumes sewn by hand over the preceding year, with the big chiefs facing off in random street meetings, singing their arcane chants and taunts and then bowing in acknowledgment of each other. (In the bad old days of the late nineteenth century, literal battles sometimes ended in bloodshed. Big Chief Allison "Tootie" Montana, who died in 2005, two months before Katrina, campaigned to make peace among the tribes starting in the 1960s, so that battles were fought with the needle rather than the knife and "the prettiest," not the most violent, won the contest.)[18]

I've spoken several times of the Indians in the course of this book, and of the local lore connecting runaway slaves to the Native American tribes that took them in, but an aura of mystery hangs over this unique cultural practice of mock confrontation. Scholars have suggested links with Buffalo Bill's Wild West show, West African initiation rites, and Caribbean carnival second lines; they also point to frequent intermarriages between Native and African Americans, both enslaved by the French and Spanish colonials of early New Orleans, as one source of the custom. At Tulane, faculty members and students have studied the roots of the Indian chants and the law school has helped some of the chiefs copyright Indian suits as works of art.

But the meaning may lie partly in the mystery—the suits and chants are a ritual that's private, encoded, and particular, meant for the in-group, not the onlookers. Ned Sublette, a musician and musicologist, says that the Indians embody resistance to erasure and obliteration; he describes a vibrant encounter on the first Mardi Gras after Katrina between Congo Nation (Big Chief Donald Harrison) and North Side Skull and Bone Gang (Big Chief "Sunpie" Barnes)—proof that the tradition still lived and that they would survive the devastation, including, specifically, the decimation of African American neighborhoods and the displacement of tens of thousands. [19] Resistance to change is the hallmark of identity, pride, personhood. Any urban renewal that simply destroys what came before is not a transformation but an obliteration.

THIS SURVEY OF CULTURAL PHENOMENA IS JUST that, a survey; no short chapter could ever do justice to the particularity, complexity, and vitality of urban life in New Orleans. But it's enough, I hope, to give you a feel of what it's like to live here. And all cities—though none, perhaps, as much as New Orleans—have an essential texture and historical identity that need preservation and continuity.

*How does a leader preserve cultural legacies while moving toward the future? Leaders embrace emotion. They cherish what is small scale, individualistic, noncommercial, and not for sale. Resisting the leveling, clean-slate impulse, they creatively repurpose and reinvent sites and structures for new uses. They recognize that resistance to change is a part of any meaningful transformation, and they respect the passing on of tradition.*

Margie and I have once again made it to Jazz Fest, though this year the rain almost kept us away. Our favorite is the Gospel Tent—I remember seeing a performance of "Never Alone" by the Zion Harmonizers in 2006, with storm imagery that pierced the heart, given the circumstances; the choir robed in shiny red, faces gleaming, voices urgent. I'm no dancer, but you couldn't help but sway and clap with the crowd, more than a thousand strong.

This year we're at the Acura Stage, the biggest venue at the festival, watching Troy Andrews, better known as Trombone Shorty, perform the closing act. Traditionally the Neville Brothers have concluded Jazz Fest, and it's a passing of the torch to have this youngster, 27 years old, do the honors.

Troy Andrews is another New Orleans prodigy, like Irvin Mayfield; the town seems to grow them in unusual quantities. Andrews, who grew up in Treme, plays trombone and trumpet; was a member of the Stooges Brass Band in his teens; has performed with Lenny Kravitz, U2, and Green Day; has appeared on HBO's *Treme*, did a New Orleans fundraiser at the Brooklyn Academy of Music, contributed to a Fats Domino tribute CD, and appeared on the *Tonight Show*; and, not long ago, received the Tulane President's Medal for his work with Horns For Schools, personally donating quality instruments for school children.

**Image 13** Trombone Shorty

Trombone Shorty, aka Troy Andrews, playing on the last day of Jazz Fest in New Orleans, May 2, 2010. Born in Treme, a neighborhood known for its musicians, he epitomizes the deep musical traditions of New Orleans. A bandleader in parades at age six, he was a member of the Stooges Brass Band in his teens, rose to national prominence in his twenties, and received the President's Medal at Tulane for his work with Horns For Schools, personally donating quality musical instruments to schoolchildren.

(*Photo credit: Sally Asher, Tulane University*)

On this last day, last moment, of Jazz Fest, he is singing and playing with his band, Orleans Avenue, in a way that does justice to the grand tradition of rhythm and blues, jazz, and funk preceding him, adding some pop and hip-hop to the mix. Even I, a musical know-nothing, get chills when he sings "St. James Infirmary Blues," and I get swept up in the rest of it too: "If You Go to New Orleans," "For True," "Backatown," and "Hurricane." They're our anthems.

As he closes out his performance, he climbs down off the stage into the sea of fans, instructing everyone to "get low"—which everyone does—and then "jump up"—which everyone does. It's one of those moments when everything coalesces and you feel the communal warmth. When he goes back up on stage he stretches out his arms, trombone in one hand, trumpet in the other, as if to embrace the whole city.

Pass it on.

# Chapter 10

# DOING GOOD

## BE TRUE TO CORE VALUES

I'M GOING TO DIVERGE FROM MY USUAL FORMAT AND START OFF not with a story but with some reflections on "the journey," that reliable old trope for the narrative arc of a book. Where have we been, and where is all this tending?

In some ways, the summing up is the hardest part. So much of what I want to say about the twin topics of leadership and community revitalization is already embedded in the stories I've told here. Those stories function as case histories, showing urban reinvention and leadership as they play out in real time. The heroic myth of the solitary leader with a pristine utopian vision doesn't apply in the real world; a leader is a given person in a set of circumstances, and both the person and what surrounds them create opportunity for change.

At this point, rather than review the principles outlined in earlier chapters, I'd like to explore one more aspect of leadership, the personal. Without waxing too autobiographical, I want to describe a few episodes in my history that I've drawn on in my time in New Orleans. The animating force of leadership comes, in the end, from within: capacities, feelings, defining moments, and beliefs that are strongly held and deeply ingrained.

And *now* I'll tell you a story—a classic one, about the army.

THE PHONE IS RINGING. IT'S MY birthday, which has become an unfavorite day, representing one more mile on the odometer. Sometimes I think I'd like a reset.

Girding myself for another congratulations in a round of calls that started at breakfast, I pick up the phone. The voice on the other end says, "Hi, Scott," and I'm instantly transported back in time, four decades ago. It has taken me only two syllables to recognize Mickey Pasquinelli, my old army buddy, even though we've been out of touch ever since we left the army 42 years ago. It turns out that Margie arranged the whole thing: found the right one out of a possible five or six Mickey Pasquinellis in the Chicago area and invited him to call me as a birthday surprise.

The years disappear and we plunge right in, reminiscing like we're back in the barracks. And of course, what comes up right away is "ten-hut." It's like a Norse edda, an oft-repeated tale that has achieved mythic dimensions.

The story goes like this. It was somewhere around 1969, the year after basic and advanced training, and we were in Officer Candidate School, a six-month course to make us into combat-ready officers. The chances of going to Vietnam were excellent, both because we were infantry and because we were going to come out of OCS as second lieutenants. The chances of being killed there were also fairly good: Infantry lieutenants had a 10 percent greater risk of dying than regular enlisted men.[1]

So it was serious business, being in the army. It was only a few weeks into the program when our commanding officer came into the bunk and shouted, "Ten-hut!"—a signal to drop whatever we were doing and stand rigidly at attention, awaiting further orders. Mickey was cleaning his rifle and was a little slow to hit his mark. The officer strode up to him, standing nose to nose, and said, "Private, do you know what ten-hut means?"

Mickey said, "Two-five huts added together, sir?"

I laughed.

And that was it. We were guilty of insubordination, a deeply serious offense because such behavior would wreak havoc in the field.

As punishment, we were put in lockers side by side, the metal doors locked tight, and we stood upright in the stifling, dark confines of those neighboring crypts for 24 hours. (Okay, maybe I've mythologized a little; maybe it was 12 and only felt like 24.) Our fellow candidates marched around the lockers every hour on the hour, an exercise that made them both witnesses and participants. After we were released, we had to spend another 24 hours on the parade ground doing military drills. It was a test of spirit: Would we quit, or would we endure?

Mickey and I got through it, somehow. In the following months, Mickey was quicker with his ten-huts, and I was disinclined to laugh at passing jokes. We worried about our futures, but it all turned out surprisingly well. We had inadvertently earned the admiration of our peers for toughing out the ordeal, and we both graduated in the top five of our class, which began with 235 members and ended with 130. A lot of people couldn't stay the course.

Mickey is telling me now, 40 years later, that our survival was all me. "I could never have gotten through it without you. You kept saying we can do this—we're not going to let them beat us."

I tell him we got through it together. "They finally realized they couldn't break us."

"No, I swear, I would have cracked. You were the one."

I'm wondering about his overestimation of me. Maybe it's just that I'm slow to anger and relatively immune to stress (or at least stress that you can see). I was born with a tough hide. Mickey was always a little more flamboyant, a little more high strung. Maybe he mistook my thick skin for something more noble. In any case, I think we both came out of the event stronger than we went in.

It's so great to talk to him, and to remember those days, even though you could say the locker episode was traumatic. As we're reminiscing, all the clichés come to mind, and they're all true: I found my inner strength. I bonded with my brothers. The army made a man of me.

At the end of our conversation, Mickey and I promise to keep up better in the coming years. We sign off with "Ten-hut!"

I NEVER DID GO TO NAM. INSTEAD, I was recruited by the Army Security Agency, a high-level military intelligence unit. There's a story there, too, about going from Germany to Turkey, in plain clothes, incognito, carrying unknown documents (plus two handguns, one in my bag and the other in a shoulder holster). During a layover in Istanbul, I had a run-in with the authorities because of a military search connected with the kidnapping of the Israeli consul and gained some familiarity with a Turkish jail.

Margie refers to this period as my spying days. Actually, it was during my three years in the military that I first really understood what leadership meant. During high school and college, despite some academic struggles associated with my undiagnosed dyslexia, I was given the "mantle" of leadership—captain of the football team, president of my class, president of the student body. But it all seemed to come to me without trying. You ran for office, you got elected; it was, basically, a popularity contest.

But in the service I began to realize that leadership is emphatically *not* a popularity contest. Though military culture is rigidly hierarchical, there is lateral power in the "band of brothers," the society of one's peers. To be a leader in that environment, you must earn respect and positive regard. And the way to do that is by performing and achieving. In OCS we had class work; we took tests; we performed physical feats. But in the end, the most important measure of who you were was how your peers rated you—not because they "liked" you but because you were exemplary; because you did your job, did the right thing, held fast to your convictions. We were there to become leaders, and it struck me, at some point, that in order to become one, you had to behave like one: be your best self and lead by example. You were a leader simply because you functioned at your highest capacity every single day.

And I felt the real weight of it. I was a young guy, 23, and I was responsible for dozens of other soldiers. I needed to step up and grow into it, right then, no excuses.

*Leaders remain true to core values of responsibility, persistence, integrity, and creative problem solving, with an eye to the ultimate good. By strengthening inner character, a leader develops the capacity to galvanize and inspire others and to take responsibility for results, showing the way forward by example.*

**Image 14**   Cowen in Army

Scott Cowen, flanked by his parents Stanley and Helen, on the day of his graduation from Officer Candidate School in Fort Benning, Georgia, in 1969, at the height of the Vietnam War. Cowen credits his military training for confirming the core values that have shaped him as a leader: setting priorities, achieving goals, holding fast to convictions, and earning the respect of peers.

I remember when I went to the draft board with my dad; I had a low number in the Selective Service lottery, meaning I was certain to be drafted, and was seeking a deferment because I'd been accepted to an MBA program at the University of Illinois. As the recruiter was going over my application, I suddenly realized I didn't want a deferment. I wanted to do the right thing. I wanted (hokey as it may sound) to serve my country. And instead of deferring, I enlisted.

Fast forward 30-some years, to a speech I gave at Central Synagogue in New York a year or so after Katrina. In that speech, I tried to answer a question often asked of me in the months after the storm: What in your prior life prepared you to deal with this crisis? I spoke then of "critical incidents" that shaped who I was and who I would become, and outlined three major cruxes: my early learning disability, which taught me how to overcome adversity and beat the odds through a combination of grit and stubbornness; the army, which taught me how to lead—how to set an example, establish priorities, achieve goals, and never say no; and finally, my religion, which I came to in early adulthood and which helped me define my code of ethics. Born into an interfaith home, I found my way to Reform Judaism and absorbed the values of integrity, inclusiveness, community, and social justice that the religion celebrates. These values, whether they stem from religious belief or philosophical conviction, make a person capable of meeting any test and assuming ultimate responsibility.

In each of the preceding chapters, I articulated a key leadership principle that informed the story I would be telling, but one underlying thread connects them all. At the heart of effective leadership is the imperative to do the right thing—perform right and moral actions. Ultimately, the purpose of leading is not to seek power, popularity, fame, wealth, or even reelection but to do good; to, as the Jewish faith puts it, "repair the world." For me, in New Orleans after Katrina, my purpose has been to help revitalize one of America's most vulnerable and resilient cities.

Which has meant, as in my army years, the day-in, day-out performance of necessary work, with the glory, if there is any, often deferred.

WE'RE HAVING BRUNCH AT THE PRESIDENT'S Mansion, in the large dining room with its ornate chandelier, a bronze sculpture of cherubim on the sideboard lit by the sun streaming in through the leaded window. Karen, our chef and very good friend, has prepared a delicious egg frittata with Pontchartrain strawberries and cream on the side. It's an elegant, if slightly ironic, setting in which to discuss the problems of the Sewerage and Water Board—which, whatever you may think of sewers, is a very big deal in New Orleans. We're a city built on water; where it goes, and how it flows, is critical to our well-being.

Unfortunately, the board has not been effectively managing the underground conduits that bring water into households and carry sewage away. With alarming frequency, the city has had to send out water advisories directing citizens to boil water for three days in order to ensure its safety for drinking and household use. It's like we're a third-world country—totally unacceptable.

Hence this meeting, with the purpose of acquainting city leaders with possible new legislation that would call for the creation of a selection committee to find the best appointees to serve on a new board of managers. Around the table are civic leaders—the presidents of seven local colleges and universities plus the chief executives of several nonprofits. The work of the city is slow and detail oriented—first a law, then the selection of a selection committee, then the recommendations of that committee, then, if all goes well, a slate of appointments to management positions. And finally, the point of the whole thing: no more boiling of water on hot July days.

I hold a lot of city meetings at my house—it's a convenient and neutral place—and often, when we get together, it's like old home week; everybody knows everybody else from countless other committees, on everything from education to crime. Today, many of the usual suspects are here: my fellow university presidents, plus Jay Lapeyre, former chairman of the board of Tulane; Ben Johnson, former head of the Greater New Orleans Foundation and currently president and chief executive of the New Orleans Chamber of Commerce; and representatives of the Business Council, led by Suzanne

Mestayer, the Chair, who have come as a group to explain the legislative process for seating the new board.

At the end of the session, we sit back over a second cup of coffee. It's at this point in the meeting—in truth, all meetings—that I pose my standard question: "So, give me your opinion on how we're doing." Though this meeting has been dedicated to the painstaking process of getting one particular thing done, what I want to hear about is on a different scale. I want to hear their impressions of how far the whole city has come since Katrina.

We go around the room, and everyone weighs in. The consensus is that we've made substantive progress on flood protection, the sine qua non of New Orleans' future. Also, everyone agrees that ethics reform has been largely successful: Most people perceive officials as more trustworthy than in the bad old days of Edwin Edwards. A three-time governor (despite persistent rumors of corruption), Edwards ran for a fourth term in 1991, winning handily against neo-Nazi David Duke. A campaign bumper sticker from that election reads: "Vote for the crook. It's important."[2] Which pretty much sums up the ethics that needed reforming.

We go around the table again, and the response to education reform is a general thumbs-up. The shake-up of the failing public school administration and the shift to autonomous charters gets high marks: More kids are graduating and more are going to college. But it's not all roses, by a long shot. Every single person at the table names crime as an intractable problem. And related to crime are problems with employment: We need workforce development, training programs, and a diversified economy in order to give people a fighting chance to avoid life on the streets.

After everyone has said their piece, I say, "Okay, agreed, crime is our chief problem. But crime is the symptom. What about the cause? We know it's poverty and everything associated with poverty—family collapse, street violence, drugs, teen pregnancies. And we also know the way out of poverty is education."

I realize it's becoming a speech. In this instance I keep my remarks brief, but I'm prone to orations on this subject. In fact, every talk I've given in the last eight or nine years hits the same theme, based on the same bedrock belief: If we provide a decent education to every child, regardless of zip code, we can change the metrics and lift up the next generation of the poor, moving them out of the underclass and into the mainstream of steady employment, stable families, and secure neighborhoods. Upward mobility is the foundational idea of our country—the American dream of equal opportunity for all. And we can revive that dream, if we have the will to do it.

The place to begin is our cities.

THE DECLINE OF AMERICAN CITIES IS A recognized fact as we move into the second decade of the twenty-first century. The soaring accomplishments of the prior century's industrial revolution are memorialized in impressive downtown skylines, while the streets below teem with blight and deterioration.

I'm thinking, of course, of Detroit, now filing for bankruptcy because it's in debt up to its ears. The demise of manufacturing, with the attendant loss of jobs and population, has led to a shrinking tax base and a radical decline in city services and urban culture. The resurgence of Detroit—and I believe there will be a resurgence—depends on two things: investment in education and a strong civic leadership that can spearhead a transformation in all vital aspects of the city.

Detroit's moment of crisis has come, not as a sudden catastrophic event like Katrina but as a long, slow slide into the abyss of debt and dysfunction. But (let me say it once again) in crisis there is the opportunity for rebirth and new freedom. Michael Hecht, CEO of GNO, Inc., the economic development group, points to the potential that exists after a great calamity, man made or natural; he says that Detroit, like New Orleans after Katrina, should focus on its inherent regional strengths—things like its manufacturing expertise, its notable universities and research enterprises, its celebrated music and arts culture—and seek to cooperate with the wider metropolitan area, with its wealthier population.[3]

These are all ways to "ambitiously optimize" what already exists—to use whatever makes a city distinctive and special. Another necessary step is to tackle the problems of persistent poverty that hollow out a city's core, using workforce development, crime prevention, and affordable housing to bring people back downtown.

But as I said earlier, we need to treat causes, not just symptoms—which means addressing the lives of our children rather than simply trying to mitigate the crime rate and housing foreclosures, boosting economic development and cultural preservation, or wrestling with a host of other urban issues. Yes, all those things are on the table too, but if you don't fix education, you will never transform a city in any large-scale, sustainable way. The root cause of inner-city problems is a generational cycle of collapse, beginning with kids whose lives are in chaos from the very beginning and who consequently are unable to learn, because they haven't developed the cognitive/emotional skills—attention, self-control, self-modulation—to negotiate the world. We need schools that will fill in the gaps of fragmented home lives, provide an alternative to street culture, and function as a safe space where young minds have the peace and security to think.

Cleveland, another hard-luck rust belt city, is of interest to me because of the more than two decades I spent there. A recent public radio piece noted two competing narratives about the city: one having to do with recent murders, grisly kidnappings, and the neighborhood collapse that allows for such crimes—a collapse that is the result of population decline, lack of investment, and vacant lots associated with concentrated poverty. At the same time, there's been a revitalization, with an influx of young people living downtown, a culinary scene that's won national recognition, rapid growth in medicine and bioscience, and a thriving arts community.[4] Signs of hope fuel more hope—a positive feedback loop of sorts, leading to self-sustaining growth and vitality.

The city already has a culture of engagement, and I believe its leadership has the will and vision to turn things around. The most promising indicator is the beginning of significant change in the public schools: For example, 25 percent of Cleveland public school students go to charter schools, and the data show some improvement in attendance, test scores, and graduation rates.[5] Certain charters are extremely high performing—places like Citizens Academy, founded in 1999 by Perry White, and the Intergenerational School, founded in 2000 by Drs. Cathy and Peter Whitehouse, both of which have been rated "Excellent with Distinction," or the Cleveland School of the Arts, which has a 100 percent college acceptance rate.

Let me be clear: I'm not a booster of charters per se. Both a centrally administered public school system and autonomous charters can work, given the right teachers, the right financial support, and the right community outreach. The kind of school isn't an end in itself but the means to an end. Detroit, Cleveland, Chicago, and many other cities are struggling to find the right means to achieve the same end, moving toward school reform that really attacks the heart of urban decline.

Everywhere I look, I see the same problems we've been confronting in New Orleans, and the solutions that are working for us may also work elsewhere: attracting young, dedicated teachers who put in long hours and extracurricular effort; supporting schools that also act as community centers, providing dental and medical care, transportation, breakfast and lunch, and "wraparound" instruction and enrichment; bringing parents and caretakers into the school community; and creating learning environments that teach not just subject matter but cognitive and emotional skills involving attention, mood regulation, self-control, persistence, curiosity, self-confidence, and hope.

AND NOW I'LL TELL YOU, BRIEFLY, A New Orleans story. The Louisiana Children's Museum, under the directorship of Julia Bland, is expanding services to children of every age, with a special emphasis on the preschool years, when many essential capacities develop in the brain.[6] The museum has developed an Early Learning Village collaborative, an innovative early childhood education resource for Louisiana that aims to change national decision making on policies that affect young children and their families. Currently the museum offers programs like Word Play, a camp with the purpose of expanding the vocabulary of very young children whose impoverished environments have dramatically impaired literacy; by the time such children enter kindergarten, they are already suffering from a huge deficit compared with children from middle-class or wealthy backgrounds.

Another museum program is a local chapter of the Zero to Three movement, founded by Dr. Ron Lally, called "For Our Babies," which advocates for services and programs aimed at the youngest of the young. And several different initiatives are designed to help parents develop parenting skills: a workshop that teaches the basics of child development; Prime Time Family Reading Time, which encourages parents to read to their children; and Family Camp and Family Fest, which help parents prepare their children for school, providing guidance on everything from health care to discipline.

All of this is education of a different sort. It's the kind of programming, along with improved public schools, that can slowly, doggedly, change the fate of the next generation of the poor. But to transform the future through better education, you need the money to do it—an investment in the human capital that turns schools (and children, and families) around. And that money is primarily state and local. The federal government has some leverage, but countless national programs, endorsed by a whole series of presidents, Democrat and Republican, have achieved very little in moving the dial on education and family support. To raise the money, you need leaders who can galvanize the communities themselves.

And we're back to leadership. Where can you find the local leaders who will change the landscape, one school, one program, one life, at a time? Where do good leaders come from?

I'M AT THE ASPEN INSTITUTE IN ASPEN, Colorado, co-chairing a meeting of the Franklin Project, an initiative to create a volunteer civilian national service on a par with U.S. military service. In front of me is a stack of paper, the project's plan of action. The plan is couched in the neutral language of a proposal but the heart of it is visionary—an idea of an American future that brings together our hundreds of millions of citizens, particularly our youth, to create a just society in which everyone serves the common good.

Through the bank of windows in the conference room, you can see a range of white-capped mountains, laced with rushing streams and framed against a piercing blue sky: It's like an ad for aspiration, hope, and striving. Climb every mountain, ford every stream.

There are only ten or so of us at the table today; it's a retreat to discuss a specific aspect of the general initiative—namely, how can we inspire and energize young adults, with a particular focus on "opportunity youth," disconnected, 16 to 24 years old, to serve our country while at the same time developing the skills and competencies that will make them engaged citizens and leaders for life? And how can we do it on a national scale by creating one million new national civil service opportunities? At the table are various educators and leaders but also two or three young people. One of them now raises his hand.

He says, "You don't remember me, Dr. Cowen. I'm Jamiel. We met in DC at the White House Council summit, and back then I thought, you understand what me and my friends are going through."

In fact, I do remember him. It was a year ago, after a panel on Community Solutions, with young people speaking out in vivid terms about their experiences of disconnection. Jamiel talked about his classic downward spiral—high school dropout, teen father, drug dealer, convict—and then his turnaround in a program like many we have New Orleans, under a mentor like many we have in New Orleans. Now he's working in a youth program in Pennsylvania as a role model and a community leader.

Whenever I see a young man with a challenging background who is achieving good things—what education activist Geoffrey Canada calls "escape velocity"—I think of all the young men I've seen in New Orleans: people like Ryan Dalton, the graduate of Café Reconcile who has become a supervisor and mentor of others and who is developing his own youth development program; like Josh Short, the promising film student and youth mentor who was shot dead in a crossfire on the street where he grew up; and like Deshawn Robinson from Grow Dat, who was on the verge of graduating from high school, a huge accomplishment, when he was booked for aiding in a robbery—but who might still make it.[7]

The ones who make it, the ones who don't, and the ones who hover on the brink. Meeting a Jamiel always reminds me that it's real lives that are at stake—that the one million the Franklin Project is aiming for, including young people like Jamiel, represent flesh and blood, not just numbers. Jamiel also reminds me of the power of one. Here's a kid you might have given up on at any point, who pulled himself up and became a beacon of hope, precisely because he's lived the life of those he's trying to help. He's a leader who seems to have come from an unexpected place, but, really, it's not so unexpected. If we tap the strength of the community and make opportunities for young people to step up to the plate, leadership will emerge naturally.

I go up to Jamiel and give him a hug. "Listen," I tell him, "come to New Orleans. I'll fly you in. You can talk at Tulane, network with some of our community service people."

Jamiel has a radiant smile. He's pleased to come.

One person, one program, at a time. Climb every mountain.

THIS BOOK IS FULL OF STORIES OF COMMUNITY and organizational transformation, but all of them are also about leadership—how we not only aspire to climb the mountain but actually get to the top. All leadership begins with vision and resolve and moves through phases of conflict and negotiation; but if it's effective, leadership ends in workable, holistic solutions that make the world better.

All the principles of leadership described in the preceding chapters can be recast as a single statement, describing a sequence of steps from the inception of a plan to its fruition: *Have a vision and identify a goal; gather facts and face realities; understand context and embrace the community; work through conflict to compromise; hold to a sense of purpose and principle; and persevere until you arrive at a holistic solution.*

It all sounds logical, simple, mainly a matter of hard work. Simplest is often truest. Really: *Just do it.* This is my story and I'm sticking to it.

But it's also true that the "hard work" is harder than you'd think. Many people, faced with an intractable large-scale problem, fall into a state of paralysis or passivity, of hoping against hope for rescue. But, as they say in management circles, hope is not a strategy. I have seen many bright ideas founder because of a lack of execution and many intelligent people falter when it came time to decide and act. Particularly after Katrina, officials at every level failed to solve the problems confronting us. Yes, those problems were staggering and complex. But a reason is not an excuse.

Leadership theory identifies two distinct kinds: direct leadership, exercised by people in positions of authority; and indirect leadership, exercised by individuals in the community who assume a take-charge role and change things. This second concept animated the White House Council for Community Solutions—the belief that the best ideas, and the best leaders, grow directly out of the local milieu. It was at a meeting of this council that I first met Jamiel, for example. Leaders can come from anywhere; talent, drive, vision, and courage are not confined to those at the top.

Courage is perhaps the operative word: the guts to imagine a future, see the current situation as it is, forge relationships, achieve consensus, and act. You lead in large measure by example; by rolling up your sleeves, committing to the process—which is messy and will inevitably entail some mistakes—and persevering over time. It's one reason I admire New Jersey governor Chris Christie's response to the catastrophe of Hurricane Sandy; he has the true grit that says Let's solve this problem *now*. It's not about who gets the credit or who's the "hero." It's about hard work and the daily grind.

When we talk about leadership, we're talking about two things, really: a process (the daily grind) and an end game. The end game is the goal, the vision of white-capped mountains. Urban revitalization requires leaders, both direct and indirect, who are committed to both the daily grind and the visionary goal. In the end, the resurgence of New Orleans is the result of people who took responsibility and took charge, of leaders from all over who did the work and found the means to achieve what looked like an impossible goal. And once again in its long, dramatic history, New Orleans has proved itself to be the inevitable city.

In closing, I'm going to get personal again. The writing of this book has coincided with the end of my tenure as the president of Tulane. One reason for this is logistical: A new strategic plan and a fundraising campaign of ten years' duration are about to go forward, and a new person, who can be there for the whole decade, should be at the helm. Another reason is good organizational governance: A thriving organization depends on an orderly succession of leadership. Alfred P. Sloan, in *My Years with General Motors*, says that you can determine the effectiveness of a chief executive by looking at how the organization is doing five years after his or her departure. You build strength that promises to endure and then hand off to the next generation of leaders.

I think of the handoff as something like Trombone Shorty performing at the end of Jazz Fest; the Neville Brothers, the closing act for 20 or more years, have essentially passed the torch to him as an exemplar and beacon for the next generation. "Pass it on."

The failure to hand off is often a disaster. As someone said about *King Lear*: bad retirement plan. It's not good for your kingdom, and it's not good for you, if you keep grasping for what was once yours. But putting Shakespearean tragedy aside, I want to speak of the generative and regenerative aspect of my retirement from the presidency. Now is my opportunity for another chapter, a space in which I can devote myself full time to everything I've written about in this book: especially education, community solutions, the revitalization of our cities, and the revival of the American dream. I know, it sounds like a speech—like rhetoric. But as I've said elsewhere about my speechifying, it's never *only* rhetoric. I believe these things. I believe in the basics: schooling, service to country, faith, commitment, and the revitalization of urban America. If these sound like truisms, they're also true.

MARGIE AND I ARE SITTING ON THE PROMENADE looking out at the Mississippi at dusk. It's a Technicolor sky. The river is moving at its slow, majestic pace. We're drinking it in together, happy to be here in a city that's come back to life. It seems we're always on planes these days, all over the map—New York, Boston, DC, Cleveland, Chicago, San Francisco, LA. But this is where we start from. This is home.

As the sky darkens and the lights on the Crescent City Connection Bridge twinkle on, I think about renting a riverboat and taking it up the

Mississippi, that huge pulsing artery that has been the scene and source of so much American history, American literature, and American abundance. The river's a good emblem for the whole country, in a way: a symbol of power and plenty. But we're more than our strength and abundance. We're a nation built on ideas—of liberty and justice, equality and opportunity. The job ahead, for all of us, is to live up to that founding vision: to rebuild our cities, open wide the doors of possibility, and revive the American dream.

# NOTES

## 1 HARD CALLS

1. No single consistent database exists on the facts of Katrina, but these figures give a sense of the order of magnitude of the event.
2. The quote is from Warren Bennis's book *On Becoming a Leader* (New York: Basic Books, 2009).
3. "1 Dead in Attic" is a phrase made famous by Chris Rose, columnist for the *Times-Picayune*, who wrote a book by that title, a collection of columns describing New Orleans in the first 16 months after Katrina. Chris Rose, *1 Dead in Attic* (New York: Simon & Schuster Paperbacks, 2007).
4. Christopher Cooper, "Old-Line Families Escape Worst of Flood and Plot the Future," *Wall Street Journal*, September 8, 2005, http://www.commondreams.org/headlines05/0908-09. htm.
5. Much of the Katrina literature—books like Douglas Brinkley's *The Great Deluge: Hurricane Katrina, New Orleans, and the Mississippi Gulf Coast* (New York: Harper Perennial, 2007), Jed Horne's *Breach of Faith: Hurricane Katrina and the Near Death of a Great American City* (New York: Random House Trade Paperback, 2008), and others—is devoted to a grim accounting of the many mistakes made not only by FEMA but by the Army Corps of Engineers, the National Guard, the city and state government, and the New Orleans Police Department. Books like Michael Eric Dyson's *Come Hell or High Water: Hurricane Katrina and the Color of Disaster: Hurricane Katrina and the Color of Disaster* (New York: Basic Civitas Books, 2007) and documentaries like *Trouble the Water* (Elsewhere Films, directed by Carl Deal and Tia Lessin, 2008) suggest racial discrimination as the root cause of all these failures. My own interpretation, based on my encounters with government authorities, is that sheer ineptitude—which, like evil, can be banal—produced a man-made tragedy above and beyond the natural disaster.
6. Bush's remark to Brown occurred on September 2, 2005. Ten days later Brown resigned from FEMA amid a hail of criticism on his handling of relief efforts after Katrina. "'Can I quit now?' FEMA chief wrote as Katrina raged: E-mails give insight into Brown's leadership, attitude," CNN.com, November 4, 2005, http://www.cnn.com/2005/US/11/03/brown.fema.emails/.
7. Ashley Morris was the inspiration for the character played by John Goodman on the HBO series *Treme*. My guess is that Morris attacked these three cities on the basis of rivalry: Houston and Dallas because of their aura of modernity and their economic success and New York because of the preeminence of 9/11 in the national consciousness. He seems to have felt that these bigger (and, in his view, luckier) cities were snubbing New Orleans as a provincial backwater unworthy of attention.
8. Many chronic medical conditions worsened after the hurricane, leading to increased illness and death. In Dan Baum's *Nine Lives: Mystery, Magic, Death, and Life in New Orleans* (New York: Spiegel & Grau, 2010), Frank Minyard, the coroner of New Orleans Parish, noticed that in the year after Katrina, many people in their thirties, forties, and early fifties were dying of what pathologists described as "natural causes"—minor conditions that don't, as a rule, kill any but the elderly. Frank felt certain that these deaths were caused by the stress of the storm (303–304).
9. Most universities have public service offerings, but Tulane is the only major research university to have a curricular public service *requirement*. A handful of liberal arts colleges have a requirement, but they represent a mix of co-curricular and curricular.

10. Dyson eloquently describes forced migrations of African Americans, both historically and in the aftermath of the hurricane, in *Come Hell or High Water*, quoting Jesse Jackson on the quality of exile felt by black people dislocated from their homes in New Orleans many of whom Jackson interviewed personally after the storm (p. 219).

## 2   CHOCOLATE CITY

1. I am indebted to Lawrence Powell's superb history of colonial New Orleans, *The Accidental City: Improvising New Orleans* (Cambridge, MA: Harvard University Press, 2012), for his description of racial complexity in the city's early years.
2. Racist groups like the Ku Klux Klan were active even at this time, and restrictive laws like the Louisiana Black Code of 1865 attempted to extend the servitude of blacks even after the official end of slavery. Still, the social and political gains in post–Civil War New Orleans African American society represent a remarkable achievement at a moment of high hopes.
3. There are numerous accounts of the Civil War and Reconstruction eras in New Orleans, but two documentaries, *American Experience: New Orleans* (PBS Home Video, written by Michelle Ferrari, 2007), and *Faubourg Treme: The Untold Story of Black New Orleans* (Independent Television Service, written and produced by Lolis Eric Elie, 2008), offer particularly potent, detailed narratives of these two periods.
4. A succinct discussion of this event, giving the particulars of the case as well as excerpts from the court proceedings, can be found in an American history lecture entitled "Separate But Equal: The *Plessy v. Ferguson* Case," from an online course at George Mason University. See http://historymatters.gmu.edu/d/5485/.
5. J. L. Chestnut, who graduated from Dillard University in 1953, later becoming a civil rights activist and founder of the first black law firm in his hometown of Selma, Alabama, is amazed at the rainbow hues of New Orleans: "[B]ack in Selma, Alabama there were only black people and white people but in New Orleans there were black people, white people, Creole people, Cajun people, and other ethnics. Make no mistake: New Orleans was Southern, but only in its own peculiar way. I often sat in the rear of a segregated city bus and tried to guess from a boarding passenger's skin color and appearance if he would sit in the front or the back of the bus. I guessed wrong as often as I guessed right. That would not happen anywhere else in the South. I was only 300 miles from home in Selma but in another world altogether and one that seemingly, in ways, was unrelated to Alabama, Mississippi and even the rest of Louisiana."

    J. L. Chestnut, Jr., "Ah, Do You Know What It Means to Miss New Orleans?" *Counterpunch*, September 14, 2006, http://www.counterpunch.org/2006/09/14/ah-do-you-know-what-it-means-to-miss-new-orleans/.

    The where-on-the-bus question is like Homer Plessy boarding the first-class car. Chestnut was dealing with the fallout of *Plessy v. Ferguson* and the Jim Crow laws of the South, but in New Orleans—in 1892 and in 1953—the intricate question of "who are you" made the binary racial division look like nonsense.
6. The exclusion of African Americans from higher education was partially rectified by the second Morrill Act of 1890, which expanded the system of land grants to include black institutions.
7. Christopher Cooper, "Old Line Families Escape Worst of Flood and Plot the Future," *Wall Street Journal*, September 8, 2005, http://www.commondreams.org/headlines05/0908–09.htm.
8. Gary Rivlin, "A Mogul Who Would Rebuild New Orleans," *New York Times*, September 29, 2005, http://www.nytimes.com/2005/09/29/business/29mogul.html?pagewanted=print. In January 2006, James K. Glassman, a conservative commentator, expressed a similar sentiment. He wrote an article suggesting that the clean slate was a blessing in disguise: Katrina had washed away the horrifying housing projects, the inadequate school system, and the wasteful public works projects that had held New Orleans back. God didn't want a chocolate city; he wanted a free market. "Back to the Future: The New New Orleans, a Land of Opportunity," *The Wall Street Journal*, January 12, 2006, http://diamondskyinc.com/Commentary.asp?sid=4&cid=22&aid=175.

9. In Nagin's memoir, *Katrina's Secrets*, he describes this meeting with Farrakhan; he also says that his introduction to the Nation of Islam while at Tuskegee University was transformative, and he was an enthusiastic participant in Farrakhan's Million Man March in Washington, DC, in 1995. C. Ray Nagin, *Katrina's Secrets: Storms after the Storm* (self-published Kindle edition, 2011; revised paperback edition, 2012.)

10. John M. Barry, *Rising Tide: The Great Mississippi Flood of 1927 and How It Changed America* (New York: Simon & Schuster, 1997).

11. BNOB Urban Planning Action Plan Final Report, Figure 30, http://www.nolaplans.com /plans/BNOB/Urban%20Planning%20Action%20Plan%20Final%20Report.pdf.

12. Kate Randall, "City Residents Denounce 'Bring New Orleans Back' Rebuilding Plan," World Socialist Web Site, January 14, 2006, https://www.wsws.org/en/articles/2006/01/newo-j14 .html.

13. Charles Babington, "Some GOP Legislators Hit Jarring Notes in Addressing Katrina," *Washington Post*, September 10, 2005, http://www.washingtonpost.com/wp-dyn/content /article/2005/09/09/AR2005090901930.html.

14. Keith Ferdinand, a cardiologist who formerly ran Heartbeats Life Center, a cardiology clinic in the Ninth Ward, had this to say about the inadequate efforts to repatriate people from the flooded neighborhoods: "The idea that people should fight with their insurance company, then fight with the Road Home, then go down to the local supply store and buy Sheetrock, pick up immigrant labor and kind of hack it out to rebuild a community like that is fairly nonsensical." Quoted by Jonathan Tilove, "Five Years after Hurricane Katrina, 100,000 New Orleanians Have Yet to Return," *Times-Picayune*, August 24, 2010, http://www.nola.com /katrina/index.ssf/2010/08/five_years_after_hurricane_kat.html.

    According to its website, the Road Home program is the largest single housing recovery program in U.S. history, with the objective of providing compensation to Louisiana homeowners affected by Hurricanes Katrina or Rita.

15. Richard Campanella, a geographer at Tulane, refers to the debate about the city's footprint as "history.... To go back and reopen the wound—it's too late. The baby's already born." (Quoted by Nathaniel Rich, "Jungleland: The Lower Ninth Ward in New Orleans Gives New Meaning to 'Urban Growth," *New York Times Magazine*, March 25, 2012, http://www.nytimes.com/2012/03/25/magazine/the-lower-ninth-ward-new-orleans. html?pagewanted=all&_r=0.

16. Dillard itself was named for its benefactor James H. Dillard, a white educator and philanthropist who championed black literacy and education. Many HBCUs have white founders, usually religious men with strong ethical convictions.

17. Xavier is the only HBCU that is both African American and Catholic; it is nationally renowned for its science curriculum, graduating more African American students who go on to medical school than any other school in the country. Its School of Pharmacy is also highly regarded.

18. *American Experience: New Orleans* (PBS Home Video, directed by Steven Ives, written by Michelle Ferrari, 2007). John Scott, a noted sculptor, since deceased, provides the concluding comment in the documentary.

## 3 THE CITY THAT CARE FORGOT

1. " 'From September of last year to February of this year,' said Mayor Mitch Landrieu in a recent speech, after reciting a litany of killings from one city high school, 'a student attending John McDonough was more likely to be killed than a soldier in Afghanistan.'" Campbell Robertson, "New Orleans Struggles to Stem Homicides," *New York Times*, December 7, 2011, http://www.nytimes.com/2011/12/08/us/new-orleans-struggles-to -stem-homicides.html?_r=0.

2. Peter Scharf, a Tulane professor of criminology, wrote an article titled "The 'Mundane' Murders of Post-Katrina New Orleans," guest blog, Tavis Smiley Reports, July 21, 2010, http://www.pbs .org/wnet/tavissmiley//reports/mundane-murders-of-post-katrina-new-orleans.html.

3. This comment comes from an interview with Robinette in *When the Levees Broke: A Requiem in Four Acts,* a documentary by Spike Lee (HBO Documentary Films, 2006), about the devastating effect of Katrina on New Orleans.

4. A slightly puzzling fact: New Orleans is worst in terms of murder rate but average in terms of violent crimes—a distinction that suggests that killing has a life of its own, apart from robbery, aggravated assault, and rape.

5. COMPSTAT combines crime analysis and geographic information systems with management principles: (1) accurate, timely information made available at all levels in the organization; (2) the most effective tactics for specific problems; (3) rapid, focused deployment of resources to implement those tactics; and (4) relentless follow-up and assessment.

6. Amanda Ripley, "The Gangs of New Orleans," *Time Magazine,* May 14, 2006, http://content.time.com/time/magazine/article/0,9171,1194016,00.html.

7. "NOLA guy" answers the question "do gangs exist in New Orleans" with a "no, not really." See http://answers.yahoo.com/question/index?qid=20120404162202AAC7yz5.

8. A. C. Thompson, "Body of Evidence," *The Nation,* January 5, 2009, http://www.thenation.com/article/body-evidence.

9. Laura Maggi, "Federal Judge Overturns Danziger Convictions of Five Former Officers Found Guilty in Danziger Bridge Shootings, Cover-up," *The Advocate,* September 20, 2013, http://theadvocate.com/home/7082617-125/story.html.

10. A three-judge panel from the 5th U.S. Circuit Court of Appeals ordered a separate retrial for Warren because of what his defense attorneys called a "spillover effect" relating to the cover up of evidence and the burning of Glover's body. Kevin McGill and Michael Kunzelman, "Ex-Cop David Warren Acquitted in Retrial Over Fatal Hurricane Katrina Killing of Henry Glover," *The Huffington Post,* December 12, 2013. See http://www.huffingtonpost.com/2013/12/12/david-warren-acquitted_n_4431693.htm

11. The changes in the NOPD reflect a marked shift in the culture of the city since Katrina. Ray Nagin's conviction on corruption charges in January 2013 is more than a long-overdue comeuppance but a sign of the times. Instead of business as usual and slipshod, oh-well ethics—the raised eyebrow, shared drink, and secret handshake of past times—the revitalized New Orleans is a brisker, more modern environment. Institutions from schools to businesses have become more transparent and trustworthy, more rational and principled.

12. I have used the crime index of nola.com, the online edition of the *Times-Picayune,* as the source of these descriptions. See http://www.nola.com/crime/.

13. Valan had written poems to his murdered girlfriend before his own death. ("Never again into her hazel eyes will I gaze. / Without her it feels like I'm trapped in a maze…Never again will I hear her say 'I love you, Valan.' / That cuts into me like an eagle talon.") Ramon Antonio Vargas, "Slain UNO Student's Mother Says Son's Killer Left Her with 'Hurtful Burden,'" *Times-Picayune,* October 25, 2012, http://www.nola.com/crime/index.ssf/2012/10/slain_uno_students_mother_says.html.

14. "'I place the blame on our mental health system for this tragedy to happen,' said Cecile Tebo, a crisis-intervention specialist and the former commander of the New Orleans Police Department's Crisis Unit….Tebo said in-patient beds in metropolitan New Orleans have decreased by 60 to 70 percent since Hurricane Katrina….She said that this problem will likely be exacerbated when Southeast Hospital closes due to the state's current round of Medicaid cuts." Naomi Martin, "Chelsea Thornton's Slaying of Children Points to Need for Mental Health Care," *Times-Picayune,* October 20, 2012, http://www.nola.com/crime/index.ssf/2012/10/chelsea_thorntons_slaying_of_c.html.

15. A minister at the funeral of Marguerite Washington, a Dillard University freshman killed by a bullet intended for her boyfriend, said of guns, "When I was Marguerite's age, I was doing the same thing she was…. The difference is that 30 years ago, there was more room for adolescent freedom and errors. If you jumped in the wrong car, or ended up at the wrong place, you assumed no one had a gun. Now assume that everyone has a gun." Jarvis DeBerry, "Murdered Dillard Freshman Was a Loyal Friend, Her Pastor Says," *Times-Picayune,* October 8, 2012, http://www.nola.com/opinions/index.ssf/2012/10/murdered_dillard_freshman_was.html.

16. Geoffrey Canada, *Fist Stick Knife Gun* (Boston, MA: Beacon Press, 2010), 35.

17. Robert Morris, "SilenceIsViolence Peace Walk and Second Line, Featuring the Original Prince of Wales Social Aid and Pleasure Club and Stooges Brass Brand," *Uptown Messenger*, January 28, 2012, http://uptownmessenger.com/2012/01/silenceisviolence-peace-walk-and-second-line-featuring-the-original-prince-of-wales-social-aid-and-pleasure-club-and-stooges-brass-band/.

18. "Second lines" are shorthand for formal parades organized by clubs; the second line is the mass of people forming behind the first line of the club members and brass band.

19. Robert Sampson, *Great American City: Chicago and the Enduring Neighborhood Effect* (Chicago: University of Chicago Press, 2013), *passim*.

20. *The Org: The Underlying Logic of the Office* (New York: Twelve, 2013) by Tim Sullivan, the editorial director of Harvard Business Review Press, and Ray Fisman, a professor at Columbia Business School, quoted in Eduardo Porter, "When Public Outperforms Private in Services," *New York Times*, January 15, 2013, http://www.nytimes.com/2013/01/16/business/when-privatization-works-and-why-it-doesnt-always.html.

21. The CeaseFire program was used in the 1990s in Boston to bring down the homicide rate, targeting gang members who represented the 1 percent of the city's youth and perpetrated 60 percent of homicides. A documentary, *The Interrupters* (directed by Steve James, PBS Frontline, 2012), shows the program in action on the streets of Chicago. See http://www.pbs.org/wgbh/pages/frontline/interrupters/.

22. The long-term success of CeaseFire New Orleans is still up in the air.

23. And one reason Tulane has been able to do it: The university is perceived as a "neutral, honest broker"—the kind of leader called for by the White House Council on Community Solutions in a Whitepaper on Community Collaborations (2012). See http://www.serve.gov/sites/default/files/ctools/CommunityCollaborativesWhitepaper_0.pdf.

24. Since 2010, Iberville has gone the way of all the other housing projects in New Orleans, and is currently being redeveloped as mixed-income housing, with one-third for public housing residents, one-third for working class families, and one-third for people who can afford the market rate.

25. Curissa "Cee Cee" Davis, former student body president at Carver High School, lost twenty friends to gun violence before she was 18 and has said she doesn't like to get close to people given the chances of their being killed. "'Why would you want to make a new friend?' she said." Quoted in Eliott C. McLaughlin, "Fed Up, New Orleans Looks to Shake Murder City Title," CNN.com, March 3, 2012, http://www.cnn.com/2012/03/01/us/new-orleans-murder.

26. Between 2008 and 2010, the New Orleans metro area had a higher percentage (10.2 percent) of Opportunity Youth than the national average (7.5 percent); of the cohort in New Orleans, 70 percent were African American. Both in New Orleans and the United States, Opportunity Youth are disproportionately African American. Greater New Orleans Community Data Center, Susan Sellers, Andre Perry, Petrice Sams-Abiodun, Allison Plyer, and Elaine Ortiz. March 2012. See https://gnocdc.s3.amazonaws.com/reports/GNOCDC_BuildingAnInclusiveHigh-SkilledWorkforceForNewOrleansNextEconomy.pdf.

27. Though opportunity youth are especially vulnerable to the stresses of poverty and to the temptations of the street, many are trying hard to do the right thing and improve their circumstances. Nearly 50 percent of opportunity youth have a high school diploma or GED.

28. Cowen Institute for Public Education Initiatives, "Reconnecting Opportunity Youth: Data Reference Guide," May 2012, http://www.coweninstitute.com/wp-content/uploads/2012/05/Reconnecting-Opportunity-Youth-Reference-Guide.pdf.

29. "StoryCorps: Melissa Sawyer," interviewed by Kathleen Whalen, produced by Eileen Fleming, WWNO. See http://wwno.org/post/storycorps-melissa-sawyer. Audio available at http://stream.publicbroadcasting.net/production/mp3/wwno/local-wwno-931550.mp3.

30. Greater New Orleans Foundation, "Q & A with Melissa Sawyer from the Youth Empowerment Project," *The Second Line*, January 21, 2010, http://old.gnof.org/qa-with-melissa-sawyer/.

31. Paul Tough, *Whatever It Takes: Geoffrey Canada's Quest to Change Harlem and America* (Boston: Mariner Books, 2008); and Paul Tough, *How Children Succeed: Grit, Curiosity, and the Hidden Power of Character* (Boston, MA: Houghton Mifflin Harcourt, 2012).

32. Paul Tough, *Whatever It Takes*, 231–232.

33. Excerpted from the unpublished essay, "From Pain to Success," by Deshawn Robinson, an intern at Grow Dat Youth Farm.

## 4 THE PROBLEM WE ALL LIVE WITH

1. William Frantz Elementary was severely damaged in Katrina. Restored in recent years, it currently houses Akili Academy, a K–9 public charter school.
2. The other three—Gail Etienne, Tessie Prevost, and Leona Tate—went to McDonogh No. 19 Elementary School, in the Lower Ninth Ward, and were, like Ruby, met with rage and abuse. By 1962 McDonogh was completely African American, the result of an Orleans Parish School Board decision to convert the school to one "for the exclusive use of Negro children"— basically, a reverse resegregation. The "McDonogh Three" went on to integrate another Ninth Ward elementary school, a middle school, and ultimately a high school against fierce opposition from white people, some of whom had formerly been friends and neighbors.
3. David L. Kirp, a professor of public policy at the University of California, Berkeley, gives evidence of this view in "Making Schools Work," *Sunday Review, New York Times*, May 19, 2012, http://www.nytimes.com/2012/05/20/opinion/sunday/integration-worked-why-have -we-rejected-it.html?scp=1&sq=Integrated%20schools&st=Search.
4. Nelson Smith, "The Louisiana Recovery School District: Lessons for the Buckeye State," Thomas B. Fordham Institute, January 2012, http://www.coweninstitute.com/wp-content /uploads/2012/01/FORINSLRSDReport.pdf.
5. Charter schools receive public monies, but spending—money per pupil, teachers' salaries, administrative costs—is at the discretion of each charter's school board.
6. Schools in New Orleans are open enrollment, a consequence of Katrina's erasure of preexisting geographic school zones; students can apply to any school no matter where they live.
7. See the description of the BNOB Commission in chapter 2.
8. The Education Committee offered a restructuring of the existing system but did not propose a specific model of governance. However, the Education Report did outline a decentralized approach that added autonomous schools to the remnants of the prior top-down system.
9. About that name: Carol Bernick, an extremely generous donor to and trustee of the university, gave a speech at the opening of the new Lavin-Bernick Center in January 2006. Carol is uncomfortable having her name on things—we were the ones who insisted—and so, as she delivered her address, she gave me a taste of my own medicine: she announced her intention of a seven-figure gift to the Institute for Public Education Initiatives, with the condition that my name be on it. So now it is, and now I know how she feels.
10. Nationally, charters aren't significantly better than public schools in terms of test scores and graduation rates. One of the distinctions of New Orleans is that the education system was essentially a do-over after the storm, so that we've had an open field for innovation.
11. See http://warreneastoncharterhigh.org/apps/pages/index.jsp?uREC_ID=196260&type= d&pREC_ID=video&showMore=1&titleREC_ID=32903. For a longer video clip, but missing some of the quoted material, see "Sandra Bullock—People's Choice Awards "Favorite Humanitarian," YouTube, January 10, 2013, http://www.youtube.com/watch?v= nJrLFwh9UFk.
12. High Schools That Work (HSTW) has been adopted by the Southern Regional Education Board to support and create programs that provide structure, motivation, and guidance for students in secondary school.
13. John Hechinger, "Oprah-Backed Charter School Denying Disabled Collides with Law," Bloomberg News, September 20, 2011, http://www.bloomberg.com/news/2011–09-21/oprah -backed-charter-school-denying-disabled-collides-with-law.html.
14. The argument often acquires political overtones. On one side, (left-leaning) teachers' union advocates decry the attack on creative, committed teachers for failing to put up good test numbers, pointing to the social collapse that impairs the whole process of education and arguing for social reforms to help vulnerable children. On the other side, (right-leaning) charter advocates say a free market environment that encourages innovation and rewards success will change lives all on its own.

15. Sci Academy has gradually added extracurriculars in the last few years, ranging from sports leagues, to arts programs, to student council.

16. Andrew Vanacore, "New Orleans Charter Schools Are Producing Success Stories," *Times-Picayune*, May 27, 2012, http://www.nola.com/education/index.ssf/2012/05 /new_orleans_charter_schools_ar.html.

17. Andrew Vanacore, "Sojourner Truth Academy to Close in May," *Times-Picayune*, November 29, 2011, http://www.nola.com/education/index.ssf/2011/11/sojourner_truth_academy_to _clo_2.html. Standardized test scores were far below state averages, with 60 percent of students failing the geometry exam and about 30 percent failing each of the other academic subjects, including English and science. Robert Morris, "Open-Admission Uptown High Schools Miss State Averages in Most Subjects," *Uptown Messenger*, July 6, 2012. See http:// uptownmessenger.com/2012/07/open-admission-uptown-high-schools-miss-state-averages -in-most-subjects.

18. Sarah Carr, "What Happens When Charter Schools Close," *Times-Picayune*, March 24, 2012, http://www.nola.com/education/index.ssf/2012/03/what_happens_when_charter_scho. html.

19. Vanacore, "Sojourner Truth Academy to Close in May."

20. Paul Tough, *How Children Succeed: Grit, Curiosity, and the Hidden Power of Character* (Boston, MA: Houghton Mifflin Harcourt, 2012.)

21. David. L. Kirp, "The Secret to Fixing Bad Schools," *New York Times Sunday Review,* February 9, 2013, http://www.nytimes.com/2013/02/10/opinion/sunday/the-secret-to-fixing-bad-schools .html?_r=0.

22. Doug Lemov, *Teach Like a Champion: 49 Techniques That Put Students on the Path to College (K-12)* (San Francisco, CA: Jossey-Bass, 2010).

23. Elizabeth Green, "Building a Better Teacher," *New York Times Magazine,* March 2, 2010, http://www.nytimes.com/2010/03/07/magazine/07Teachers-t.html?pagewanted=all&_r=1&.

24. *Waiting for Superman* (directed by Davis Guggenheim, Warner Brothers, 2011).

25. Larry Abramson, "As NOLA Charter Schools Thrive, Tensions Grow." *NPR*, March 3, 2009, http://www.npr.org/templates/story/story.php?storyId=101355913.

26. David L. Kirp, "Making Schools Work," *New York Times Sunday Review,* May 19, 2012, http:// www.nytimes.com/2012/05/20/opinion/sunday/integration-worked-why-have-we-rejected-it .html?_r=0.

27. "Suppression of Quality Education," *Vigilant Vote,* n.d., http://www.vigilantvote.com/american -education.html.

28. Altman, together with Anthony "Tony" Recasner, a former psychology professor at Loyola University, pioneered the charter movement in New Orleans in the early 1990s, educating one hundred inner city schoolchildren in the New Orleans Charter Middle School (which was formally chartered in 1998) and in the process proving that, with adequate instruction, poor students can perform at grade level.

## 5   MAKE IT RIGHT

1. The natural levee—alluvial soils deposited along the river's bank—influenced the founding of New Orleans as a wilderness outpost for the French in 1717; the site gave them a vantage point to see potential enemies rounding "the English Turn" of the river below the city. (It was called "English Turn" because, in 1700, the French rebuffed English forces trying to invade Louisiana at that bend in the river.) The site was also chosen as a backdoor route to the Mississippi, with an easy two-mile portage from Lake Pontchartrain via Bayou St. John to the river, avoiding a hundred miles of treacherous travel up the lower Mississippi from the coast. Lawrence N. Powell, *The Accidental City: Improvising New Orleans* (Cambridge, MA: Harvard University Press, 2012), 1–2 and *passim*.

2. Two recent books on the subject of New Orleanians' return to their houses: Daniel Wolff, *The Fight for Home: How (Parts of) New Orleans Came Back* (New York: Bloomsbury USA, 2012), and Tom Wooten, *We Shall Not Be Moved: Rebuilding Home in the Wake of Katrina* (Boston: Beacon Press, 2012). Wooten's book focuses on the neighborhoods that have had

astonishing rebirths , including Hollygrove, Broadmoor, Village de L'Est, and the Lower Ninth Ward.

3. In my testimony to Congress on the repair of school buildings after Katrina, I made the case for continued relief from FEMA, extending the Stafford Act beyond the deadline for "temporary repairs" in order to ready schools for the 2007 calendar year. "U.S. House of Representatives Committee on Education and the Workforce, Testimony of Scott S. Cowen—President, Tulane University, April 26, 2006," http://tulane.edu/administration/president/speeches_letters/house-commitee-education.cfm.

4. Years after this, in August 2010, the New Orleans City Planning Commission approved a master plan, "Plan for the 21st Century: New Orleans 2030," focused on the city's future beyond the recovery, including a comprehensive zoning ordinance with legal penalties for noncompliance.

5. Ed Blakely, *My Storm: Managing the Recovery of New Orleans in the Wake of Katrina* (The City in The Twenty-First Century) (Philadelphia: University of Pennsylvania Press, 2012).

6. "Remember when he called us lazy, racist, and backward?" Clancy DuBos, a WWL-TV political analyst, said of Blakely in a 2012 commentary when Blakely's name was in the news again as a possible expert on Hurricane Sandy. James Gill of the *Times-Picayune* has written columns (2009 and 2012) describing Blakely as an inept blowhard; Michelle Krupa, also of the *Times-Picayune*, criticizes the self-congratulatory slant of Blakely's memoir (2012).

7. In "City Neighborhoods: A Matter of Evolving Perception," *The Lens*, June 1, 2011, geographer Richard Campanella refers to this magic number as "The 73," the figure conventionally cited across a range of sources, but suggests not reading "too much reality" into it. Neighborhoods, he says, tend to be strong at their cores and ambiguous at their peripheries, dissipating into contested spaces. He also suggests that people's perceptions of "neighborhood" are highly local and tend to vary, and that major boulevards and avenues, often used to demarcate boundaries, actually bind neighborhoods together rather than divide them. See http://thelensnola.org/2011/06/01/new-orleans-neighborhoods-the-73-census-tracts-creole-treme-marigny-sixth-ward/.

8. These numbers are drawn from the Greater New Orleans Community Data Center census of 2010. One of the biggest losses of population occurred (no surprise) in the Lower Ninth Ward, which plunged from 14,000 people in 2000 to 2,800 in 2010. See http://www.gnocdc.org/PopulationLossAndVacantHousing/index.html.

9. During the fall of Saigon, it was the priests who protected congregants from persecution by the communists and helped them flee.

10. Karen J. Leong, Christopher A. Airriess, Wei Li, Angela Chia-Chen Chen, and Verna M. Keith, "Resilient History and the Rebuilding of a Community: The Vietnamese American Community in New Orleans East," *Journal of American History* 94 (December 2007): 770–79, http://www.journalofamericanhistory.org/projects/katrina/Leong.html, paragraph 14.

11. Originally this statement came from the school's website, http://www.interculturalcharterschool.org/. However, the site has since become a non-working link, because the RSD did not renew its charter for 2013

12. Veronica Barberini, "New School Year in Eastern New Orleans Bring Many Changes; Growing East," *Times-Picayune*, August 22, 2013, http://blog.nola.com/new_orleans/2013/08/new_school_year_in_eastern_new.html.

13. Purists might insist my shotgun was a "townhouse" because of its two stories. (True shotguns have only one, or, if it's a camelback, one and a half—or that's what the academicians say.) But I'm sticking to my story (as it were). The rooms were lined up shotgun fashion, and the windows and the porch were also derived from the shotgun, which is good enough for me.

14. I am indebted to Doug MacCash of the *Times-Picayune* for this description of the Picots' house, which coincides with my own memories of touring Make It Right. Doug MacCash, "Make It Right at a Crossroads Halfway through its Lower 9th Ward Rebuilding Project," *Times-Picayune*, March 9, 2012, http://impact.nola.com/katrina/print.html?entry=/2012/03/make_it_right_at_a_crossroads.html.

15. William McDonough and Michael Braungart, *Cradle to Cradle: Remaking the Way We Make Things* (New York: North Point Press, 2002).

16. Kevin Fox Gotham, "Make It Right? Brad Pitt, Katrina Rebuilding, and The Spectacularization of Disaster," in Sarah Banet-Weiser and Roopali Mukherjee, eds., *Commodity Activism: Cultural Resistance in Neoliberal Times* (New York: New York University Press, 2012), 99. See http://www.tulane.edu/~kgotham/Papers/Make%20It%20Right.pdf.

17. Ibid., 101.

18. The argument continues about the virtues and defects of Make It Right, as the project extends its offerings not only to original residents of the Lower Ninth but to other New Orleanians, including schoolteachers, firefighters, and emergency workers. An article in the *New Republic* by Lydia Depillis, March 13, 2013, criticizes the project for wasting money in the wrong ways, in the wrong place, and not considering the lack of amenities and services in the neighborhoods (http://www.newrepublic.com/article/112620/brad-pitts-make-it-right-houses-drag -new-orleans). An article in the *Times-Picayune* by Doug MacCash, "Make It Right a Drag on New Orleans? The New Republic Says So," March 26, 2013 (http://www.nola.com/arts /index.ssf/2013/03/make_it_right_a_drag_on_new_or.html) and a statement by Tom Darden, executive director of Make It Right, March 18, 2013 (http://makeitright.org/new-orleans/our -response-to-the-new-republic/), present rejoinders to the New Republic attack, defending the real contribution of these homes, as shelter and as templates, and predicting that amenities and services would develop over time, now that the houses are there.

19. NORA has also partnered with Make It Right, giving the program grant money under the Neighborhood Stabilization Program; NORA also sold Make It Right 40 lots for a second phase of development. See http://www.nola.com/homegarden/index.ssf/2009/07/post_40 .html.

20. "Mayor Landrieu and Leonard and Louise Riggio Announce Partnership to Build 100 New Homes in Gentilly," press release, The City of New Orleans, October 17, 2012, http://new.nola .gov/mayor/press-releases/2012/20121017-mayor-landrieu-and-leonard-and-louise-rig-en/.

21. Todd A. Price, "Noble Cause," *New Orleans Living Magazine*, December 9, 2009, http://www .livingneworleans.com/?p=3575.

22. "Barnes & Noble's Founder to Build 100 More Homes in New Orleans," November 20, 2012, http://www.bncollege.com/news/barnes-nobles-founder-to-build-100-more-homes-in-new -orleans/.

23. New Orleans Habitat Musicians' Village, http://www.nolamusiciansvillage.org/residents/.

24. TCC's website describes its mission as follows: "University/Community Design Partnerships (UCDP) [the consortium at Tulane City Center focused on urban renewal] take on many forms, from small design/build projects, to pre-design project definition and analysis, to site design and planning. Each project however, also shares common structural elements, specifically that a TSA [Tulane School of Architecture] faculty member plays the coordinating role and is supported by a small group of students." See http://www.tulanecitycenter.org /programs/universitycommunity-design-partnerships.

25. A food desert is an inner city neighborhood that lacks access to fresh produce and whole foods; residents of these areas very often rely on convenience stores or fast food franchises for food.

26. I am indebted to Brad Edmondson's article, "A Comeback Story in New Orleans: The Hollygrove Neighborhood Rises from Katrina's Destruction, Better than Ever," *AARP Bulletin*, August 23, 2010, for the details of what happened in Hollygrove. See http://www.aarp.org /home-garden/livable-communities/info-08–2010/a_comeback_story_in_new_orleans.html.

27. Ibid.

# 6  FIGHT, FIGHT, FIGHT

1. The Greater New Orleans Foundation (http://old.gnof.org/about/overview/mission-history/) describes this kind of community activism as the basis of "civil society."

2. An internal study done by HUD had concluded that renovation would be a cheaper option than new construction. Tram Nguyen, "Pushed Out and Pushing Back in New Orleans," *Colorlines: News for Action,* April 7, 2010, http://colorlines.com/archives/2010/04/pushed _out_and_pushing_back_in_new_orleans.html.

3. Since Katrina, it's been hard to get precise numbers about population, and statistics vary depending on the source. A blog called NO Projects, written by Jenny Sklar (http://noprojects.blogspot.com/), offers numbers on each of the housing projects and on people displaced, citing as sources the Housing Authority of New Orleans and the Department of Housing and Urban Development as well as Road Home and the Greater New Orleans Community Data Center. The numbers cited for the HANO rental voucher waiting list come from an article by Kalima Rose, "Bringing New Orleans Home: Community, Faith, and Nonprofit-Driven Housing Recovery," in Amy Liu, Roland V. Anglin, Richard M. Mizelle Jr., and Allison Plyer, eds., *Resilience and Opportunity: Lessons from the U.S. Gulf Coast after Katrina and Rita* (Washington, DC: Brookings Institution Press, 2011), 113.

4. Brad Heath, "Katrina's Wrath Lingers for New Orleans' Poor," *USA Today*, December 13, 2007, http://usatoday30.usatoday.com/news/nation/2007–12-13-katrinapoor_N.htm.

5. Jenny Jarvie, "A Fury in New Orleans as Housing Demolition OKd," *Los Angeles Times*, December 21, 2007, http://articles.latimes.com/2007/dec/21/nation/na-neworleans21.

6. "HUD Chief Resigns Amid Ethics Investigations," CNN.com, March 31, 2008, http://www.cnn.com/2008/POLITICS/03/31/hud.resignation/index.html; Libby Lewis, "HUD Secretary Jackson Steps Down Amid Probe," NPR.com, March 31, 2008, http://www.npr.org/2008/03/31/89248516/hud-secretary-jackson-steps-down-amid-probe; Edward T. Pound, "Katrina Aftermath: Questionable Contracts," *National Journal*, October 4, 2007, http://news.nationaljournal.com/articles/071004nj2.htm; Edward T. Pound, "Firms Tied to HUD Chief's Wife," *National Journal*, February 5, 2008, http://news.nationaljournal.com/articles/080205nj2.htm. Jackson denied wrongdoing, and the Department of Justice closed its investigation in 2010 without pursuing charges. His wife was not a target of the federal probe. Leah Nylen, "Investigation of Former HUD Secretary Ends," *Main Justice*, May 3, 2010, http://www.mainjustice.com/2010/05/03/investigation-of-former-hud-secretary-ends/.

7. Rose, "Bringing New Orleans Home: Community, Faith, and Nonprofit-Driven Housing Recovery," 113–114.

8. Katy Reckdahl, "New C. J. Peete Complex Is Solid, Shiny—but Not as Social, Some Residents Say," *Times-Picayune*, August 21, 2011, http://blog.nola.com/politics/2011/08/new_cj_peete_complex_is_solid.html.

9. Raquel Rolnik, "Report of the Special Rapporteur on Adequate Housing as a Component of the Right to an Adequate Standard of Living, and on the Right to Non-Discrimination in This Context," UN Human Rights Council, February 4, 2009, http://www.refworld.org/docid/49a54f4a2.html.

10. Statistics are from the Greater New Orleans Foundation, http://old.gnof.org/programs/housing/.

11. Nguyen, "Pushed Out and Pushing Back in New Orleans."

12. Another story has it that Long was upset because Tulane denied him the honorary doctor of laws degree he wanted.

13. To clarify: the UMC will continue to serve people who are uninsured, but will also provide services for private patients.

14. I myself issued an optimistic statement about UMC for the press release on the groundbreaking, preserving my cordial relations with LSU and politicians at every level.

15. Michelle Levine, a storeowner who was forced out of the neighborhood by the UMC construction said, "After the storm, some Tulane-Gravier home owners used their federal Road Home and other recovery money to rebuild. Some of them were elderly...there were a few community meetings about the new hospital but all along the plan was to tear down the neighborhood." Susan Buchanan, "Hospital Building Accelerates in New Orleans After Homes Were Moved," *The Blog, Huffington Post*, August 8, 2012, http://www.huffingtonpost.com/susan-buchanan/hospital-building-acceler_b_1748384.html.

16. Christopher Tidmore, "Demolition by Neglect: Historic Homes Left to Rot by LSU-UMC," *Louisiana Weekly*, January 23, 2012, http://www.louisianaweekly.com/demolition-by-neglect-historic-homes-left-to-rot-by-lsu-umc/.

17. Today, it is still unclear whether the new UMC facility, now under construction, has a commitment for full funding. The hospital has now been leased to the LCMC, which will control and operate it, increasing the probability for a more successful medical center.

18. And it wasn't only Charity, the public hospital, that experienced such extremities. A recent book on Memorial Medical Center, southwest of the French Quarter, catalogues these horrors and more, including the euthanizing of suffering patients with overdoses of morphine when rescue was delayed for days. Sheri Fink, *Five Days at Memorial* (New York, NY: Crown Publishers, 2013).

19. Karen DeSalvo, "Delivering High-Quality, Accessible Health Care: The Rise of Community Centers," in Liu et al., *Resilience and Opportunity*, 50.

20. An innovative payment method is critical in providing full-spectrum care: Providers are paid a prospective multi-month lump sum that's risk adjusted, so that serious illness can be covered for those who need it, with lesser amounts going to routine care.

21. DeSalvo, "Delivering High-Quality, Accessible Health Care," 51–57.

22. We ten were the founders; the group, formally known as The Times-Picayune Citizens' Group, ultimately acquired 70 members.

23. Kevin Allman, "The Fight to Save *The Times-Picayune*," *Gambit*, September 18, 2012, http://www.bestofneworleans.com/gambit/the-fight-to-save-the-times-picayune/Content?oid=2072666.

24. Ibid.

25. Quoted by Cain Burdeau, "Times-Picayune to Cut Paper to 3 Days a Week," *Bloomberg Businessweek*, May 24, 2012, www.businessweek.com/ap/2012–05/D9UVFPR80.htm.

26. Ibid. According to *Bloomberg Businessweek*, the *Times-Picayune*'s average paid circulation was 133,557 in the six months through March 2012, down 49 percent compared to March 2005, a few months before Hurricane Katrina hit.

27. A report from LSU surveying more than 1,040 respondents uncovered some serious concerns about the impact this change would have on the community:
    - More than two out of five residents—42 percent—report the loss of the daily *Times-Picayune* will have a major impact on their ability to keep up with news and information about their local community.
    - Nearly one out of two residents—46.6 percent—believe the loss of the daily *Times-Picayune* will have a major impact on the diversity of views represented in discussing community issues.
    - Two out of five—41.4 percent—said the loss of the daily *Times-Picayune* would have major impact on the ability of local news media to serve was a watchdog over local government.
    - One in five respondents think the loss will cause a major increase in both business (20.5 percent) and government (21.8 percent) corruption.
    "LSU PPRL Surveys the State of Newspapers in New Orleans: Citizens React to the Loss of the Daily *Times-Picayune*," LSU Media Center, October 4, 2012, http://www.lsu.edu/ur/ocur/lsunews/MediaCenter/News/2012/10/item53424.html.

28. According to a 2010 report from the Kaiser Foundation, 36 percent of residents in New Orleans still did not have Internet access at home. "Both my subjects and my neighbors are always looking for a print copy of what I do," said one reporter. The reporter added: "One of the charms of New Orleans is that we are 10 years behind in everything, and that includes the Web." Quoted in David Carr and Christine Haughney, "New Orleans Newspaper Scales Back in Sign of Print Upheaval," *New York Times*, May 24, 2012, http://www.nytimes.com/2012/05/25/business/media/in-latest-sign-of-print-upheaval-new-orleans-paper-scaling-back.html.

29. Tania Dall, "Save *The Times-Picayune* Movement Takes Off," WWLTV Eyewitness News, June 4, 2012, http://www.wwltv.com/home/Citizens-group-of-business-leaders-activists-forms-to-try-to-save-Times-Picayune-157035525.html.

30. As David Manship put it, "We just got a lot of inquiries from New Orleans about the fact they wanted a daily newspaper—and we just decided, heck, let's give it a shot. We believe the advertisers will follow." Quoted in Allman, "The Fight to Save *The Times-Picayune*."

31. Ryan Chittum, "The Louisiana Newspaper War: *The Advocate* Picks Up 23,500 Readers in Less Than Three Months in New Orleans," *The Columbia Journalism Review*, December 21, 2012, http://www.cjr.org/the_audit/the_louisiana_newspaper_war.php.

32. Kevin Allman, "John Georges Talks about His Purchase of *The Advocate*," *Gambit*, May 1, 2013, http://www.bestofneworleans.com/blogofneworleans/archives/2013/05/01/john-georges-talks-about-his-acquisition-of-the-advocate.

33. Quoted by Christine Haughney, "*Times-Picayune* Plans a New Print Tabloid," *New York Times*, April 30, 2013, http://www.nytimes.com/2013/05/01/business/media/times-picayune -plans-a-new-print-tabloid.html.

34. John Georges comes from an old New Orleans family that has run Imperial Trading, a food distribution company, for over a century. Allman, "John Georges Talks about His Purchase of *The Advocate*."

35. St. Joseph's Day, an Italian holiday akin to St. Patrick's Day, always occurs on March 19. Why the Mardi Gras Indians come out on (or close to) an Italian saint's day is anybody's guess, but practically speaking, it's a last opportunity to show off the costumes that these men have spent an entire year designing and creating before the weather turns too hot for feathers and beads.

# 7   GROW DAT

1. Emilie Taylor, Tulane City Center design project manager for Grow Dat, says architecture matters but community engagement matters more: Making a beautiful object won't change the world, but collaborating with a community can be "transformative." SEEDocs-Grow Dat, *How Our Work Promotes Love and Forgiveness* (video interview), http://tellusworld.org/entry /tulane-university.

2. Muffin's remarks, slightly edited, are drawn from an NPR interview by Eve Abrams, "Grow Dat Farm Nurtures Leaders," WWNO, December 11, 2012, http://www.wwno.org/post/grow -dat-youth-farm-nurtures-leaders.

3. A book on this subject by Michelle Alexander, *The New Jim Crow: Mass Incarceration in the Age of Colorblindness* (New York: New Press, 2010), describes the shockingly high rate of incarceration of young African American males, often for minor offenses, leading to a lifetime of second-class citizenship in which they are disenfranchised and unemployed— a recurrence of Jim Crow practices under the guise of criminal justice.

4. Ed Lavandera, "New Orleans Café Breaking Chains of Poverty," *Eatocracy*, CNN.com, August 15, 2011, http://eatocracy.cnn.com/2011/08/15/new-orleans-cafe-breaking-chains-of -poverty/.

5. This remark and others are drawn from a video interview of Cuccia by Alfred Edmond Jr. at the New Jersey Summit on Social Entrepreneurship held at the New Jersey Performing Arts Center in Newark on October 19, 2011. The video can be seen on YouTube: http://www.youtube .com/watch?v=oOgL7y2Q4Sw.

6. In Cuccia's words: "A bunch of other denominations got involved. We went into a neighborhood that had 30 churches in 30 blocks, and none of them were working together. So we pointedly gathered those who were really down in the neighborhoods doing something." Kerry Weber, "Craig Cuccia, Co-founder and Executive Director of Café Reconcile, New Orleans, Louisiana," *Catholic Digest*, October 1, 2007, http://www.catholicdigest.com/articles/good _works/making_a_difference/2007/10–01/craig-cuccia-co-founder-and-executive-director -cafeacute-reconcile-new-orleans-louisiana.

7. Karen M. Lozinski, "Reconcile New Orleans—Everyone at the Same Table: A Conversation with Glen Armantrout of Reconcile New Orleans," *Food Dat*, January 14, 2013, http://fooddat .com/2013/01/reconcile-new-orleans-everyone-at-the-same-table/.

8. Cuccia describes the long-term positive effects of "making contact": "We got together and developed a program where kids from the inner city came in and had a fine dining experience. They learned how to be waiters and waitresses, to work in the kitchen, and they got a little stipend. They learned how to have dinner conversation. That went over really well, and we had all these different volunteer groups come in and just share with the kids and do artwork. And we introduced them to African-American doctors, and firemen, and policemen. We were somebody that cared and was concerned about them, and it broke down a lot of barriers and perceptions and we built a lot of trust with the neighbors." Weber, "Craig Cuccia, Co-founder and Executive Director of Café Reconcile."

9. The Emeril Lagasse Foundation, Shell Oil, and Credit Suisse, among others, have donated money and support.

10. Michel Martin, host, "From Dishwashers to Head Chefs," *Tell Me More*, NPR interview, April 8, 2013, www.npr.org/2013/04/08/176570806/from-dishwashers-to-head-chefs.

11. This material is quoted from http://cafereconcile.org/about/staff/ryan-dalton, a non-working link; staff portraits remain online for only a brief period.

12. The quoted remarks also come from the staff profile on the Café Reconcile site. See also "The Push Project: Education and Recreation for a Better Tomorrow," http://sparkaction.org /content/push-project-education-recreation-better-t.

13. Tulane University's Disaster Resilience Leadership Academy and University of Haiti, Haiti Humanitarian Aid Evaluation, January 2011, http://drlatulane.org/groups/haiti-humanitarian- aid- evaluation/Haiti%20Humanitarian%20Aid%20Evaluation%20Tulane%20University%20 DRLA%20and%20University%20of%20Haiti%20Structured%20Analysis%20January%20 2011.pdf.

14. Ibid.

15. DRLA carried out a social impact assessment of the BP oil spill on gulf communities, funded by Oxfam America, to identify effects on vulnerable members of the Native American, Vietnamese, and immigrant communities, oil and gas workers, and members of the fisheries industry as well as to identify local leaders who are effectively engaging with those communities. *Social Impact Assessment of the BP Oil Spill Disaster on Gulf Communities*, Tulane DRLA, 2010–2013. See two reports: "DRLA DCFS Deep Water Horizon Oil Spill Resilience Framework: Phase I," October 2010, http://drlatulane.org/groups/community-resiliency-deep-water-horizon -oil-spill/eadership%20Academy%20Deep%20Water%20Horizon%20Oil%20Spill%20 Phase%20I%20Report%20October%202010.pdf/view; and "Deep Water Horizon Oil Spill Phase II Report," December 2010, http://drlatulane.org/groups/community-resiliency-deep -water-horizon-oil-spill/Tulane%20University%20Disaster%20Resilience%20Leadership%20 Academy%20Deep%20Water%20Horizon%20Oil%20Spill%20Phase%20II%20Report%20 December%202010.pdf/view.

16. The truth is, many major American cities—not just a post-Katrina New Orleans but Detroit, Cleveland, Chicago, Oakland; the list goes on—are zones of disaster, marked by violence, hunger, homelessness, illness, and suffering. An effective social innovation, on the international or the national level, inevitably has to address the deeply intertwined issues of trauma, families, poverty, and social justice.

## 8   INFLECTION POINT

1. Some details of this conversation were reconstructed from an article in the alumni magazine of Tulane's A. B. Freeman School of Business, "A Bicycle Built for Business," *Freeman Magazine* (Summer 2013), http://freemanblog.freeman.tulane.edu/freemanmag/index.php/2012/08/a -bicycle-built-for-business/.

2. Some of these references, along with other top rankings, can be found in the December 2013 STARs (Statistics, Testimonials, Awards, and Rankings) report on the GNO, Inc website: http://gnoinc.org/uploads/GNO_Inc_STARs.pdf. See also http://gnoinc.org/wp-content /uploads/2010_Year_In_Review.pdf.

3. Film New Orleans, Mayor's Office of Cultural Economy, "Filmography," http://www .filmneworleans.org/for-the-local-community/filmed-in-new-orleans/filmography/.

4. Adam B. Kushner, "Forget Hollywood. Filmmakers are Flocking to New Orleans," *Atlantic Cities*, April 11, 2013, http://www.theatlanticcities.com/jobs-and-economy/2013/04/forget -hollywood-filmmakers-are-flocking-new-orleans/5268/.

5. A description of *Shell Shocked* (Scrub Brush Productions, directed by John Richie of New Orleans Video Access Center), can be found on a cached page dated February 2, 2011 at the NOVAC website, http://www.zoominfo.com/CachedPage/?archive_id=0&page_id= -208169319&page_url=//novacvideo.org/scrub-brush-productions/comment-page-1/&page

_last_updated=2011–02–02T01:07:23&firstName=John&lastName=Richie. See also http://www.shellshockeddoc.com/.

6. The conventional measure of a city's economic well-being has been tied to the gross domestic product and the poverty rate, but a new set of metrics, the "Opportunity Index," takes into account many of the topics addressed in this book, including education, housing, health, crime rate, community engagement, and employment. New Orleans rated a C on the index in 2012, but education, community engagement, and overall opportunity are slowly improving; the city received a grade of C+ in 2013. See http://opportunityindex.org/#9.00/29.951/-90.072/Orleans/Louisiana. Also see http://www.measureofamerica.org/wp-content/uploads/2012/09/2012_Opportunity_Index_Findings1.pdf.

7. From the GNO, Inc. website: "An unprecedented level of business development activity in our region suggests that a profound economic resurgence is occurring. More than $20 billion is being invested in six target sectors: three foundational—building on our existing strengths—and three diversifying—leveraging regional assets to create new opportunities. There should be no question that the 10-parish Greater New Orleans region is open for business and is firmly focused on welcoming and supporting new investment and development in these industry sectors." http://gnoinc.org/industry-sectors/.

8. Derek Thompson, "The Big Comeback: Is New Orleans America's Next Great Innovation Hub?," *The Atlantic*, April 8, 2013, http://www.theatlantic.com/business/archive/2013/04/the-big-comeback-is-new-orleans-americas-next-great-innovation-hub/274591/.

9. US Patent 5919426 A, "Products of apatite-forming-systems," publication date July 6, 1999, http://www.google.com/patents/US5919426?dq=nakamoto+theobromine&ei=DPn8TrbkMOnnsQKzoY2eAQ.

10. New Orleans BioInnovation Center: http://www.neworleansbio.com/about_us/tenants/; http://www.neworleansbio.com/about_us/clients/services/nola_mobile_health/; and http://www.neworleansbio.com/about_us/clients/diagnostics/chosen_diagnostics/.

11. The Propeller website (http://gopropeller.org/news/365/) lists semifinalists in the PitchNOLA competition in two categories: Community Solutions, devoted to ventures that address New Orleans' most pressing social and environmental challenges, and Lots of Progress, specifically devoted to renewal efforts on vacant lots.

12. Kathy Finn, "Startups Flourish in New Orleans: Building Enterprises from the Ground Up," *New Orleans Magazine* (January 2013), http://www.myneworleans.com/New-Orleans-Magazine/January-2013/Startups-Flourish-in-New-Orleans/.

13. As the mSchool website puts it: "Students who previously lacked access to the hardware, bandwidth, or home supervision necessary for online learning become first-class digital citizens." See http://mschools.org/how/.

14. Mark Waller, "Kickboard School Data Startup Leads the Growing Field of Educational Entrepreneurship in New Orleans," *Times-Picayune*, April 12, 2013, http://www.nola.com/business/index.ssf/2013/04/kickboard_school_data_start-up.html.

15. Ibid.

16. "Iconic Circle Food Store Coming Back," news segment, WDSU New Orleans, January 15, 2013, http://www.wdsu.com/news/local-news/new-orleans/Iconic-Circle-Food-Store-Coming-Back/-/9853400/18136464/-/7x8pn4/-/index.html.

17. Alex Woodward, "Circle Food Store to Reopen Summer 2013," *Gambit*, January 14, 2013, http://www.bestofneworleans.com/blogofneworleans/archives/2013/01/14/circle-food-store-to-reopen-summer-2013.

18. Peirce Lewis, *New Orleans: The Making of an Urban Landscape*, 2nd ed. (Center for American Places, 2003).

19. Mary Landrieu, U.S. Senator for Louisiana, "Energy Security," 2013, http://www.landrieu.senate.gov/?p=issue&id=14.

20. Mary Landrieu, U.S. Senator for Louisiana, "Justice for the Gulf Coast: RESTORE ACT," 2013, http://www.landrieu.senate.gov/?p=general&id=81.

21. Joe Epstein and Nate Hindman, "Swamp Savior: Can a 72-Year-Old Inventor Rescue the Sinking Bayou?," *Free Enterprise*, June 24, 2013, http://www.freeenterprise.com/free-enterprise-tour/swamp-savior-can-72-year-old-inventor-rescue-sinking-bayou.

22. Blade Dynamics has its factory in NASA's Michoud Assembly Facility in New Orleans East.

## 9 LET THE GOOD TIMES ROLL

1. Ron Marks, dean of the School of Social Work, has been taking graduate students to northern India for the past twelve years.
2. These remarks, slightly edited, were drawn from the Dalai Lama's Commencement Speech, "The Dalai Lama at Tulane Commencement 2013," YouTube, http://www.youtube.com /watch?v=M5GgNebzUss.
3. 2013 Commencement Remarks, May 18, 2013, http://tulane.edu/administration/president /speeches_letters/commencement2013.cfm.
4. To quote Irvin Mayfield, cultural ambassador of New Orleans (among many other titles and honorifics): "Jazz is as ubiquitous as gravity. New Orleans' improvisational and multicultural style is directly linked to the way we interact, cook, worship, celebrate and mourn. Jazz provides the city's character."
5. A fuller list of Mayfield's board memberships includes, among others, the African American Museum, Louisiana State University's Department of Psychiatry and Health Science, the New Orleans Jazz and Heritage Foundation, Tulane University's School of Architecture, and the Youth Rescue Initiative.
6. "On Turning Ten: Trumpeter Irvin Mayfield's New Orleans Jazz Orchestra," October 8, 2012, http://blogs.artinfo.com/blunotes/2012/10/on-turning-ten-trumpeter-irvin-mayfields-new -orleans-jazz-orchestra/.
7. From "Artistic Literacy," a public lecture delivered at the University of New Orleans, Thursday, January 26, 2012, http://irvinmayfield.com/blog/?cat=4.
8. "Statement from the Original Big 7 Social Aid and Pleasure Club on Mother's Day Secondline Shooting," Louisiana Justice Institute, posted May 12, 2013, http://louisianajusticeinstitute .blogspot.com/2013/05/statement-from-original-big-7-social.html.
9. Helen Freund, "Mother's Day Parade 'Re-do': 'These Are Our Traditions...Our Culture,'" Times-Picayune, June 1, 2013, http://www.nola.com/living/index.ssf/2013/06/mothers_day _second-line_parade.html.
10. Some other famous food products from New Orleans also have family stories; consider the Reily Foods Company's French Market Coffee (chicory), Luzianne Coffee and Luzianne Tea, and Zatarain's Jambalaya Mix. And then there are Magic Seasoning Blends (creation of homeboy chef Paul Prudhomme) and Southern Comfort (concocted by a bartender in a tavern just off Bourbon Street in 1874).
11. Dave Walker, "Janette Desautel Shares 'Treme' Screen Time with One of Her Inspirations, New Orleans Chef Susan Spicer," Times-Picayune, July 4, 2011, http://www.nola.com/treme-hbo/index.ssf/2011/07/janette_desautel_shares_treme.html.
12. Rich Cohen (another Tulane grad) has written a fascinating book on Zemurray, The Fish That Ate the Whale: The Life and Times of America's Banana King (New York: Farrar, Straus and Giroux, 2012), detailing his flamboyant, and occasionally illegal, adventures.
13. The quote comes from an interview by William Vitka, "Fats Domino, 'Alive and Kicking,'" CBSNews.com, February 25, 2006, http://www.cbsnews.com/stories/2006/02/25/eveningnews /main1346150.shtml.
14. Doug MacCash, "Unusual Flood-Resistant 'Steamboat House' Helped Keep the Neighborhood Afloat," Times-Picayune, August 28, 2010, http://www.nola.com/homegarden/index .ssf/2010/08/unusual_flood-resistant_steamb.html.
15. Richard Rainey, "Mayor Mitch Landrieu Planning to Move New Orleans City Hall, Civil Court to Old Charity Hospital," Times-Picayune, July 3, 2013, http://www.nola.com/politics /index.ssf/2013/07/mayor_landrieu_planning_to_mov.html.
16. Allan Katz and Danae Columbus, "Moving City Hall to Former Charity Site Has Many Challenges," July 25, 2013, http://uptownmessenger.com/2013/07/allan-katz-and-danae -columbus-moving-city-hall-to-former-charity-site-has-many-challenges/.
17. During the 1960s, civil rights activists protested what they perceived as self-mockery, black men in blackface—satire is tricky at times of active social change—but the Zulus survived to continue their tradition of knowing parody in a city known for its embrace of complex forms of identity and self-expression. Louis Armstrong was Zulu king in 1949, before he exiled

himself from his beloved city in frustration and anger at Jim Crow practices that kept him from full citizenship in his hometown, even while he was receiving accolades and acceptance in Europe.

18. "Mardi Gras Indians History and Tradition," Mardi Gras New Orleans, http://www.mardi-grasneworleans.com/mardigrasindians.html.

19. Ned Sublette, *The World that Made New Orleans: From Spanish Silver to Congo Square* (Chicago: Lawrence Hill Books, 2009), 295–311.

## 10   DOING GOOD

1. Dr. Arnold Barnett, "MIT Study of the Vietnam Death Rates," cited in Vietnam War Myths and Facts, LZ Center. A version of this article appeared in *MIT Tech Talk* 37, no. 8 (September 30, 1992), http://www.lzcenter.com/Myths%20and%20Facts.html#MIT%20Study%20of%20 the%20Vietnam%20Death%20Rates%20by%20Dr.%20Arnold%20Barnett.

2. Edwards later spent almost nine years in prison for graft and corruption but on his release from prison still hoped to return to public life; he'd been forgiven often enough in four terms to believe he could go for a fifth at age 80. In October 2013, a reality television show, "The Governor's Wife," debuted on A&E; the show catches up with Edwards since his release from prison, mainly confining itself to family matters (and another crack at fatherhood with his new 35-year-old wife). As Alessandra Stanley of the *New York Times* puts it, "The show is hardly a bid for political rehabilitation by Mr. Edwards. Louisiana is a state with an elastic view of disgrace and Mr. Edwards, who won four terms, is famous for having said that the only way he could lose an election was to be caught in bed with a 'dead girl or a live boy.'" Alessandra Stanley, "Real Politician of Louisiana, At Home: 'The Governor's Wife, on A&E, Follows Life of Edwin Edwards," *New York Times*, October 25, 2013, http://www.nytimes.com/2013/10/26/arts/television/the-governors-wife-on-ae-follows-life-of-edwin-edwards.html?_r=0.

3. Adriana Lopez, "D.O.A.: Detroit? Think Again. Motor City Has a Chance at New Life," *Forbes*, July 23, 2013, http://www.forbes.com/sites/adrianalopez/2013/07/23/d-o-a-detroit-think-again-motor-city-has-a-chance-at-new-life/.

4. The Cleveland Museum of Art, which has free admission, has recently undergone a major expansion, and the Cleveland Orchestra remains the world-class organization it's always been.

5. Terry Ryan and Aaron Churchill, "Searching for Excellence: A Five-City, Cross-State Comparison of Charter School Quality," Thomas B. Fordham Institute, March 2013, http://www.edexcellence.net/publications/searching-for-excellence.html.

6. The website of the Louisiana Children's Museum describes numerous programs aimed at every phase of child development, from birth to 11 years of age. See "Where We Are Going" (http://lcm.org/going) and the programs listed under "Community Engagement" (http://lcm.org/community-engagement).

7. I realize I've mentioned only young men here. Of course young women also need help and mentoring, and many are also achieving escape velocity. I've emphasized young men because it's a fact, statistically, that young African American males are at greater risk of dysfunction, disconnection, and early death than females.

CPSIA information can be obtained at www.ICGtesting.com
Printed in the USA
BVOW11s0620140114

341463BV00005B/31/P